THE
SENTENC
GUIDEL

THE U.S. SENTENCING GUIDELINES

Implications for Criminal Justice

Edited by
DEAN J. CHAMPION

PRAEGER

New York
Westport, Connecticut
London

Library of Congress Cataloging-in-Publication Data

The U.S. sentencing guidelines : implications for criminal justice /
    edited by Dean J. Champion.
        p.   cm.
    Includes bibliographies and index.
    ISBN 0–275–93324–5   (alk. paper)
    1.   Sentences (Criminal procedure)—United States.
KF9685.U25   1989
345.73'0772—dc20
[347.305772]   89–16092

Library of Congress Catalog Card Number: 89–16092
ISBN: 0–275–93324–5

First published in 1989

Praeger Publishers
One Madison Avenue, New York, NY 10010
A division of Greenwood Press, Inc.

Printed in the United States of America

The paper used in this book complies with the
Permanent Paper Standard issued by the National
Information Standards Organization (Z39.48–1984).

10 9 8 7 6 5 4 3 2 1

Contents

Preface

On October 12, 1984, the Comprehensive Crime Control Act, Public Law 98–473, became effective. Among other things, this act included enabling legislation for the establishment of a United States Sentencing Commission with the statutory authority to change existing federal district court sentencing policies and procedures and to create a new and, ideally, more equitable sentencing system. The United States Sentencing Commission, hereafter referred to as the Commission, was vested with many duties and powers. Some of these duties and powers are summarized in Appendix C.

The Comprehensive Crime Control Act of 1984 foresaw guidelines that would further the basic purposes of criminal punishment, including (1) deterring crime, (2) incapacitating offenders, (3) providing just punishments, and (4) rehabilitating offenders (U. S. Sentencing Commission, 1987:1.1). With these general objectives functioning as orientations for subsequent actions, the Commission undertook the task of extensively revising existing federal sentencing practices. Perhaps the most influential or dominant objective was the provision for "just punishments" for those convicted of violating federal criminal laws. The primary result of the Commission's deliberations, investigations, and recommendations was the creation of a new set of federal sentencing guidelines. These guidelines became effective and binding on all federal judges on November 1, 1987.

The development of sentencing guidelines is not unique to the federal government. Several states, particularly Minnesota, had established sentencing guidelines in the 1970s and early 1980s. The principal reason for establishing sentencing guidelines was to eliminate or at least reduce sentencing disparities according to extra-legal factors such as gender, race, ethnicity, and socioeconomic status. Sentencing disparities occur whenever offenders with similar histories commit identical crimes and receive widely different sentences. Such disparities are most apparent where particular jurisdictions and judges are identified.

A blatant example of a sentencing disparity is as follows. Two convicted male offenders appear before the same judge during the same week or month. Both offenders have been convicted of the same crimes, both have strikingly similar criminal records and histories, and the aggravating and mitigating circumstances surrounding their crimes are likewise identical. Both offenders are represented by the same defense attorney. Both offenders had elected bench rather than jury trials. However, the judge sentences offender A to three to five years in prison, while offender B is sentenced to probation for a term of three years. Offender A is black, whereas offender B is white. Other than the obvious racial difference, nothing else exists to explain this sentencing discrepancy.

The disparity described above occurs at the front-end of criminal processing. Disparities also exist at the back-end and involve discrepancies in parole board decision making that can only be explained by citing racial, ethnic, gender, or socioeconomic variables.

In addition to the issue of sentencing disparities, serious questions have been raised within the legal community, among scholars and researchers, and among the general public about the "fit" between the seriousness of the crime committed and the accompanying punishment, the deterrent effect of current judicial practices and correctional programs and operations, and the rehabilitative value of existing educational, vocational, and therapeutic programs for offenders both within and without prison walls. The Commission was established for the purpose of targeting these problem areas and reviewing and rationalizing the entire federal sentencing process.

This book is an in-depth examination of the U. S. Sentencing Guidelines developed by the Commission. It seeks to determine both the short- and long-range implications of these guidelines for three major criminal justice system components: law enforcement, prosecution and the courts, and corrections.

Readers are advised that the views, speculations, opinions, and conclusions of each contributing author in the sections to follow are theoretically and/or empirically grounded. Furthermore, by yearend 1988, lawsuits from various sectors had been filed in all federal circuits, in over half of the states, challenging the constitutionality of the guidelines and the Commission as well as several other important legal issues. Some federal judges have refused to comply with these guidelines when sentencing convicted offenders in their districts. Needless to say, these guidelines are highly controversial and were spawned in such a milieu.

It is hoped that this book will be received in the same spirit it was conceived. It is our collective intent to render an objective appraisal of these guidelines and to stimulate a productive dialogue among both theoreticians and practitioners in criminal justice and criminology. Among the contributing authors there are diverse views about these guidelines and their potential effectiveness for promoting more equitable punishments for those convicted of federal crimes. Some contributing authors are on record as having virgorously opposed the implementation of these guidelines. We believe that the diversity of opinions, theories, and evaluations represented here will not only be of interest to most scholars, but that additional questions, discussions, and controversies will be generated. This is the healthy result of academic inquiry.

Finally, this book is dedicated to the Academy of Criminal Justice Sciences, an interdisciplinary community of scholars continually seeking answers to all questions which relate to criminal justice and criminology.

Part I

The U. S. Sentencing Guidelines: An Overview

U. S. Sentencing Guidelines in Perspective:
A Theoretical Background and Overview

Kay A. Knapp   Denis J. Hauptly

INTRODUCTION

The story of substantive and penal law reforms in the United States has been written in state jurisdictions. This is not surprising since the U. S. Constitution reserves jurisdiction over common law crimes to the states absent some special federal jurisdictional connection (U. S. Constitution, Amendment X). Each state enacts its own criminal code and penal structure. The last thirty years have been a particularly fertile period of state-initiated substantive and penal law reform. Beginning in the early 1960s, states began revising their criminal codes in light of the Model Penal Code published in 1962 (American Law Institute, 1962). By 1985, three-fourths of the states had revised their codes coinciding with Model Penal Code guidelines (American Law Institute, 1985).

States also took the lead in initiating sentencing reforms. As policy makers grew disillusioned with indeterminate sentencing and its accompanying lack of structure and accountability, states began experimenting with more structured sentencing. In the 1970s several states had adopted legislatively established determinate sentencing (Shane-DuBow, Brown, and Olsen, 1985). The shortcomings of those determinate sentencing systems led other states in the 1980s to move toward the more effective structured-sentencing approach of pre-

Ed. Note: The views expressed are those of the authors.

sumptive sentencing guidelines (Tonry, 1988). During this same period, states developed and implemented a wide array of innovative correctional programs for offenders deemed too serious for standard probation, but for whom prison was also considered unnecessary for public safety and counterproductive to offender rehabilitation (Petersilia, 1985; Tonry, 1988).

In contrast to the substantive and penal reform innovations among the states, the federal government has led in reforms only with respect to procedural law [See Endnote 1]. As suggested above, one reason for the federal government's general lack of leadership in substantive and penal law reform lies in the federal context itself [see Endnote 2]. Substantive law reform advocates in the 1950s through the 1980s focused primarily on common law crimes. Federal jurisdiction over crimes is limited to those offenses such as tax and immigration that directly impinge on federal interest, and to those offenses that affect interstate commerce. The federal government has used the interstate commerce base to increase its involvement in handling common law crime with the enactment of such "jurisdictional" crimes as the Travel Act, the Hobbs Act, wire and mail fraud, and Racketeering Influenced and Corrupt Organizations (RICO) [see Endnote 3]. Still, relative to the states, the federal government has very limited responsibility for and jurisdiction over common law crime. By and large the commonlaw-oriented substantive law reform movement was less relevant to the federal government than it was to the states, where the vast majority of codes were revised.

In addition to the uniqueness of federal crimes, the limited role of the federal government relative to the states in law enforcement, code enactment, penalty setting, and correctional management, and the remoteness of Congress from the day-to-day real problems of the criminal justice system have fostered actions that are primarily symbolic with respect to substantive and penal law issues. For example, the federal government was among the first jurisdictions to react to the U. S. Supreme Court decision in *Furman v. Georgia* (1972), which required special procedures before the death penalty could be imposed. However, the federal government's reaction was largely symbolic. The Congress enacted a Constitutional death penalty provision that met these standards but applied it only to certain murders during the course of aircraft hijackings [see Endnote 4]. In the 15 years since that statute was enacted, there have been rare occasions where the federal death penalty might theoretically have been applied but it has not been pursued by the Department of Justice, despite that Department's consistent advocacy of capital punishment as an appropriate penalty. Similarly, following the acquittal of John Hinckley in his assassination attempt on former President Ronald Reagan, Congress abolished the separate insanity defense. Yet, the types of offenses in which such a defense is typically offered are rarely found in federal courts. While some states have acted symbolically relative to crime and justice matters, the ratio of symbolic to nonsymbolic content is much lower. Most states enacting the death penalty provisions to meet the *Furman* standards, for example, were not acting symbolically.

In addition to the federal government's unique jurisdiction over crime and the tendency to take largely symbolic action in crime and justice matters, the federal government enjoys a fiscal freedom relative to law enforcement, penalty setting, and correctional management unknown to most states. Efficient and cost-effective management of systems and institutions is a significant issue in most state-initiated legal and penal reforms (Strasser, 1989). This concern derives from an acute awareness of resource constraints and of competing interests for limited resources (Randall, 1989). Deficit spending has spared the federal government from such concerns.

Recent federal efforts to reform sentencing are best understood in this general context of unique and discretionary federal jurisdiction over crimes, the tendency toward symbolic action, and the fiscal freedom enjoyed by the federal government. The Sentencing Reform Act was first introduced in Congress in 1977 as part of a major substantive reform that included a revised federal criminal code and revisions to bail and procedural laws as well (S.1437, 95th Congress). After seven years of debate, the sentencing reform legislation finally passed after having been stripped of the major substantive criminal law reform provisions (Title II, Public Law 98–473). Sentencing Commission members were appointed in September 1985. The Commission worked on guidelines during 1986 and 1987, and it published three different drafts of guidelines. Despite widespread criticism of these guidelines and a guaranteed constitutional challenge, the guidelines were implemented November 1, 1987.

During the same time frame, states were developing innovative sentencing structures. The first legislatively mandated sentencing guidelines were developed and implemented in Minnesota in 1980. Discretionary release by paroling authorities was eliminated and judges began to impose real-time sentences (minus legislatively defined "good time"). In 1982, Pennsylvania implemented a more limited sentencing reform. Guidelines for judges were imposed, although discretionary release by a paroling authority continued to determine the actual time served. In 1984 the State of Washington implemented more comprehensive guidelines which addressed not only prison sentences, but set forth rudimentary guidelines for jail and non-incarcerative sanctions. Presumptive sentencing guidelines took effect in Florida in 1983, but inadequate correctional resources prevented their full implementation. In 1985, legislatures rejected guideline proposals in New York and South Carolina. By the end of the 1980s, guidelines proposals were either under development or under legislative review in Tennessee, Oregon, Louisiana, New Mexico, and the District of Columbia. Several other states were considering legislation which would establish sentencing commissions.

This chapter examines and contrasts the development of the U. S. Sentencing Guidelines and state sentencing reform efforts with respect to (1) the sentencing reform's relation to substantive criminal law, (2) the prosecutorial role, (3) correctional resources, and (4) guideline implementation.

SUBSTANTIVE CRIMINAL LAW AND SENTENCING REFORM

Neither the antiquated federal criminal code nor the more modern state criminal codes based on the Model Penal Code were created with structured sentencing systems in mind. No existing codes are adequate to support contemporary structured sentencing systems (Robinson, 1988; Tonry, 1982, 1988a). Absent the development of a model code designed for structured sentencing systems, the problem for structured sentencing is to identify the code's particular inadequacies and provide the non-statutory distinctions and structures necessary for an effective structured sentencing system.

The Model Penal Code, for example, is a very general document designed for the indeterminate, rehabilitation-oriented sentencing systems that were dominant in the 1940s and 1950s. Offenses involving similar types of conduct are differentiated primarily on the basis of culpability levels. This is useful in determining the degree of blameworthiness, but it is less helpful in distinguishing between degrees of resulting or intended harm. Additionally, the range of behaviors and harms encompassed in a single provision tends to be extremely broad (e.g., assault may include a barroom brawl or severe physical abuse of an infant; forgery or fraud may include passing bad checks for small amounts as well as sophisticated schemes to take large sums from vulnerable elderly) (Model Penal Code, Articles 211 and 224, American Law Institute, 1962). The penalty structure in the Model Penal Code is similarly broad, dividing felonies into only three punishment categories (Model Penal Code, Section 6.01, American Law Institute, 1962). The penalty classifications establish statutory maximum sentences based on the worst-case scenario, by definition, an extreme case.

State guideline efforts have developed several methods to deal with the inadequacies of codes derived from or resembling Model Penal Code provisions. The methodology has grown increasingly sophisticated over the decade of state efforts in states such as Oregon and Louisiana. Offenses (both statutory and *de facto*) are examined and analyzed with respect to culpability, harms, and interests protected. Weights are assigned to offenses based on types and levels of harms, levels of culpability, and priorities established by a state commission with respect to interests protected. The analysis provides the basis for a detailed ranking and classification of offenses by criteria the commission designates important for differentiating sentences.

State commissions differentiate the general penal code provisions in several ways. First, they make offense distinctions based on elements not found in the codes. Thus, they may separate assault cases involving very young victims from other assaults and analyze each offense separately according to the classification methodology. More specific monetary distinctions than appear in the code might be added; or monetary distinctions might be added where none exist in the code (e.g., burglary offenses) [see Endnote 5]. State commissions consider the frequency of behavior or harm and the difficulty in proving the behavior or harm in adding offense differentiations to the classification. If a behavior or harm occurs infrequently, it is usually reserved for sentence departure. Offense differentiations that are easy to establish (e.g., age of the victim) are preferred to those requiring more elaborate evidence (e.g., extent of victim injury). Depending upon the frequency of occurrence and range of behavior, the latter type of differentiations may be accomplished through commission-initiated code revisions, the use of sentencing ranges, or departures.

With limited success, a second means whereby states differentiate codes is to draw thresholds below the statutory maximum sentence and require findings before each threshold can be crossed. Minnesota requires substantial and compelling circumstances to increase or diminish the sentence from the presumptive range. A second threshold was established by the court decision to limit aggravated departures to double the presumptive sentence except in rare cases (*State v. Evans,* 1981). The Washington state commission included the Minnesota standard for departure and appellate review in an unsuccessful attempt to incorporate the Minnesota case law and the court-imposed departure threshold in the Washington guidelines (State of Washington, 1988). The Pennsylvania commission incorporated two levels of aggravation, an "aggravated range" which the judge can impose if reasons are provided, and an aggravated departure which exceeds the "aggravated range." Only aggravated departures are reviewable (State of Pennsylvania, 1986). The guideline proposal submitted to the Oregon legislature in 1989 included an absolute double the presumptive sentence limit for aggravated sentences [see Endnote 5]. These devices were developed to address the over-broad penal structures in the current criminal codes and to reserve the statutory maximums for those cases that the legislature intended them for—the very worst cases.

A third method used by some states to address the inadequacies of code structures is to classify offenses based on the usual case. The Model Penal Code classifies offenses based on the worst case. The statutory maximum penalties are needed only to ensure that the worst cases can be dealt with appropriately. The appropriate penalty for a less serious case (i.e., virtually all cases) was to be established by the judge and the parole board. The "usual case" classifications created by state commissions do not necessarily correlate well with the statutory "worst case" classification systems. For instance, the "usual case" of auto theft might deserve a punishment that is a very low fraction of the statutory maximum because the range of conduct that can be found in auto theft is very broad. On the other hand, the "usual case" of aggravated sexual assault might deserve a punishment that is a significant portion of the statutory maximum because the range of conduct found in such cases is narrower.

The focus on usual case results in emphasizing *de facto* as well as *de jure* elements. *De facto* elements are not as clearly articulated or specifically defined as *de jure* elements. Nonetheless, *de facto* elements are often very relevant to the sentencing decision and are often too subtle to build into a sentencing scheme in a more mechanical way. Thus, they are built in conceptually through the notion of "usual case." This approach relies upon the judgment and experience of the sentencing commission to incorporate *de facto* elements into the sentencing guidelines and relies upon the judgment and experience of the trial and appellate courts to incorporate *de facto* elements into specific sentences. In situations where no usual case is discernable, because of infrequent prosecution coupled with a wide range of behavior, the offense is generally left out of the classification scheme. Each case is then handled by the court in light of general guideline policies and principles.

Not all state criminal statutes are modeled after the Model Penal Code. A minority of the state codes, and the federal criminal code, are "unrevised." These codes tend to be a hodgepodge of statutes enacted at various times for various purposes and without any reference to each other or without any standard form of drafting. The unrevised codes generally lack uniform language concerning either conduct, harms, or culpability. Instead of the four states of mind typically used in Model Penal Code jurisdictions, for example, the federal criminal code contains literally dozens of different labels for mental states. Also, one section may refer to a serious assault as "aggravated" while another may punish the imposition of "serious bodily injury." Statutes generally proliferate in these codes. There are, for example, nearly 200 separate federal theft offenses and nearly as many separate false statement offenses.

Because these offenses may have been drafted at different times and by different legislators on different committees, the penalty structure in unrevised codes is equally disparate. Statutory sanctions generally display a bewildering range of maximums. A false statement to any agency of the federal government, for example, is punishable by up to five years' imprisonment under 18 U.S.C. Sec. 1001 (1989). But in 18 U.S.C. Sec. 1010, a false statement to the Department of Housing and Urban Development (HUD) is punishable by a term of up to two years. In a case involving a false statement to HUD, a federal prosecutor could simply charge a conspiracy to defraud the federal government under 18 U.S.C. Sec. 371 (with a maximum sentence of five years) and treat the false statement as an overt act. If the mails were used, a fourth alternative charge (mail fraud) would be available.

The fact of an unrevised code and its concomitant lack of organization and consistency does not fundamentally change the nature of the sentencing commission's task. Depending on the specific code, more extra-statutory elements may need to be incorporated into the sentencing classification scheme to effect appropriate structured sentences. And the commission may need to recommend a greater number of revised penalty provisions to the legislature—erratic maxima for similar behavior allow the prosecutor to inappropriately "cap" sentences below the guideline sentence by negotiating a charge with a very low maximum.

The general problems of unrevised codes are exacerbated in the federal code because of the limitations placed on federal criminal jurisdiction. The federal government may not proscribe common law crimes generically. Despite this constitutional limitation, there are consistent political demands for federal coverage (largely for symbolic purposes) of offenses with high public visibility. For instance, there was no federal coverage of kidnapping until 1934, when the Lindbergh infant was kidnapped. The public outcry led to the passage of 18 U.S.C. Sec. 1201, creating a federal crime of kidnapping when interstate transit was involved.

The use of these jurisdictional bases to create federal crimes out of common law crimes often serves to mask the underlying conduct. For example, 18 U.S.C. Sec. 241 prohibits a conspiracy to injure or intimidate any citizen in the free exercise of their constitutional rights. This statute, aimed primarily at the Ku Klux Klan, has been used to prosecute murder, kidnapping, rape, voting fraud, and a host of other forms of conduct. The jury hears a murder case and then is instructed to determine if a civil rights case has been established.

Similarly, 18 U.S.C. Sec. 1341 prohibits the use of the mails in a fraud scheme. What was designed to reach simple scams which no state could investigate or prosecute has been creatively used to prosecute political officials whose dishonest public service included an incidental use of the mails. The jury hears a political corruption case and then is instructed on a mail fraud charge.

These two features, the unrevised nature of the criminal code and the "jurisdictional" nature of many federal crimes, combine to confound the drafters of federal sentencing guidelines with an illogical set of statutes and a contradictory set of maximum sanctions. Nonetheless, as noted above, states have devised several mechanisms to compensate for these code deficiencies. And like state commissions (and in the tradition of federal parole guidelines), the U. S. Sentencing Commission used the mechanism of extra-statutory factors to provide for adequate offense differentiations.

While the U. S. Sentencing Commission adopted a mechanism to deal with the inadequate elemental base of the federal criminal code, the Commission did not adopt other mechanisms used by state commissions to address code deficiencies. The Commission, for example, did little to "smooth" the especially erratic sentencing maxima through guideline and departure policies or through recommended statutory revisions. And unlike state commissions, the Commission did not incorporate a "usual case" methodology which serves to incorporate *de facto* elements and which builds upon the judgment and experience of commissioners and trial and appellate courts. Rather, the Commission adopted a "minimal" or "base case" approach. A point value is given to the barest elements of the offense required to be shown for a conviction. Points are added for numerous aggravating factors and points are occasionally subtracted for various mitigating factors. This approach is more mechanical and less conceptual than the usual case approach used by state commissions. It also enhances the power of the prosecutor in sentencing. The prosecutor may or may not bring forth evidence to show the presence of aggravating factors and thereby effect the guideline sentence. The usual case approach, with its incorporation of *de facto* elements and its experiential base, enhances the judge's sentencing power.

It might be argued that the application of the usual case concept would be peculiarly difficult in the federal context. Federal prosecutors operate in 95 geographic areas with nearly as many unique cultures. The "usual" cocaine case in Miami may involve 25 kilos, while the "usual" cocaine case on an Indian reservation in South Dakota may involve less than an ounce. However, such an argument, while applicable to certain types of crimes, is generally overbroad. There are typical bank robberies, typical perjuries, typical false statements, typical tax evasions, typical immigration cases, and even typical drug importation cases. As state commissions have done, offense typicality can be enhanced with the addition of significant non-statutory offense differentiations. Indeed, a significant bulk of federal sentences involve crimes where defining the typical is entirely possible.

The makeup of the Commission might also have contributed to the departure from the tradition of usual case methodology. The Commission differs from state commissions in that most of its members have very limited experience with sentencing. One served as a federal prosecutor many years ago. Another was briefly a federal trial judge, while one served for a short time as a regional federal parole officer. The others have no significant background in the federal criminal justice system. This group lacks the experiential base to define the usual case. State commissions consist almost exclusively of those with extensive experience with their states' criminal justice systems. State commissions have had little difficulty reaching consensus around usual case content.

Whatever the reason, the Commission chose to adopt a very rudimentary, quasi-elemental offense methodology instead of building on the increasingly sophisticated usual case methodology used by state commissions. The Commission's approach might grow in sophistication with additional thought and experience, in the same way as the usual case approach became more sophisticated in the states. Ancillary revisions necessary in the federal criminal justice system with the retention of an elemental approach include the development of independent fact-finders to enhance judicial sentencing independence and addressing the proliferation of erratic sentencing maxima.

However, the enhanced power accruing to prosecutors under the current approach, absent any revision of the erratic penalty statutes and absent independent fact-finders, cannot be justified. Prior to the implementation of the U. S. Sentencing Guidelines, it would have been fair to ask if the code structure did not already give too much power to federal prosecutors. After the sentencing guidelines went into effect, the answer seemed self-evident, as will be seen in the following section.

THE ROLE OF THE PROSECUTOR IN SENTENCING REFORM

Any structured sentencing effort that eliminates the releasing authority of the parole board and transfers that discretion to the front of the sentencing system will undoubtedly enhance the power of prosecutors and judges. A structured sentencing system that becomes more "lawful" relies more heavily on findings based on evidence, and that can further enhance the power of prosecutors in sentencing. The challenge for sentencing commissions with respect to substantive criminal law is how best to compensate for inadequacies in current criminal codes; the challenge for commissions with respect to the distribution of discretion is how to appropriately limit prosecutorial power in structured sentencing systems and to balance prosecutorial power with appropriate judicial sentencing authority. Judges are uniquely placed to consider all policy-relevant factors in their sentencing decisions. Many areas of judicial decisions are subject to appellate review, and sentence review is not different in kind or nature than many other areas of review. The long tradition of record-keeping and appellate review make judicial decisions accountable in a way that prosecutorial decisions are not.

The position of federal prosecutors is quite different from that of state prosecutors. The abundance of common law crime in the states and the limited resources of police and state prosecutors requires the exercise of considerable discretion in selecting cases for prosecution. However, the discretion prosecutors exercise in case selection is channeled and directed to a significant extent by their political constituents. State prosecutors are responsive to the perceptions of the people who live in their jurisdiction. This channels and limits their discretion significantly. They cannot generally decline prosecution of cases involving clear violations of the law. If the citizens in their communities are concerned about gambling or pornography, prosecutors will prosecute such alleged offenses. Otherwise, they may not be inclined to do so. State prosecutors have more latitude in processing cases (e.g., charging and negotiating), once cases are selected for prosecution. Discretion in processing cases is particularly significant under "unrevised" codes. But priorities for selecting cases for prosecution in states are fairly well established by the community.

Federal prosecutors operate under a different set of constraints. In some instances they may be the only possible source of prosecution for offenses alleged. But these instances are very limited. Immigration cases (which are found in only a few of the 95 federal districts) are a good example. In this class of cases, prosecutorial discretion is not overbroad. Generally they must prosecute or institute civil actions such as deportation proceedings. In another relatively small category of cases, largely civil rights violations and political corruption, federal prosecutors are under a strong obligation to act because local officials cannot or are unwilling to do so.

In all other matters, federal prosecutors operate in a totally discretionary manner. While this view may appear extreme to some critics, there is virtually no crime, including convenience store stickups or juvenile purse-snatchings which, because of their respective effects on interstate commerce, do not have some federal criminal statute covering them. Yet, little policy exists to guide the selection of cases and there is very little effective centralized control (Beck, 1978). Without such control, the exercise of discretion becomes a prerogative of each of the 95 U. S. Attorneys. These officials are not subject to electoral review and are only very rarely removed because of dissatisfaction with their performance.

Even investigators may be said to have less discretion than prosecutors in the federal system or to have their discretion effectively controlled by the prosecutors. Since federal investigators (from the FBI, DEA, INS, U.S. Marshal's Service, BATF, U.S. Postal Service, and Customs, to mention only a few of the major agencies) could theoretically investigate almost any crime in the United States, they have policies which determine where their resources will be expended. A major determinate of these policies has been the willingness of prosecutors to prosecute. If the Department of Justice will not prosecute, the agency will exercise its discretion not to investigate. Local police departments obviously do not have this luxury.

In addition to the extremely broad discretion in choosing whether to proceed in any given case, the environment of a confounding criminal code offers prosecutors a wide range of charges from which to choose, with various sentencing maxima, for many types of criminal conduct. Thus, prosecutors often have discretion to choose among multiple statutory "base" offenses under the guidelines. The Commission's decision to incorporate additional offense differentiations in an additive approach rather than a usual case approach exacerabates an already severe problem of prosecutorial discretion. Aggravating factors must be proved by prosecutors. The decision to present such factors or withhold them is discretionary with prosecutors. Thus, by selecting a charge, often from among a range of possible charges, the prosecutor determines what the base value will be. It is then also the prosecutor's decision as to which aggravating factors can or will be presented to the court for consideration.

In short, the prosecutor controls not only the statutory maximum available, but also the base offense value and all aggravating circumstances. The prosecutor's decisions lead directly to a single guideline which, if imprisonment is involved, is statutorily limited to a range of time whose maximum may not be more than 25 percent greater than its minimum (28 U.S.C. Sec. 994(b), 1989). The judge's role is limited to selecting specific sentences from within certain ranges. If judges choose to depart from these guidelines and sentence offenders to terms above or below these maximum or minimum ranges, they, having exercised the most narrowly circumscribed discretion in the system, are subject to appellate oversight (18 U.S.C. Sec. 3742, 1989). The Commission handed the bulk of the discretion in sentencing to the prosecutors, an advocacy group with neither political accountability nor centralized control [see Endnote 6]. The imbalance in sentencing discretion between judges and prosecutors will be difficult to rectify under the guideline structure chosen by the Commission.

CORRECTIONAL RESPONSES

Another key difference between states and the federal government with respect to sentencing policy is the traditional fiscal freedom enjoyed by the federal government. Most states involved in guidelines development are very concerned about the impact of sentencing proposals on correctional resources (Strasser, 1989). The tradition is to look carefully at the correctional costs of sentencing proposals and to assess cost and policy trade-offs in the development of guidelines. Most state legislatures instruct their sentencing commissions to consider correctional costs in developing their guideline proposals and to recognize the scarcity of their correctional resources.

Two states, Florida and Pennsylvania, departed from that state guideline tradition. Florida's failure to assess adequately the impact of their sentencing guidelines on correctional resources and the failure to provide for sufficient additional correctional resources prevented the full implementation of sentencing guidelines. The Pennsylvania commission did not engage in the cost assessment trade-offs common to other state commissions. The Pennsylvania guidelines also differ from other state guidelines in the limited nature of sentencing reform. The parole board, which sets the actual sentence duration for most prison inmates, is not covered by the sentencing guidelines. The limited nature of the reform precludes the use of structured sentencing to coordinate sentencing and correctional resources.

Recent guidelines legislation in Tennessee and Oregon mandates the development of more comprehensive state-structured sentencing policies that address the use of sanctions such as local jails for sentenced offenders and the use of nonincarcerative sanctions such fines, probation, or other sentencing alternatives. Legislation also mandates correctional impact assessments of sentencing proposals on the full range of correctional sanctions. States developing sentencing guidelines are increasingly reluctant to mortgage their future with "time bomb" sentencing schemes (e.g., longer sentences), the costs of which are not realized for five, ten, or even fifteen years. And guidelines states are increasingly unwilling to pay the price for sentence mortgages that were incurred by prior legislatures.

Compared with state guidelines efforts, the Commission was profligate with respect to correctional resources. The Commission focused almost exclusively on prison as the punishment. Fines were essentially included as a discretionary add-on to primary prison sentences (U. S. Sentencing Commission, 1987d). A relatively small proportion of federal offenders are eligible for probation under the guidelines. Nonincarcerative sanctions are largely ignored. Apparently, the painstaking cost assessments of a wide range of policy options so critical to state guideline efforts did not occur at the federal level.

Despite the seeming unconcern with correctional costs during the development of the U. S. Sentencing Guidelines, the Commission adopted an innovative methodology to understate the guidelines' contribution to prison population projections [see endnote 7]. The Commission's gymnastics in understating the guidelines' impact suggests some recognition that the days of fiscal freedom at the federal level are limited.

Unlike guidelines states, the federal government's tradition has been to fund any and all correctional increases regardless of the source. If the federal government takes deficit reduction seriously, then that tradition might change. Certainly the Commission took a calculated risk on the willingness of a future Congress to pay the bill incurred by the 100th Congress. If a future Congress decides not to pay the bill, it could ask the Commission to revise the guidelines. However, Congress is more likely to take the easier route and reinstate discretionary, back-door release.

THE PROBLEM OF IMPLEMENTATION

Sentencing commissions represent something of a hybrid. Since sentencing authority has never been the exclusive province of any particular branch of government, commissions which seek to structure sentencing discretion have themselves generally been comprised of persons from more than one governmental branch. Under state constitutions as well as the U. S. Constitution, such a structure inherently raises questions about the separation of powers. Indeed, such questions appeared about the Commission in its embryonic stage and culminated in an onslaught of litigation once the guidelines had been promulgated and went into effect (*Mistretta v. United States*, 1989). States faced with the expectation of similar litigation resolved the matter by having their legislatures adopt guidelines into positive law. Congress did not take such action with regard to the federal guidelines despite being urged to do so in an article by a lawyer who ultimately litigated the matter before the U. S. Supreme Court (Morrison, 1987).

The litigation on the federal guidelines consumed 14 months. Eventually, the Supreme Court clearly and unambiguously affirmed the structure of the Commission and the validity of the guidelines on separation of powers grounds in the *Mistretta* decision. While less broad-based challenges are expected, it is reasonable to say that the overall validity of the Commission structure has been established.

However, a significant by-product of the litigation remains. Nearly 150 federal judges found the guidelines unconstitutional, and for the most part, they coupled their rulings and sentences with a general refusal to be bound by the guidelines even during the pendency of the appeals. Thus, for fourteen months the federal courts operated under two different sets of sentencing standards. While increased emphasis was placed on drug prosecutions, the Attorney General of the United States, the Deputy Attorney General, and the head of the Criminal Division of the U. S. Department of Justice were replaced. A new head of the FBI came into office and George Bush became President of the United States. This interregnum destroyed any possibility of an immediate and sound evaluation of the guidelines.

The offender population also changed during that time interval. The unbiased population of pre-guidelines sentences begins in 1985 and ends in 1986. Even some of those data are problematic because those still incarcerated at the time the guidelines took effect may be affected by the guidelines if the U. S. Parole Commission takes them into consideration in determining their release dates. An offender population against which this group must be compared does not begin until early 1989 nor end until early 1990. Therefore, at least three years, and as much as five years, separate the cases in the two groups. Comparisons between two groups so widely separated in time raises profound and unresolvable methodological problems.

The replacement of so many criminal justice policy makers during this same time period compounds the offender population problem. If prosecutors are plea bargaining more or less, is this the direct result of the guidelines or rather, a change in the attitude of Department of Justice officials? If more drug dealers are serving prison sentences, is that because the guidelines call for longer sentences and prosecutors find it more attractive to prosecute drug dealers, or because the new Attorney General calls for more drug dealer prosecutions and devotes more resources to proving the full extent of their crimes in sentencing hearings? These questions and hundreds of others cannot be answered, and therefore, no one can evaluate adequately the impact of the sentencing guidelines themselves [see endnote 8].

This is doubly unfortunate since the Commission operates on an annual budget of over $6 million per year and has scores of staff persons. This contrasts with state commissions which generally operate with annual budgets of $150,000–$300,000 and a only a fraction of Commission staff proportionately. The possibility of a first-class evaluation of the impact of sentencing guidelines was at least monetarily possible in the instance of the federal guidelines. That opportunity has vanished and can never be reclaimed.

The only comfort derived from this analysis is that the peculiar federal context of the guidelines limits the general utility of even a methodologically sound evaluation. Nonetheless, a sound evaluation of the impact of the guidelines might have been of assistance to the Congress in considering whether the billion-dollar prison construction program resulting from the guidelines will return good value in terms of general sentencing goals.

ENDNOTES

1. See, Order of the Supreme Court of the United States, December 26, 1944 (promulgating the Federal Rules of Criminal Procedure).
2. The U. S. federal context is similar to that found in Australia. There, too, state jurisdictions will likely lead in the implementation of structured sentencing reform. See *Sentencing Report of the Victorian Sentencing Committee*, Vols. I, II, and III, Melbourne, Victoria, April 1988.
3. See 18 U.S.C. Secs. 1951, 1952; 18 U.S.C. Secs. 1341, 1343; 18 U.S.C. Sec. 1961 et seq.
4. 49 U.S.C. Sec. 1472(i).
5. See draft of "Proposed Rules for the Implementation of Sentencing Guidelines Appendix C," Oregon Criminal Justice Council, Portland, Oregon, November 1988.
6. See the Memorandum of November 3, 1987, from Associate Attorney General Stephen S. Trott to all United States Attorneys, which discusses the issue of prosecutorial control over sentences.
7. The Commission attributed to Congress all sentence increases for drug offenses over pre-guideline practices. Congress "owned" all increases because they had adopted mandatory sentences for various drug offenses. However, that attribution to Congress was overbroad. The usual, logical methodology for attributing mandatory minimum costs in a guidelines environment is to assess the difference between the mandatory minimum sentence and the expected sentence absent the mandatory minimum sentence. If there is no difference, no costs are attributed to the mandatory minimum provision. The Commission assigned all of the mandatory value to Congress even when its guidelines exceeded that minimum. The implications of this method are either that, left to its own devices, the Commission would have sentenced drug dealers much less severely than Congress, or

that the Commission did not want to take responsibility for what it had done. Actually, the Commission's methodology got even sillier. It assigned the mandatory minimum level to drug cases not covered by the law and attributed those increases to Congressional action as well.

8. Even if there had been no time lapse and even if there had been no change in policy makers, evaluation of the guidelines might still be very difficult. Departures are allowed almost at will with little or no guiding standard so a large group of cases will be sentenced in an effectively standardless way. In addition, Congress has shown itself to be either unaware of the guidelines or unwilling to accept them as a fact of life. Since the implementation of the guidelines it has enacted a number of mandatory minimum sentences, effectively overruling the guidelines, and, in one instance, has actually written a guideline with instructions to the Commission to adopt it. See e.g., Public Law 100–690, Sec. 6454.

Part II

Law Enforcement

2

The U. S. Sentencing Guidelines and Police Officer Discretion

W. Clinton Terry III

INTRODUCTION

If the criminal justice system is viewed as a system having a beginning and an end, it may be argued that discretion is more prevalent at the ends of the system rather than in the middle of it (Kadish, 1962). At the front end of the system, police officers are dispatched to answer calls daily, and they must constantly make decisions about how such calls will be handled. Many of these calls are service calls. While such calls do not involve the application of criminal laws, they nevertheless require some action from responding officers. Calls and events involving crime require decisions and actions, the most serious of which is effecting arrests of suspects. As with calls for service, making arrests requires the exercise of judgment.

At the back end of the system, particularly at the post-adjudication stage, is the sentencing process [see Endnote 1]. Judicial discretion at this stage of the criminal justice process involves determining whether those found guilty of offenses, either through confession, plea bargaining, or a jury trial, will be sentenced to prison or placed on probation. In making these decisions, judges consider the seriousness of the conviction offense, the offender's prior record, recommendations from probation officers contained in presentence investigative reports, and the overall impact that incarceration may have on the offender's family and other dependents. With the passage of state and federal sentencing guidelines (designed, in part, to reduce or eliminate sentencing disparities and judicial discretion), judges also assess the requirements and applications of these guidelines for particular offenders. Although the discretionary powers of police and judges are located at different ends of the criminal justice system, each shares several similarities. These commonalities are the focus of this chapter.

Sentencing Guidelines

One of the earliest efforts to develop sentencing guidelines was conducted in 1972 by the U. S. Parole Commission. In order to increase the level of predictability of parole decisions, **empirical guidelines** were devised. These were based, in part, on previous parole decision-making patterns. These measures gradually evolved into a matrix that contained "scales of offense severity and 'parole prognosis' (the probability of recidivism) on one axis, and on the other a range of prison terms from which the prisoner's release date could be chosen" (Block and Rhodes, 1987:5).

In 1974, the Vermont District Courts and the District Court in Denver, together with Chicago, Phoenix, and Newark, experimented with **voluntary sentencing guidelines** [see Endnote 2]. In November 1976, Denver judges adopted voluntary sentencing guidelines on a more or less permanent basis. In 1979, Maryland and Florida explored the feasibility of their voluntary guidelines only to discover that their sentencing guidelines did not have much impact upon sentencing outcomes. In 1980, Minnesota put forth the first **sentencing commission** model based upon its own sentencing priorities. This represented a departure from previous empirical approaches based upon past practices and was based on the principle of retribution (Block and Rhodes, 1987:5; Knapp, 1984; Levin, 1984; Griswold, 1985, 1987).

The development of federal sentencing guidelines was long in the making (Forst and Rhodes, 1982; Lowe, 1987). As Eskridge (1986:71) comments: "Senate Bill 1437, which included a sentencing guidelines provision, first passed the Senate in 1978, but died in the House. The bill was reintroduced as S.1722 in 1979, but the Senate adjourned without voting on it. The bill was reintroduced in 1981 as S.1555 and in 1982 as S.2572, but the measure failed each time. Finally, in October 1984, sentencing guidelines were mandated at the Federal level. The notion was included as a provision of the Comprehensive Crime Control Act of 1984."

As the result of this legislation, a United States Sentencing Commission was formed. The legislation also included the abolition of parole by 1992, and limited the amount of time prisoners could have taken off their sentences for good behavior. The Commission guidelines, as subsequently developed, prescribed sentences for different crime categories and for different categories of offenders. The nature of the crime, the public concern about the category of crime in question, the deterrent effect sentencing guidelines might create, and the defendant's criminal history were considered (U. S. Sentencing Commission, 1987).

The Commission's guidelines went into effect November 1, 1987. By late 1988, 244 federal district judges had ruled on their constitutionality. In 140 of those cases, judges declared the guidelines unconstitutional. In the remaining 104 cases, federal judges found the guidelines to be constitutional [see Endnote 3] (ABA Journal, 1987, 1988; Silets, 1986; Robinson, 1986; Miethe and Moore, 1988).

Police Discretion

Unlike efforts to limit judicial sentencing disparities and discretion vis-á-vis the passage of state and federal sentencing guidelines, there has been little organized effort to limit police discretion. However, there has been considerable public debate on the disparities surrounding certain police practices, including the use of deadly force.

Prior Studies. Numerous studies have examined police discretion. Among the first researchers to acknowledge the different processes and variables involved in deciding when to make arrests was LaFave (1965:75–82). Of particular importance was offense seriousness; police are more likely to make arrests when offenses involve felonies rather than misdemeanors (Piliavin and Briar, 1964; Black, 1970, 1971, 1980; Lundman et al., 1978; Smith and Visher, 1981; Sykes et al., 1976). Not only does offense seriousness highlight the importance of police discretion, it also indicates the constraining influence of the law upon police behavior generally (Sherman, 1985; Sykes et al., 1976). The stronger the evidence, the greater the likelihood of arrest (Black, 1971; Lundman et al., 1978).

Goldstein (1969) has observed that line officers exercise a considerable amount of discretion because most of their calls cannot be directly supervised by others, and because much of their work involves low visibility from the general public. Responding to calls such as disputes between neighbors, loud parties, and lost animals, police exercise virtually unlimited discretion, since these are the types of calls that are least likely to come to the attention of others. While the very organization of police work provides many opportunities for discretion, departmental policy and structure also influence police decision-making (Wilson, 1968; Sykes et al., 1976).

Among the factors affecting police discretion, significant attention has been given to the relationship between complainants and suspects (Black, 1971). It has been noted that arrest practices disclose the preferences of citizen complaints (Black, 1971; Lundman et al., 1978).

Particularly, the greater the relational distance between complainants and suspects, the greater the likelihood of arrests; events involving strangers are more likely to lead to arrests compared to events involving those related by blood or by bonds of close friendship (Black, 1980; Pepinsky, 1976a; Sherman, 1985). Black (1971) says that police do not discriminate on the basis of race. Other researchers suggest that police sometimes treat lower-class persons and blacks differently compared with upper-class persons and whites (Piliavin and Briar, 1964; Goldstein, 1977:102; Pepinsky, 1976a; Sherman, 1985; Smith and Visher, 1981).

Since the mid-1960s, it has become increasingly apparent that citizen respect toward the police is strongly related to police officers making arrests or writing reports. For example, Piliavin and Briar (1964) found that cooperative juveniles tend to be released, while uncooperative juveniles tend to be arrested. These researchers also found that only 13 percent of those juveniles passing informal "attitude tests" were arrested compared with 90 percent of those juveniles who flunked such "tests." They also determined that prior record, style of dress, and group membership influenced police decisions to arrest.

In similar studies, Black (1971) found that disrespectful suspects were more likely to be arrested than respectful suspects. In examining minor misdemeanants, Sykes et al. (1976) found that one out of ten polite offenders were arrested compared with 41 percent of those offenders who exhibited less than average politeness. Interestingly, Black and Reiss (1970) found that overly polite suspects were as likely to be arrested as antagonistic youths. Other researchers support these findings as well (Lundman et al., 1978).

In an examination of the relation between adult crime victims and police report writing, Black (1970) found that polite victims had reports written more frequently compared with impolite victims. As with studies correlating juvenile demeanor and police arrests, Black also found that 96 percent of the citizenry exhibited politeness when interacting with police.

Discretion as Effective Use of Power. What then is police discretion? According to Davis (1969:4), ". . . a public officer has discretion whenever the effective limits on his power leave him free to make a choice among possible courses of action or inaction . . . . Especially important is the proposition that discretion is not limited to what is authorized or what is legal but what is within the effective limits of the officer's power' . . . . An officer who decides what to do or not to do often (1) finds facts, (2) applies law, and (3) decides what is desirable in the circumstances after the facts and law are known. The third of these three functions is customarily called 'the exercise of discretion'. . . . " [see Endnote 4].

Davis's definition of discretion as the effective use of power appears to be a rather open-ended treatment of police decision-making. There are numerous actions that are covered within the rubric of the effective use of power, including legal and illegal actions. Although Davis is a lawyer, his definition seems to treat the law as only one variable, albeit an important one, among other variables influencing police decision-making. After all, when all of the facts are known, it may be found that no criminal law is applicable; nevertheless, police officers must consider the law in deciding what to do.

Discretion as a Variable. Pepinsky (1978:28) argues that Davis's view of discretion defines "legitimate discretion as the power of officials to choose among courses of action or inaction consistent with the terms of the law" [see Endnote 5]. While Pepinsky's statement may be a fair representation of the general legal reasoning on the issue of police discretion, it is unclear whether Davis wishes to restrict the discussion of police discretion to "terms of the law." Nonetheless, Pepinsky's statement allows him to discuss police discretion as a variable.

In an effort to operationalize the concept of discretion, Pepinsky (1978:29) defines "legitimate discretion" as "variation among official applications of the law, consistent with the law's terms, that an observer cannot explain or predict." Unlike Davis's definition, this definition confines the notion of police discretion to the law. From this perspective, the empirical question is less whether police officers exercise discretion in such matters as making arrests and/or writing reports as it is the degree to which they make discretionary decisions. In writing police reports, for instance, Pepinsky (1976b) has found that officers invariably report particular offenses when police dispatchers have mentioned those particular offenses while sending the officers out.

Discretion as a Constant. Virtually every area of police behavior and performance has received some form of empirical attention. Although the following list is certainly not exhaustive, studies of police discretion have included areas such as domestic and violent disputes (Berke and Loseke, 1981; Smith, 1985; Smith and Visher, 1987), child abuse (Tobias et al., 1980; Willis and Wells, 1988), traffic offenses (Gardiner, 1969; Lundman, 1979), patrol work (Reiss, 1971; Rubinstein, 1973), skid row (Bittner, 1967), juveniles (Piliavin and Briar, 1964; Black and Reiss, 1970; Lundman et al., 1978), and report writing (Pepinsky, 1976b). As a consequence, there is a great deal known about the variability of police conduct. Pepinsky is right to conclude that police behavior, as with other forms of behavior, is variable. However, whether it is germane to consider police discretion as a variable is another question.

If discretion is treated as a subset of behavior (i.e., action), then it may be fruitful to consider it as a variable. However, if discretion is viewed as decision making (i.e., as a process), then it is perhaps better to view it as a constant rather than as a variable. The question here is not whether one decides to engage in particular actions, but rather, whether one has the choice to decide. Is the act of decision-making itself a fundamental aspect of every social action? The answer to this question is yes.

One way to address these questions is to examine briefly the nature of rules, an example of which is law. Although people often believe that many laws are precise and clear, the fact is that they are not always precise and clear. This distinction between clear and vague laws, a distinction frequently noted in the literature, is misleading. It is misleading because it implies that it is possible to write clear and precise laws. From an interpretive perspective, no law or any other written or oral rule is literally specific. One never knows what the laws mean until they are placed within specific contexts, because it is these contexts that give specific laws their meaning, a meaning which, parenthetically, is always subject to change, depending upon the circumstances within which they are placed. Obviously, one of the simplest illustrations of this principle is disturbing-the-peace laws.

Police officers may respond to two loud party calls, one in a suburban neighborhood and one in the student ghetto near a major university. In the suburban neighborhood, the music being played may be heard from only nearby homes. The responding officers may ask that the party-givers turn their music down. At the other party, students are playing the William Tell Overture at maximum volume and hollering "High Ho Silver." Their music and noise may be heard from a distance of several blocks. Reminding themselves that these students are merely having a good time, the responding officers decide to check on the party in a half hour, at which time they will do something if things have not quieted down a bit. What disturbing the peace means depends upon the situation within which it is placed (i.e., interpreted).

Klockars (1985:96–98) presents a comparable illustration dealing with speeding laws. Whereas disturbing-the-peace laws are intentionally nonspecific, posted speed limits appear to be unquestionably clear-cut. If the speed limit is exceeded, by definition, the driver is speeding. When drivers are stopped for speeding, however, they might say, "I am a volunteer ambulance driver responding to a call." Or they might explain, "My wife just called and told me to rush home. She is starting to have a baby." Or they might argue, "I am on my way to the hospital. There has been an accident. My child was badly hurt."

All of these statements might be found acceptable to police officers making the traffic stops; but they may also be found unacceptable.

Klockars couches his discussion of speeding laws in terms of laws overreaching their intended objectives. This is an interesting and novel way of saying that a 35-mile-per-hour speed limit was never intended to preclude "speeding" by volunteer ambulance drivers, husbands rushing home to wives who have begun labor, or fathers rushing to hospitals when their children have been injured. To avoid trivializing this illustration, Klockars (1985:98) is careful to indicate that "every law has the property of overreach."

One lesson that may be drawn from Klockar's discussion of laws overreaching their intended objectives is that laws, even those laws that appear crystal clear, are subject to diverse interpretations. There is nothing mechanical about the application of the law to concrete situations. It is through such applications of individual laws within the context of their specific usages that laws take on a congeries of meanings. Such meanings, however, tend to be rather open-ended. As situations change, the complex of heretofore meanings given to particular laws are reexamined in the light of new circumstances in order to determine the appropriate interpretation of the law within the context of a then-and-now situation. What a 35-mile-per-hour speed law means, therefore, is that drivers should not exceed 35 miles per hour, except under a set of circumstances that has not as yet been fully articulated.

Abandoning Police Discretion. The current debate over police discretion has had two principal consequences: (1) it has impeded police self-assessment, change, reform, and police-community relations, and (2) it has contributed to the misunderstanding of police discretion as a process rather than as an action.

Much of the debate surrounding police discretion has focused upon the myth of full law enforcement. Remarking about the Chicago Police Department, for example, Davis (1975:iii) says that "the central fact is that the police falsely pretend to enforce all criminal laws; the reason for the pretense is that they believe the law requires them to enforce all criminal law but they are unable to. The false pretense is pervasive and has many consequences. Written instructions from top officers (general orders, special orders, and training bulletins) provide for full enforcement, with slight exceptions. But all officers readily acknowledge that some law is never enforced and that some is only sometimes enforced."

The consequence of the police attempt to maintain the myth of full enforcement is the inability to openly examine police practices and behaviors for fear that the myth of full enforcement would be exposed. As such, the process of police self-study, change, and reform is often nipped in the bud. Moreover, police departments committed to the notion of full enforcement can never really reveal to the communities they serve the actual promises and shortcomings of policing those communities. It would be very difficult for these departments to argue for open selective enforcement, which has been a goal advocated by such scholars as Davis (1969, 1975) and Goldstein (1977) for years. Illustrative of these difficulties is the following comment from Davis (1975:iii–iv): "The false pretense (of full law enforcement) prevents open selective enforcement, prevents top officers from making and announcing enforcement policy, prevents special studies of enforcement policy, prevents the use of professional staffs for making enforcement policy, prevents enlistment of public participation in policymaking, and discourages efforts of the police to coordinate their enforcement policy with the policy of prosecutors and judges."

In addition to impeding the professional development of police work, the current discussion over police discretion accentuates certain misconceptions about the process of discretion itself. It is believed, for instance, that discretionary practices among police officers could and should be eliminated [see Endnote 6]. This follows naturally enough from the premise of full enforcement which would prohibit the exercise of any (discretionary) actions that are contrary to full enforcement of the law.

One avenue to its elimination (or at least to its mitigation) is the refinement of existing rules in order to make them more precise. Another way is to write additional rules to cover contingencies apparently not contemplated or covered by original rules. Both of these approaches misconceive the nature of discretion itself. Rather than aiding the situation, they exacerabate it. The addition of more rules or the refinement of earlier regulations creates more rules that must be interpreted during the course of their implementation, hence increasing the level and complexity of decision-making rather than simplifying and making it easier. Moreover, it misconceives the very nature of discretion itself. Discretion is not a product that can be refined or fine-tuned, nor can it be eliminated as easily as certain actions or behaviors. In fact, discretion is not a behavior per se; rather, it is an ever-present process, a constant, underlying actions and behaviors.

As a constant, police discretion is devoid of any analytical power; consequently, it may be abandoned. Inasmuch as this may impact the world of policing, it may open up the traditionally closed police world, to some greater extent at least, to a closer scrutiny of police organizational practices and behaviors by both police and nonpolice. Obviously, most organizations are somewhat nervous whenever they are subjected to close study or inquiry. Nevertheless, with the notion of discretion firmly benched on the sidelines, police departments need not fear the accusation that they fail to provide full enforcement of the law, poor management, or are in other ways involved in wrongdoing because of their failure to provide full enforcement.

SENTENCING GUIDELINES AND POLICE DISCRETION

Judicial and police behavior, especially prior to the passage of sentencing guidelines, exhibit considerable degrees of variability. In the case of police work, much of this behavior occurs in the low visibility world of police encounters with citizens and suspects outside the framework of the criminal justice system. For judges, however, their actions often become a part of the public record. Nevertheless, variability in their actions is still in evidence [see Endnote 7].

It is doubtful whether sentencing guidelines have any significant impact upon police behavior. Given the current state of disagreement over the constitutionality of these guidelines, especially at the federal level, they would seem to have had little effect upon federal law enforcement officers. Moreover, sentencing processes in general are too far removed organizationally from the everyday work of police officers to have much effect.

If the argument were put forward that sentencing guidelines strengthen the role of prosecutors within the criminal justice system, and if it were argued, in addition, that such increase in prosecutorial activity also increases the influence of police with whom prosecutors work, it would still seem unlikely that sentencing guidelines would have much impact upon the work of police officers. One of the primary reasons for this is that police departments depend upon information for the performance of their duties. Most of this information comes from citizens, largely through the use of the telephone. Only a very small fraction of information comes into police departments through selected informants, popular beliefs to the contrary. It is this information around which departmental policies are shaped, including of course, the situations within which it is put into effect, that shapes the nature of police behavior.

CONCLUSION

Despite their divergent locations and interests in the criminal justice system, there are some commonalities between judicial and police behavior and decision-making worthy of note. Both judges and police officers are forced to act upon information provided them. They decide which actions to implement based upon this information, and upon prior experience in similar or related matters. Furthermore, they share accusations of exercising unwarranted disretion whereby sentencing disparities and inequities are incurred by offenders. Both are subject to efforts to limit the degree of these disparities and alleged inequities. Attempts to curb judicial decision-making have taken the form of sentencing guidelines. Attempts to curb police discretion often take the form of clarifying or creating new rules governing their behavior. Neither of these efforts is likely to offer much success, inasmuch as they misinterpret the nature of discretion.

There is no choice about discretion. It is an ever-present or constant feature of human interaction. To argue that sentencing or policy discretion should be abolished is to misunderstand these fundamentally different interpretive processes. To argue that sentencing disparities for identical crimes should be reduced or eliminated or that police responses to identical calls for assistance should receive identical or at least similar responses, including the use of deadly force in these situations, is not to argue for the elimination of discretion. Rather, it is more an argument of bringing greater uniformity into official behavior based as much upon a value orientation driven by a sense of justice and/or fair play as it is upon a sense of indignation that officials are engaged in some form of wrongdoing.

ENDNOTES

1. Probation, parole, and corrections also lie past the adjudicatory stage of the criminal justice system, thus according to this analysis, they, too, are subject to high levels of discretionary decision-making. Because the focus of this paper is upon police and sentencing discretion, discussion of discretionary decision-making among probation, parole, and corrections is omitted.
2. Vermont eventually dropped out.
3. *Corrections Digest*, September 7, 1988:4.
4. Similar definitions and discussion of police discretion may be found in Wilson (1968:7–10) and Goldstein (1977:93).
5. Pepinsky recognizes that the use of police discretionary powers involves illegal activities as well, as does Davis (1968).
6. Ironically, Davis (1975:iii), who has otherwise written perceptively about the nature of police discretion, writes at the beginning of his introduction to the study of discretion among Chicago police officers: "This is a study of police discretion in selective enforcement. The purpose is to try to find or invent better ways to control police discretion in determining whether and when to enforce a particular law."

7. That certain aspects of judicial and police behavior appear beyond the pale of legal processes is not suggested by the law, as internalized by judges and police officers. Furthermore, it fails to play a role in these gray areas of the criminal justice system. Certainly judicial and police behavior are affected by both legal and extra-legal considerations.

3

Potential Deterrent Effects of the Guidelines

Steven P. Lab

INTRODUCTION

Throughout the enabling legislation and the related sections of the U. S. Code pertaining to the establishment of the sentencing guidelines, a variety of goals is espoused. Among these diverse goals is the provision for sentences which reflect the immediate offense, the rehabilitation of the offender, the future protection of society, and deterrence. Each of these goals is admirable and desirable. Unfortunately, there is considerable conflict implicit in these goals, and the extent to which each is provided for in the guidelines varies greatly.

This chapter explores the potential of the U. S. Sentencing Guidelines for providing crime control through deterrence. Crime control through incapacitation will be examined in Chapters 7 and 12. The present discussion is as follows: First, the conflicting nature of the guidelines will be examined. Second, the deterrence doctrine will be discussed. Finally, the guidelines will be compared to various issues in deterrence in an attempt to predict the deterrent potential of the guidelines for crime control.

COMPETING GOALS OF THE GUIDELINES

The disparate goals in the new U. S. Sentencing Guidelines appear throughout its related documents. The U. S. Sentencing Commission expressly notes that "the Comprehensive Crime Control Act of 1984 foresees guidelines that will further the basic purposes of criminal punishment, i.e., deterring crime, incapacitating the offender, providing just punishment, and rehabilitating the offender" (U. S. Sentencing Commission, 1987:1.1). Beyond this, the Commission notes that the basic objective of Congress "was to enhance the ability of the criminal justice system tò reduce crime through an effective, fair sentencing system" (U. S. Sentencing Commission, 1987:1.2). Implicit in these statements is the call for both crime control, particularly in the form of deterrence and incapacitation, and for "just deserts" in sentencing.

The primary assumption made by the enabling legislation and the U. S. Sentencing Commission's guidelines is that both crime control and "just deserts" may be achieved simultaneously. Unfortunately, these goals may be incompatible. Von Hirsch (1987a) notes that different factors must be considered when working toward different goals. For example, factors relevant in crime control may include prior work record, family relationships, age, and other social characteristics. The Salient Factor Score System, used by the U. S. Parole Commission to predict possible future criminal activity, includes many of these types of factors because of their relationship to recidivism and success on parole [see Chapter 12] (Gottfredson et al., 1975). A "just deserts" approach, however, seeks to punish all convicted offenders in direct relation to the seriousness of the offense or harm done. Demographic and social characteristics of offenders have no demonstrable bearing on the amount of harm inflicted or the criminal statute which has been violated. Consequently, the only relevant information for the "just deserts" rationale is offense-related information.

While the basic ideas of crime control and "just deserts" may be incompatible, there may be a means whereby both sets of relevant factors may be considered simultaneously. Such an approach would be multidimensional in nature, and it would necessarily outline a wide variety of alternate scenarios. What would evolve would be a sentencing system whereby all convicted offenders who committed the same type of offense and who shared certain demographic and social characteristics would be sentenced in an identical fashion. The guidelines would need to consider both the legal and individual factors at the same time. Von Hirsch (1987a) does not regard the goals of "just deserts" and deterrence as completely dissonant. However, he suggests that one rationale should have priority over the other and provide the basic driving force in sentencing.

Even a cursory reading of the U. S. Sentencing Guidelines shows which rationale is dominant. While the Commission has paid lip service to the goals of deterrence and incapacitation, their primary aim is the promulgation of sentences that sanction offenders according to the offense, the harm they have inflicted upon victims, and their criminal history. In essence, the focus is almost exclusively on "just deserts." There is no explicit consideration given to other social or demographic factors which have a proven or theoretical relationship to deterrence, incapacitation, or recidivism. Therefore, to what extent will these guidelines deter present or future offenders? Before we can answer this question, we must examine the deterrence doctrine.

DETERRENCE

The deterrence philosophy is a major source of support used by those individuals espousing policies for "getting tough" on offenders. Their argument is that stronger penalties will cause potential offenders to refrain from crime. Andenaes (1975), a leading authority on deterrence, defines deterrence as **influencing by fear**. The fear is of apprehension and punishment. According to Andenaes, the level of offending will decrease as the potential for punishment increases. It is important to note that potential offenders do not have to actually receive punishment to be deterred. Rather, the potential or threat of punishment may bring about the desired outcome.

The potential of deterrence may vary because of differences in the type of deterrence desired as well as the degree to which various factors are satisfied. Two types of deterrence will be considered here: specific and general deterrence. **Specific deterrence refers to punishments which keep offenders from recidivating.** The emphasis is upon sole offenders. Punishment of any one offender is not expected to have an impact on anyone other than that offender. The second type of deterrence is general deterrence. Unlike specific deterrence, **general deterrence aims to have an impact on individuals not related to the offense or offender.** In essence, the punishment of one offender should serve as an example and prompt other prospective offenders to refrain from offending.

Three requirements must be met for either type of deterrence to be successful. First, the punishment must be of such a magnitude that offenders (or potential offenders) see little benefit in the activity. This idea of severity assumes that potential offenders will not act in ways which bring enough punishment or pain to offset the pleasure related to their behavior. The second feature of deterrence is certainty of punishment. An absence of certainty would mean that potential offenders could act with impunity. Severity of a sentence has little value if the odds of ever being caught and punished are low. Celerity or swiftness is the final requirement for deterrence. The assumption is that any punishment must be applied in a reasonably proximate time to the offense if offenders are expected to equate the punishment with the action. The more remote the punishment from the act, the less chance that potential offenders will equate the two actions. It is assumed that the existence of these three factors will bring about deterrence.

Despite interest in deterrence and an extensive body of literature on the subject, there is little demonstrable evidence of a deterrent effect resulting from the actions of the criminal justice system. This is true in studies investigating both specific and general deterrence. Specific deterrence has received comparatively little attention in the literature and generally investigates the influence of imprisonment on subsequent offending. These studies provide little support for specific deterrence. Various investigations note that over 50 percent of all released prisoners will be reincarcerated for new crimes (Gibbs, 1975; Witte, 1980).

Similar analyses of the length of confinement in prison and success on parole also show little relation between the punishment and subsequent recidivistic behavior (Babst, Koval, and Neithercutt, 1972; Berecochea and Jaman, 1981; Gottfredson, Gottfredson, and Garofalo, 1977). Indeed, one study reported that longer periods of confinement in prison (more punishment) are related to higher levels of post-incarcerative deviance (Beck and Hoffman, 1976). Other studies of specific deterrence using corporal punishment (Clarke, 1966), different penalties for traffic offenses (Shoham, 1974), and arrests in domestic disputes (Sherman and Berk, 1984) disclose similar results. While some of the studies make claims that specific deterrence is effected, serious methodological flaws (e.g., unrepresentativeness of samples and random assignment of conditions) make the conclusions of these investigations highly suspect.

Most research has focused upon the general deterrent influence of punishment, particularly the death penalty. One method of investigating deterrence is a cross-sectional approach where two jurisdictions with differing laws or procedures are compared with one another. Ehrlich (1977), a leading advocate of the deterrent effect of the death penalty, has claimed that each execution deters approximately 20 homicides. However, the adequacy of Ehrlich's argument has been severely criticized, particularly on methodological grounds (McGahey, 1980). Where simple investigation of the death penalty points to the severity of the sanction, other studies attempt to examine the influence of the certainty of apprehension and punishment (Forst, 1977; Geerken and Gove, 1977; Tittle and Rowe, 1974) or a combination of severity and certainty (Gibbs, 1968; Passell, 1975; Sampson, 1986; Tittle, 1969). However, most of the support is for certainty of apprehension and punishment and not the severity of the sanction.

Deterrence has also been examined through longitudinal research. These studies attempt to determine the effect of changes in the law or differences in application of the law over time within the same jurisdiction. Such an analysis eliminates any confounding differences which may appear in cross-sectional studies. As is the case with cross-sectional studies, most longitudinal investigations fail to find any significant effect of severity of punishment on subsequent reoffending (Decker and Kohfeld, 1984; McFarland, 1983; Passell and Taylor, 1977; Phillips, 1980). Conversely, deterrent effects do appear in longitudinal studies of changes in the certainty of apprehension and punishment (Phillips, Ray, and Votey, 1984; Ross, 1982). In sum, studies of deterrence tend to show that the severity of punishment has little, if any, impact on criminal behavior. However, certainty of apprehension and punishment does appear to have at least a minimal influence on the rate of offending. Research has generally ignored the issue of celerity.

The failure of studies to find any great deal of deterrent impact in the law or the application of legal sanctions may be due to problems in perception. There is an implicit assumption in most studies that potential offenders know about the law and the criminal justice system. Prospective offenders who are ignorant of the law, the punishments, and the imposition of those sanctions cannot be expected to refrain from offending simply because of the existence of laws. Most of the early deterrence research ignored this perceptual issue. However, recent studies have focused closely on offender perceptions and their relation to criminal behavior.

Interestingly, most studies of perception look primarily at perceived certainty of punishment. Two studies (Erickson, Gibbs, and Jensen, 1977; Jensen, Erickson, and Gibbs, 1978) have found that the perceived certainty of apprehension and punishment are negatively related to self-reported deviance. Hollinger and Clark (1983) and Pestello (1984) have examined certainty and severity at the same time. Both studies show that perceived certainty of apprehension leads to lower levels of deviance. Perceived severity also appears to inhibit deviant conduct.

One problem underlying most of these studies of perception is the lack of attention given to past experiences and their effects on perception and deterrence. Some researchers question whether the perception of risk (i.e., apprehension and punishment) deters crime or whether actual apprehension and punishment raises the perception of risk (Bishop, 1984a; Bishop, 1984b; Paternoster et al., 1982; Paternoster et al., 1985; Saltzman et al., 1982). Indeed, much of this research fails to show which comes first—the perception or the deviant conduct. The idea that experience may increase the perception of risk is called the "experiential effect." In analyses which simultaneously examine the deterrence and experiential effects, the latter effect seems to have the most influence on deterring prospective offenders.

But these studies do not show that perceived risk of apprehension and punishment (deterrence) exert no effects. Rather, deterrence is not as important as an offender's previous experience in terms of shaping behavior. For example, Bishop (1984b) found that while higher levels of perceived risk of apprehension resulted in reduced future behavior, past delinquent activity had a larger impact on perceptions of certainty of apprehension and punishment. Another study similarly reports that perceptions of certainty and severity are secondary to the impact of prior experiences on behavior and perceptions (Lanza-Kaduce, 1988).

An overall inspection of the deterrence literature provides only qualified support for the claim that legal sanctions, regardless of whether they are applied, have any impact on crime. The greatest support appears in evaluations of certainty of apprehension and punishment. Severity of punishments have less influence on deviant behavior. Perhaps one of the most important findings relates to perceptions and deterrence. Research suggests that perceptions are based more on past experiences rather than on present interpretations of the law and events. Therefore, deterrence has lower priority compared with experience in future behavioral forecasts. Lack of experience may mean less significance is attached to possible legal sanctions accompanying law violations and from the criminal justice system generally.

THE DETERRENT POTENTIAL OF THE GUIDELINES

The deterrent potential of the U. S. Sentencing Guidelines may be evaluated in the context of several assumptions. First, we may assume that the diverse goals of the enabling legislation and the Commission can be accommodated by a single set of guidelines. Second, it may be assumed that deterrence is a viable possibility. This means that past failures to generate deterrence and the inconclusive results of deterrence studies are more the result of failures to provide adequate severity, certainty, or celerity than the failure of the basic premises of deterrence. The unanswered questions are (1) to what extent have the guidelines included factors related to deterrence? and (2) to what extent have the guidelines altered the severity, certainty, and celerity of punishments? Answering these questions will provide us with an indication of how successful these guidelines may be at deterring future criminal conduct.

Meeting the Deterrent Goal

As we have seen, two primary goals or philosophies underlying the new guidelines are "just deserts" and deterrence. While both of these goals are laudable, each suggests different elements for enhancement which are somewhat incompatible (von Hirsch, 1987b). "Just deserts" prompts consideration of offense-related factors, while deterrence suggests offense and socio-demographic variables for inclusion. This does not preclude the possibility that the guidelines could conceivably include elements relevant for both goals. To what extent has the Commission attempted to include factors that are relevant for deterrence? The answer to this question is clear—the Commission has not allowed for such provisions.

Individual variables which have been shown in past research to be related to participation in criminal and deviant behavior as well as to recidivism have been excluded by the Commission from the guidelines. Chapter 5, Part H of the guidelines explicitly states that age, education and vocational skills, race, sex, socio-economic status, employment, and other demographic factors "are not relevant in the determination of a sentence" or are "not ordinarily relevant in determining whether a sentence should be outside the guidelines" (U. S. Sentencing Commission, 1987:5.29–5.31). This determination does not question the relevance of these factors as influential in determining sentences for deterrence. Indeed, it could be interpreted that the Commission violated its mandate by excluding these items.

The Commission's enabling legislation directed it to "consider whether the following matters, among others, with respect to a defendant, have any relevance to the nature, extent, place of service, or other incidents of an appropriate sentence, and shall take them into account only to the extent that they do have relevance" (29 U.S.C., Sec. 994(d), 1988). This is followed by a list of factors including the demographic variables listed above. The federal guidelines do not question the utility of these variables in determining appropriate penalties for convicted offenders. Rather, the Commission has justified the elimination of these items on the grounds that the guidelines would become overly specific and cumbersome if all relevant factors were considered. While this may be true, the choice of factors to include or exclude clearly is consistent with the "just deserts" philosophy. In its own words, "the Commission has developed these guidelines as a practical effort toward the achievement of a more honest, uniform, equitable, and therefore, effective sentencing system (U. S. Sentencing Commission, 1987:1.4).

Precisely what constitutes an "effective" sentencing system is unclear, but it would appear that the Commission intended "effective" to mean a system where similar criminal behaviors are punished similarly rather than one which functions as a deterrent to future criminal conduct. The Commission's neglect of these excluded factors cannot be overstated from the point of view of crime control. Such factors as employment history, family relationships, educational achievement, and age have been found closely related to success on probation and parole (Gottfredson et al., 1975; Greenwood, 1982). These factors are given some consideration only when federal judges consider departing from the sentencing guidelines. However, these departures are exceptions and require written justification from the judge.

It would appear that the Commission has adopted a single goal in their development of the sentencing guidelines. Granted, the "just deserts" goal is easier to address compared with the deterrence/crime control objective. This is true because there are considerably more combinations of individual and social factors which may be relevant for the latter rather than the former goal. Von Hirsch (1987b) and others have argued for the legitimacy and importance of both objectives, despite the fact that one goal will dominate all others. However, the Commission seems to have written guidelines where only one goal has been emphasized to the exclusion of all others.

Changes in Deterrent Factors

Recognizing that the guidelines have failed to consider theoretically important individual and social variables for deterrence, it is still possible that the guidelines may affect the severity, certainty of apprehension, and punishment. If this is the case, the deterrent capacity of law and the criminal justice system may still have been enhanced by the Commission. At this point, we will assume that the guidelines will be applied as written. Therefore, to what extent have these guidelines altered the severity, certainty, and celerity of punishment?

Severity of Sanctions

Even a cursory reading of the guidelines discloses that the severity of sanctions in the pre- and post-guidelines period has changed only imperceptibly. The Commission developed the guidelines using an empirical approach. This approach was presumably based on existing sentencing practices [see Chapter 4, for further commentary concerning the formulation of these guidelines]. The information used in this assessment came from "data drawn from 10,000 presentence investigations, crimes as distinguished in substantive criminal statutes, the United States Parole Commission's guidelines and resulting statistics, and data from other relevant sources, in order to determine which distinctions are important in present practice" (U. S. Sentencing Commission, 1987:1.4). Using this approach, the Commission sought to identify the most common or "average" sentence imposed by the courts. What this means is that the Commission made its initial determinations of sentencing ranges by considering previously established judicial sentencing practices. Although the Commission departed from the established practices in some instances, the new guidelines for the most part reflect previous sentencing ranges as penalties associated with most federal criminal statutes.

The Commission justified such an empirically based approach on the grounds that the result would reflect "established distinctions" in offenses and penalties which "the community believes, or has found over time, to be important from either a moral or crime control perspective" (U. S. Sentencing Commission, 1987:1.4). This argument presupposes that the beliefs of the community and the prior actions of the courts are sufficient to bring about deterrence and crime control. There is little question that the establishment of guidelines based on prior sentencing norms would promote some equality in future sentencing, provided that the guidelines are followed explicitly. There is no basis for the argument that crime control will be improved by these new guidelines beyond the previous level of crime control attained by earlier sentencing practices, however.

The methods used in developing the guidelines do little to increase the severity of punishments for most offense categories. The norms of past sentencing have now become mandated punishments. While some convicted offenders may now receive harsher sentences than they would have received in the pre-guidelines era, an equivalent number will also receive less severe sentences for the same offenses prior to the development of the guidelines. The average or typical is now the normative guideline. It is reasonable to conclude that the lack of any real change in severity of sanctions will be accompanied by little, if any, alteration in the deterrent impact of the law.

Certainty of Sanctions

Previous deterrence research suggests that certainty of apprehension and punishment is perhaps the most important element in deterrence. Accordingly, the impact of any sentencing changes will be intensified as the certainty of punishment increases. The issue of certainty and the guidelines must be considered in terms of specific and general deterrence. The new sentencing guidelines may have some impact on certainty of punishment for specific deterrence. However, they do little or nothing to increase the certainty of punishment for general deterrence.

Specific deterrence may be enhanced to the extent that the guidelines mandate greater certainty of punishment compared with previous practices. Those offenders who are apprehended may anticipate greater certainty of punishment, particularly some amount of incarceration, under the new guidelines, compared with a more varied array of outcomes under previous sentencing schemes. To the extent that past analyses of specific deterrence have shown little relation to actual punishment since there was greater uncertainty of punishment, the new guidelines have remedied this situation by increasing punishment certainty. This remedy may only reflect minor changes, however, and the specific deterrent influence of the new guidelines may remain largely unrealized.

Similarly, there is little reason to expect any general deterrent impact of the guidelines relating to changes in the certainty of punishment. In order to increase the certainty of punishment, there must also be an increase in the apprehension of offenders. Punishments cannot be meted out unless the offenders are brought to trial. The court has little or no power to apprehend offenders. Most offenders enter the courts through arrests by police and other law enforcement officers. Present weaknesses of these agencies to detect and apprehend criminals are unaddressed by the guidelines. The guidelines themselves cannot be faulted for this oversight, however. The Commission had no vehicle by which it could assess the practical problems of detection and apprehension or to suggest improvements in the ability of law enforcement agencies to increase their apprehension abilities. Such an endeavor would be beyond the scope of the Commission's express mandate. However, the issue of certainty is central to any viable attempt at deterrence. Without a corresponding change in apprehension, there should be little or no change in general deterrence. General deterrence assumes that unapprehended offenders would be deterred as the result of the increased level of apprehension of others. If the current level of crime can be attributed to the failure of present law enforcement practices to apprehend and make examples of offenders, then the new guidelines cannot be expected to improve the certainty of apprehension and punishment. In short, general deterrence will not be enhanced through Commission actions.

Celerity of Sanctions

Celerity is perhaps the easiest element of deterrence to consider. The due process rights outlined in the U. S. Constitution and in various court cases have established that there is little the system can do to eliminate the often lengthy delays in processing. The guidelines do nothing to improve the speed with which offenders are tried and sentenced. While plea bargaining is addressed later in this chapter and elsewhere throughout this book [see especially Chapter 6], the Commission has done little to limit such actions. Bargaining between the prosecution and defense may still appear. The apprehension and trial stages have been largely unaffected in terms of speed. Deterrence, therefore, has not been enhanced through any change in celerity.

The basic tenets of deterrence have received little support from the new federal sentencing guidelines. Severity of punishment, the single deterrent element which the guidelines could impact the most, has not been substantially altered. By the Commission's admission, most of the punishments are the result of establishing the average accepted federal sentencing practices as guidelines. Some of the sentences have been modified from previous practices, although these are rare and do not stand out. Certainty has received limited indirect attention to the extent that the mandated sentences are imposed on those offenders reaching the sentencing stage. On the other hand, certainty of apprehension, the basic concern for most offenders, is unattended to by the guidelines, as would be expected in view of the scope and mandate of the Commission. Celerity of punishment appears to have been unaltered by the guidelines as well.

Despite these deficiencies, is it possible that the changes appearing in the guidelines could have a deterrent impact? That is, could the alterations in sentencing severity, certainty (from a specific deterrence viewpoint), and the expected uniformity in sentences bring about a change in crime and deviance? In order to address these questions, it becomes necessary to consider the issues of public perceptions of punishments, the impact of plea bargaining, and related issues.

Public Perceptions of Deterrence

As noted previously, perceptions of severity and certainty may mitigate the impact of actual alterations in these factors. Assuming these factors have been altered to some degree by the guidelines, should we necessarily expect that they will have a deterrent effect? In general, the answer is no. The reason for this response rests on past research about public knowledge and perceptions about sanctions.

Although the Commission has altered the sentencing structure, there is little reason to believe that the offending public is aware of these changes. Past research has shown that the public has little knowledge about the law. For example, Zimring and Hawkins (1973) reported that 41 percent of the Nebraska respondents they surveyed believed that writing checks with insufficient funds was not illegal if they eventually made arrangements to pay their debts. Indeed, the public appears to be unaware of minimum and maximum penalties for most offenses. Similarly, it has been found that the public is ignorant about the possible punishments associated with the most common felonies (Social Psychiatry Research Associates, 1968).

Lack of knowledge about existing penalties should also be mirrored in the knowledge about changes in the law and the lack of deterrence. Simple alternations in the severity of punishment will probably have minimal influence on people's perceptions. The reasons for this are simple. The fact that the general public is uninformed about established penalties suggests that they would know even less about minor modifications in the sentencing structure, especially in the federal system. Assuming that many current offenders are not deterred by existing punishments, minor modifications (especially in terms of increased seriousness of sanctions) would probably exert little impact. For instance, if a current sentence of 10 years of incarceration does not deter prospective offenders, there is little basis for assuming that increased severity to 12 or 15 years' incarceration will function as more of a deterrent than 10 years. Without a corresponding increase in apprehension or perceptions of apprehension, perceptions of severity would remain relatively ineffective. Indeed, Williams and Hawkins (1986) question whether criminals are capable of making such fine distinctions about the possible incarcerative consequences of their actions which deterrence arguments would require.

The perceptual issue surfaces in another problem related to the jurisdiction of the guidelines. The new guidelines are only binding on federal district courts. To what extent do offenders make distinctions between federal- and state-level offenses? It is reasonable to assume that most perceptions of certainty and severity are based on local and state actions and laws and not federal actions, especially given the relatively limited scope and jurisdictions of the federal statutes. Doerner and Wright (1990) note that the federal courts deal with only a small proportion of the total number of offenders in the United States. They say that the federal courts handled about 47,000 criminal defendants in 1984–1985 out of all approximately 13 million arrested. Arguably, the greatest impact on perceptions should appear from changes in local and state codes, not federal statutes. The only point at which the federal actions should induce a noticeable change is where potential offenders are in violation of one or more federal statutes. This would constitute a very small portion of all offenders.

One final factor to consider is the large number of recent legal challenges to the guidelines. Many jurisdictions have questioned the constitutionality of the guidelines or have simply refused to abide by them. Other jurisdictions have challenged them in court, and there appears to be serious legal bases for the opposition. Indeed, the Ninth Circuit Court of Appeals, representing nine western states, has ruled that the guidelines are unconstitutional. While the reasons for this ruling involve the separation of powers between Congress and the executive branch in the origination of the U. S. Sentencing Commission rather than the guidelines themselves, the end result is the same. The guidelines are not being used by nearly half of all federal district judges, or they are being applied sporadically. Both of these factors inevitably detract from the deterrent potential of the guidelines by eliminating any perceived certainty of sanctions.

Plea Bargaining and Deterrence

The extent to which the new guideline sentences may enhance deterrence can be affected by any actions that may mitigate the application of the accompanying sanctions. Plea bargaining is one activity which may alter the impact of the guidelines. While the question of plea bargaining is examined more extensively in other chapters in this book [see Chapters 4, 5, and 6], it is important to address here the possible impact of such actions on deterrence.

Earlier literature on the deterrence doctrine has rightly indicated that plea bargaining jeopardizes any potential deterrent effect of the law. Plea bargaining means that offenders do not necessarily receive those sanctions corresponding with the statutes they have violated. Neither do offenders necessarily receive the condemnation which is deemed appropriate by the law. Some experts argue that the failure of past sanctions to deter crime is partially the result of plea bargaining and less severe sentences associated with subsequent plea agreements. These critics might contend that the simple application of existing sanctions should be sufficient to provide a proper degree of deterrence. In essence, this viewpoint holds that sanctions imposed as the result of plea bargaining are insufficiently severe and that there is a reduction of certainty associated with the application of federal criminal statutes.

To what extent have the guidelines eliminated existing plea bargaining? "The Commission has decided that these initial guidelines will not, in general, make significant changes in current plea agreement practices" (U. S. Sentencing Commission, 1987:1.8). In general, guilty pleas may be negotiated to the extent that the resulting conviction offenses and sentences are representative of the crime seriousness. This would seem to mean that plea bargaining would have little effect on the sentence imposed by the court, since the sentencing range would remain largely unchanged as the result of a guilty plea. To some extent, this suggests that there is now a greater chance of receiving the prescribed sentence (or one within the same general range), compared with the possible sentences imposed in the pre-guideline period.

However, plea bargaining may simply be altered in style and not eliminated entirely. For example, several writers have suggested that mandatory sentencing guidelines may bring about more **charge reduction bargaining** (Alschuler, 1988; Kramer and Lubitz, 1985; Miethe, 1987; Tonry, 1988). Charge reduction bargaining includes reducing the original charges filed by arresting officers. While defendants may not be able to plead guilty in exchange for sentences outside of the prescribed ranges for more serious offenses, they may enter guilty pleas to lesser charges which directly lower the severity of the prevailing sentencing range. Tonry's (1988) examination of sentencing guidelines in Minnesota, Pennsylvania, and Washington suggests that such charge reduction bargaining has increased under the new guidelines. In terms of these new guidelines, Tonry says that the requirement that the "remaining charges adequately reflect the seriousness of the actual offense behavior" is a poor limitation on such bargaining. The principal problem is the vagueness of what "adequately" reflects the seriousness of the offense. Charge reduction bargaining poses obvious problems for both certainty of punishment and sentencing severity under the new guidelines.

The extent to which the system is willing to adhere to the guidelines is also questioned in view of the system's "going rate." The going rate refers to the idea that actors in the criminal justice system have established informal standards for what should be done with various types of offenders and the number of offenders the system will and can handle (Walker, 1985). The deterrent effectiveness of the sentencing guidelines is partly a reflection of the view of those who impose the sentences. A lack of compliance by system members to increase the level of system activity or to alter the normal routine results in an accommodation of the guidelines without any real change in sentencing or operations. To some extent, the Commission recognized this problem when it attempted to write guidelines which would not greatly affect the size of the existing federal prison population. They recognized the implicit "going rate" of the system. Tonry and Coffee (1987) have warned that attempts to change existing operations of the system will encounter resistance from the system in various forms. Analyses of state sentencing guidelines have supported this prediction with short-term changes reverting to the earlier sentencing norm over time (Tonry, 1988). In essence, attempts to alter the operations of the system and its personnel will meet with resistance, and any adherence to the status quo will limit the deterrent potential of the guidelines.

SUMMARY

This chapter has examined the crime control/deterrent potential of the new U. S. Sentencing Guidelines. Such a discussion is replete with side issues which must be given proper consideration in order to evaluate this potential. Through a discussion of the goals of the Commission and the guidelines it formulated, the various key factors of deterrence and the adherence of the guidelines to the needs of deterrence are disappointing. It has been effectively demonstrated that the guidelines hold little promise for enhancing crime deterrence.

The guidelines fail to address most of the crucial issues related to deterrence. First, the guidelines fail to live up to the goal of deterrence by eliminating variables and factors known to be related to deterrence. Instead, the Commission has chosen to focus almost exclusively on offenses and "just deserts" issues. Second, the Commission has relied heavily on past sentencing practices in formulating new sentencing sanctions. The resulting sentences have not resulted in a categorical escalation in severity of punishment. Certainty has been addressed only as it pertains to receiving specific sentences. The chances of being apprehended (a more relevant and influential factor for many offenders) and the celerity of sanctions are not addressed by the guidelines. Third, the public's perception of the severity, certainty, and celerity of punishment are similarly unaffected. Indeed, actions of the system (such as plea and charge reduction bargaining as well as the going rate) and of the courts (constitutional challenges) have the potential of seriously undermining any perceived risks from the guidelines.

The bottom line of this discussion is that the guidelines have done little or nothing to increase the deterrent efficacy of the law or the criminal justice system. Quite frankly, there are too many unaddressed issues and concerns to expect the guidelines to alter deviant or criminal behavior to any significant degree by those already violating the law or by potential offenders. While the guidelines may provide more uniformity in sentencing, they should not be considered as the primary vehicle whereby crime control can be achieved through deterrence.

Part III

The Courts

4

The Selling of the Sentencing Guidelines:
Some Correspondence with the U. S. Sentencing Commission

Albert W. Alschuler

INTRODUCTION

The American criminal justice system undoubtedly will survive the U. S. Sentencing Guidelines, just as it has survived other disasters that have befallen it. One cannot predict with much confidence, however, what adjustments the system will make. Perhaps Congress, despite the Commission's failure to fulfill its statutory obligation to recommend needed increases in the capacity of federal prisons [see Endnote 1], will approve the large-scale prison construction proposed by President Bush. Perhaps parole will reappear under a new name; Congress or courts remedying violations of the cruel and unusual punishment clause may authorize "pity committees" to select deserving inmates for early release from crowded federal prisons. Perhaps a U. S. Sentencing Commission with changed membership will abandon the present guidelines and draft new ones. Perhaps executive clemency will assume a larger role in determining when federal prisoners are released.

Perhaps courts will frequently depart from guidelines, finding "aggravating or mitigating circumstance[s that were] not adequately taken into account by the Commission in formulating the guidelines" [see Endnote 2]. Perhaps courts will frequently find "extraordinary and compelling reasons" for modifying sentences at the request of the Director of the Federal Bureau of Prisons [see Endnote 3]. Perhaps prosecutors, defense attorneys, probation officers, and judges will learn that "creative interpretation" of the guidelines can afford them substantial sentencing discretion. Perhaps lawyers and judges will make frequent use of the loopholes for plea bargaining that the guidelines afford. Perhaps federal prosecutors, by declining to prosecute, will thrust larger numbers of cases upon overburdened state systems. Perhaps prosecutors will abandon some areas of federal prosecution altogether.

Some years after implementation of the guidelines, researchers may report that neither the hopes of the guidelines' proponents nor the fears of their opponents have been realized. As researchers usually do, they may suggest that not very much has changed. The researchers are likely to note some signs of progress and some areas of concern. If these researchers duplicate the Commission's emphasis on formal offense categories and its general disregard for offender characteristics, they will probably find that sentences have become more uniform. They may also infer that plea bargaining pressures have increased [see Endnote 4]. Finally, they may report that, although sentences have become more severe, their severity has not grown as much as some observers anticipated; they may note in addition that increased severity reflects the temper of the times and might have occurred in any event.

Someday, however, even if observers look back upon discretionary pre-guidelines sentencing with astonishment, they may view the first federal sentencing guidelines as a symbol of some disturbing trends in American penology—a mark of an increasing dehumanization of offenders; of more incessant political appeals to our fear of crime; of a more impatient search for simple, mechanistic solutions to difficult human problems; and of a deepening failure of leadership in an ever less republican system of government. These observers may wonder how the guidelines happened, and the purpose of this chapter is to offer a footnote on this issue.

The history offered by this chapter is a largely personal tale told by a peripheral player who was never an "insider." To tell the story, I have accepted the invitation of the editor of this volume to reproduce some correspondence that I wrote concerning the guidelines and the responses that this correspondence engendered. I have added some narrative to describe events that occurred before, "in between," and following the letters.

* * *

The U. S. Sentencing Commission submitted its guidelines to Congress in April 1987. Under the Sentencing Reform Act, these guidelines were to become effective on November 1 unless Congress rejected them, modified them, or delayed their implementation [see Endnote 5].

When the Commission submitted its guidelines, I suggested to my colleague Norval Morris that we might usefully assemble a study group composed of people who had voiced general reservations about sentencing guidelines and of people who had been enthusiastic proponents. This group might review the guidelines to determine whether it could reach agreement on some successes and failures of the Commission's work (and possibly even on the appropriate action for Congress to take). People who had studied sentencing might be able to offer some collective guidance as Congress considered an important change in the federal criminal justice system.

At Morris's behest, the Edna McConnell Clark Foundation agreed to host a small conference on the guidelines in New York City. (My suggestion to Morris was apparently only one of many spurs for this conference; Professor Daniel Freed opened the conference by noting that it had many parents). The conference was successful in crystallizing my own view of the guidelines. Most speakers noted defects of the guidelines; and although the guidelines had a thoughtful and articulate defender in Judge Jon Newman, Newman so frequently responded to criticisms of the guidelines by suggesting departures that many of us wondered whether the game could be worth the candle. During the conference, members of the group received page proofs of some parts of the Commission's *Supplementary Report on the Initial Sentencing Guidelines and Policy Statements,* and this report indicated that the guidelines were likely to restrict greatly the use of non-incarcerative sanctions and to increase significantly the population of federal prisons (although the report apparently sought to minimize this effect by calculating the guidelines' impact from a very high "base").

At the conclusion of the conference, all but a few members of the study group favored a joint statement expressing concerns about the guidelines. Although drafts of this statement were later circulated to the group, the process of refining the statement was not completed before the deadline for Congressional action. Fearing that a group statement might encounter some snags and concluding that a more personal statement would be useful in any event, I prepared remarks that I later presented before the Criminal Justice Subcommittee of the House Committee on the Judiciary. I circulated copies of my statement to several criminal justice scholars and federal judges, and I secured the signatures of 68 of these knowledgeable people to a letter that concluded, "Implementation of the guidelines would be a retrogressive rather than a progressive measure and would render the federal sentencing system less just."

My statement before the House Criminal Justice Subcommittee (with footnotes omitted) follows:

STATEMENT OF ALBERT W. ALSCHULER, PROFESSOR OF LAW, THE UNIVERSITY OF CHICAGO, BEFORE THE CRIMINAL JUSTICE SUBCOMMITTEE OF THE COMMITTEE ON THE JUDICIARY, UNITED STATES HOUSE OF REPRESENTATIVES, July 23, 1987.

My name is Albert Alschuler. I teach law at the University of Chicago. I hope that the Congress will not allow the *Sentencing Guidelines and Policy Statements* submitted by the United States Sentencing Commission to go into effect (as they will automatically if Congress fails to act before November). The Commission, in my view, has failed to do the job that Congress directed it to do. Despite the defects of the current federal sentencing system, this system remains preferable to the system that the guidelines would create.

This statement discusses four deficiencies of the Commission's guidelines—their overuse of imprisonment, their contribution to an increased federal prison population, their effective transfer of sentencing discretion from judges and parole authorities to prosecutors, and the crudity of their sentencing standards—standards that neglect offense and offender characteristics that virtually all sentencing judges have considered important.

* * *

Many American jurisdictions currently are experimenting extensively with noncustodial sanctions, and commentators whose views of criminal justice differ as substantially as those of Edward Kennedy and Edwin Meese have favored a broader use of these sanctions. The federal courts, which benefit from a well-trained, adequately funded probation service, ought to be in the forefront of the development of effective nonincarcerative punishments. Nevertheless, the chart that follows, drawn from the Sentencing Commission's Supplementary Report to Congress, indicates that the use of alternatives to imprisonment will decline very substantially under the guidelines:

Percentage of Defendants Receiving Probation

Offense Type	*Under Current Practice*	*Under Guidelines*
Person Offenses	31.4%	14.6%
Robbery	18.0%	3.0%
Burglary	64.0%	43.0%
Property offenses	60.1%	33.1%

Offense Type	Under Current Practice	Under Guidelines
Drugs	20.8%	5.1%
Fraud	59.0%	24.0%
Income taxes	57.0%	3.0%
Firearms	37.0%	9.0%
Immigration	41.0%	30.0%

This chart reports only the percentage of offenders sentenced to what the Sentencing Commission calls "straight" probation; it does not include sentences to both probation and imprisonment.

The foregoing figures, suggesting a dramatic increase in the use of incarcerative sanctions, do not rest on the assumption that every future offender will receive the sentence that the guidelines appear to prescribe. The Commission has assumed that only a small minority of future offenders—the 15 percent convicted at trial—will be sentenced as severely as the guidelines appear to mandate. Although the guidelines authorize only a "two-level" reduction in sentence (in most cases about a 20 percent reduction) when a defendant "affirmatively accepts responsibility" for his or her crime, the Commission's predictions assume that defendants who plead guilty will receive discounts of 30 or 40 percent from their probable post-trial sentences (the same "percentage reduction" that guilty-plea defendants currently receive). This assumption underscores the Commission's recognition that its guidelines will not significantly limit plea bargaining. If judges and prosecutors were to apply the guidelines as written, the reduction in the use of probation would be more striking than the chart suggests.

The Commission has limited not only the use of probation as an alternative to imprisonment but also the use of fines. Although the Commission has provided for the imposition of fines "in all cases," it has authorized these fines only as a supplement to other punishments and not as an alternative to them. The guidelines thus effectively mark the end of the fine as an independent sanction. The Commission has taken this action without explanation—at a time when commentators of varying persuasions have concluded that fines often can be as effective as imprisonment and that, when they are, they are far more cost-efficient.

The Sentencing Reform Act of 1984 provides, "The Commission shall insure that the guidelines reflect the general appropriateness of imposing a sentence other than imprisonment in cases in which the defendant is a first offender who has not been convicted of a crime of violence or an otherwise serious offense." A

Commission whose guidelines would reduce the proportion of fraud offenders who receive probation from 59 to 24 percent, the proportion of property offenders who receive probation from 60 to 33 percent, and the proportion of tax offenders who receive probation from 57 to 3 percent seems not to have paid much heed to this directive.

* * *

The Commission's *Supplementary Report* declares, "To a large extent, the reduction in straight probation results from the reduction of disparity in sentence length, rather than from an increase in average sentence length." Nevertheless, the Commission does anticipate a great increase in average sentence length. It has attributed this increase primarily to the Anti-Drug Abuse Act of 1986 and to the Sentencing Reform Act's directive to set guidelines at or near the statutory maximums when cases involve career offenders. Again, the Commission's projections rest on the assumption that the guidelines and other sentencing provisions will apply as written only to defendants convicted at trial, and that defendants who plead guilty will be sentenced much less severely. The projected sentence increases noted in the following chart would be greater in the absence of this assumption.

Average Time Served (Imprisonment—In Months)

Offense type	Under Current Practice	Under Guidelines
Robbery	44.8	75.4
Person	37.7	75.2
Drugs	23.1	57.7
Firearms	14.1	15.2
Burglary	7.7	16.5
Fraud	7.0	8.0
Property	6.8	6.5
Immigration	5.7	5.2
Income tax	5.5	11.9

The human costs of unnecessary imprisonment are of greater concern than the economic costs, but the fiscal impact of the Commission's proposals do merit serious attention. Even under what the Commission calls its "low growth scenario," the federal prison population will more than double within the next 10 years—from 42,000 at present to 92,000 in 1997. The Commission attributes most of the projected increase to an increase in the number of federal prosecutions, to the impact of the sentencing provisions of the Anti-Drug Abuse Act of 1986, and to the impact of the Sentencing Reform Act's directive concerning guidelines sentences for career criminals. Using as its "base" the vastly increased prison population that it expects these developments to trigger, the Commission has concluded, "There is no scenario under which the guidelines will have no more than a 10 percent impact on prison population."

A large projected "base" can make a significant increase in prison population appear relatively small, and the Anti-Drug Abuse Act and the other developments emphasized by the Commission may not have the effects that the Commission expects. When prisons are overcrowded, for example, federal prosecutors may respond to the sentencing provisions of the Anti-Drug Abuse Act, not by increasing the number of drug prosecutions as the Commission anticipates, but by leaving a greater number of drug prosecutions to the states.

Estimating the effect of sentencing guidelines on prison populations is extraordinarily difficult, however. I offer only the following conclusion, one that seems safe and conservative: Under each of its alternative "scenarios," the Commission expects a massive increase in the number of federal prisoners. It nevertheless has taken actions that will aggravate rather than ameliorate the expected crisis. These actions appear to contravene another admonition of the Sentencing Reform Act: "The sentencing guidelines . . . shall be formulated to minimize the likelihood that Federal prison population will exceed the capacity of the Federal prisons."

* * *

The Sentencing Reform Act directs the Commission to promulgate policy statements concerning the acceptance or rejection of plea agreements by federal judges, and the legislative history of this provision reveals Congress's concern that prosecutorial plea bargaining might undermine the objectives of the guidelines. Nevertheless, the guidelines declare, "The Commission has decided that these initial guidelines will not, in general, make significant changes in current plea negotiation practices."

The Commission's assessment of its guidelines' plea bargaining provisions may be incorrect. These provisions, cast in vague and ambiguous language, require (among other things) a determination whether the charges remaining after a plea agreement "adequately" reflect the offender's conduct. Some judges might read these provisions to mandate a close review of plea agreements to ensure that they do not lead to sentences substantially different from those prescribed by the guidelines. Other judges (like the Commission) might assume that plea negotiation remains essentially unregulated. Disparity in sentencing practices might result from differing interpretations of the guidelines. Nevertheless, the Commission's judgment that its guidelines will not significantly restrain current plea bargaining practices does seem plausible.

If this judgment were to prove correct, the effects would not all be unfortunate. Unrestrained plea bargaining might well ameliorate the defects of the guidelines noted earlier in this statement. Bargaining by prosecutors could cause the guidelines to yield a less severe reduction in the use of nonincarcerative sanctions and a smaller growth in the population of federal prisons than the Commission anticipated. If plea bargaining did have these effects, however, the reason would be simply that the Commission had allowed plea bargaining to undercut its guidelines. These effects would materialize only if the reduction in punishment awarded to defendants who pleaded guilty became even greater than the "30 percent off" that the Commission expects these defendants to receive. In my view, effectively transferring sentencing discretion from judges and parole authorities to prosecutors (and at the same time increasing the sentence disparity between guilty-plea and trial defendants) would not be progress; to the contrary, it would be a perverse and regrettable development.

When guidelines mandate imprisonment but a prosecutor concludes that the defendant merits probation, plea bargaining may provide the only means of imposing the sentence that the prosecutor (and frequently the trial judge) considers just. Indeed, a system of sentencing guidelines that on its face prescribes severe sentences but that leaves plea bargaining unconstrained creates a prosecutor's paradise. In such a system, sentencing guidelines masquerade as the Sentencing Commission's determination of appropriate penalties. In reality, the guidelines are merely bargaining weapons—armaments that enable prosecutors, not the Sentencing Commission, to determine sentences in the overwhelming majority of cases. In operation, the guidelines rarely set sentences; they merely augment the power of prosecutors to do so.

Police interrogation manuals have described the "good-cop, bad-cop" stratagem for obtaining confessions. After a police officer acting the role of a "bad cop" has threatened a suspect with harsh treatment, another officer appears as a sympathetic "good cop" and agrees to save the suspect from the actions that the "bad cop" has threatened. The "good cop" offers to help the suspect, however, only if the suspect cooperates. Sentencing guidelines that appear to mandate "tough" sentences but that leave plea bargaining unconstrained are likely to have a similar effect. The Sentencing Commission plays the role of the "bad cop," threatening the accused with harsh treatment. The prosecutor, the "good cop," then agrees to protect the defendant, but only if he or she abandons the right to trial.

* * *

A more specific illustration of the plea bargaining leverage that the guidelines provide may illustrate another defect of the guidelines as well—the crudity of their sentencing standards. The Commission's guidelines begin by prescribing sentences for homicide cases. Although homicide prosecutions in the federal courts are relatively rare, this initial section of the guidelines provides a clear example of how the guidelines are likely to operate. The guidelines direct federal courts to impose determinate sentences of imprisonment within the following ranges when first-offenders are convicted of homicide:

	Absent any "Adjustments" or "Departures"	*Following an "Affirmative Acceptance of Responsibility"*
First-degree murder	life without parole	324–405 months
Second-degree murder	135–168 months	108–135 months
Voluntary manslaughter	57–71 months	46–57 months
Involuntary manslaughter	5–21 months if the conduct was reckless; 6–12 months if the conduct was negligent	10–16 months if the conduct was reckless; 2–8 months if the conduct was negligent

Under the guidelines, a prosecutor who offers to reduce a charge from one grade of homicide to another (say, from first-degree to second-degree murder or from second-degree murder to manslaughter) apparently can provide an enormous reduction in the defendant's sentence. Typically, the prosecutor can offer a sentence about one-third as severe as the sentence that the defendant would have received if convicted of the greater charge at trial. For example, the basic guidelines sentence for a first-offender convicted of first-degree murder is life without parole, but a defendant charged with first-degree murder who pleads guilty to second-degree murder apparently can expect to be sentenced to about ten years' imprisonment.

The prosecutor's bargaining power under the guidelines results in part from the Commission's failure to differentiate among offenses and offenders in any but the crudest terms. The commentary to the guidelines recognizes that first-degree murder includes many cases in which defendants have not killed intentionally or knowingly. It suggests that "departures" from the guidelines may be appropriate in these cases of unintentional killing, adding that "the Commission does not envision that departure below that specified in Section 2A1.2 (Second Degree Murder) is likely to be appropriate." The Commission, in other words, simply has not provided meaningful guidelines for cases of unintentional first-degree murder. The commentary further declares, "The Commission has concluded that, in the absence of capital punishment, life imprisonment is the appropriate punishment for . . .'willful, deliberate, malicious, and premeditated killing.'"

A "willful, deliberate, malicious, and premeditated killing" may be a killing by a hired "hit-man," by a political terrorist, or by a robber who has decided not to leave a witness to his or her crime. It also may be a killing by a battered spouse not currently threatened with imminent harm; a killing by a lover who has been jilted; a killing during a barroom quarrel; or even the mercy killing of a terminally ill relative. One might have expected a Commission charged with drafting sentencing guidelines for homicide cases to have differentiated among these different offenses. When Congress provided, "If the sentence specified by the guidelines includes a term of imprisonment, the maximum of the range established for such a term shall not exceed the minimum of that range by more than the greater of 25 percent or 6 months," it surely expected the Sentencing Commission to draw finer lines than those provided by the offense categories of the federal criminal code.

For the most part, the Commission has not drawn these finer lines. It has relied primarily on statutory offense categories, sometimes refining these categories on the basis of the harm inflicted (for example, the value of the property that an offender has stolen or the quantity of drugs that the offender has sold). The members of the Commission apparently did not attempt to remedy their own lack of sentencing experience by consulting extensively with people who had greater experience. The Commission instead simply compiled aggregate statistics on past sentences. In the words of Daniel Freed, the Commission studied sentences, not sentencing. It apparently made little effort to understand either the way in which judges have determined sentences or the world of conduct governed by its guidelines. Focusing simply on offense categories, it failed to treat sentencing as "a human process."

Consider, then, an offender who had led a law abiding life until one day when a person whom he or she loved abandoned him or her for someone else. This offender now has been charged with first-degree murder for killing his or her former lover in a state of grief and anger during a confrontation in which the victim recounted the offender's perceived failings. Unless the conduct that provoked the killing could be described as "wrongful," the Commission has not expressly invited any "departure" from its guidelines. The guidelines say only, "Life without parole." Nevertheless, a prosecutor who believed that so severe a sentence should be reserved for a criminal who posed a serious, continuing threat to society might offer to permit the defendant to plead guilty to second-degree murder.

In evaluating the prosecutor's offer, a good defense attorney would consider the likelihood that a judge would impose a sentence other than the guidelines sentence even were the offender convicted of first-degree murder at trial. The Sentencing Reform Act authorizes such a "departure" when a judge "finds that an aggravating or mitigating circumstance exists that was not adequately taken into consideration by the Sentencing Commission in formulating the guidelines and that should result in a sentence different from that described."

A trial judge might conclude that, because the Sentencing Commission failed to consider—either adequately or at all—any mitigating circumstances in homicide cases, its guidelines should not constrain his or her sentencing discretion. The defense attorney, however, probably could not anticipate so bold a ruling. Even were the attorney prepared to gamble that some "departure" from the guidelines was likely, he or she might not anticipate a great departure. A first-degree murder sentence as low as the guidelines sentence for second-degree murder, for example, might prompt an appeal that the judge might wish to avoid. The attorney might conclude that his or her only choice was to accept the prosecutor's offer—in effect, the prosecutor's determination of sentence. The risk of "life without parole" or of something close to it might seem too great to run. The attorney might reach this conclusion although a "manslaughter" sentence appeared more appropriate in the circumstances of the case and although the attorney believed that a jury might convict the offender only of this lesser crime at trial.

One cannot be certain what effect the guidelines would have on the determination of sentence in this far from abberational case; but whatever the guidelines' effect, it seems likely to prove unfortunate. When the best that can be said of sentencing guidelines is that judges may "depart," that prosecutors may "bargain," and that the guidelines therefore may not significantly change current practice, those guidelines do not merit adoption.

* * *

With the implementation of federal sentencing guidelines, the United States Parole Commission will disappear. This agency has minimized the effects of both judicial and prosecutorial sentencing disparities by applying uniform standards for release on parole throughout the nation. Insofar as the effective operation of the Commission's guidelines would depend on the willingness of judges to "depart," the guidelines might not greatly limit judicial sentencing disparity. Sentence review by a dozen United States Courts of Appeals, moreover, would seem substantially less likely to reduce disparity than the application of uniform parole guidelines by a single national agency.

More importantly, the sentencing guidelines provide no significant control of *de facto* sentencing decisions by prosecutors, and the Sentencing Reform Act authorizes no control of these informal prosecutorial decisions by the United States Courts of Appeals. With the implementation of the guidelines, the corrective that the Parole Commission has provided for disparate prosecutorial practices would disappear, and no substitute would be provided. On balance, the replacement of the current parole guidelines with the Commission's sentencing guidelines might aggravate rather than minimize sentence disparity. Rather than sacrifice justice in the individual case for the sake of certainty in sentencing, the guidelines might yield both injustice and uncertainty.

The Parole Commission, which determines only the date of a prisoner's release, obviously has been unable to reduce disparity in the most important component of the sentencing decision—the choice between prison and probation. The Sentencing Commission's guidelines might reduce disparity in this phase of the sentencing process—but only by mandating a far more common use of imprisonment. Disparity might be preferable to the unreflective use of imprisonment as the "standard" criminal punishment. Moreover, the guidelines seem more likely to transfer broad discretion to impose nonincarcerative punishments from judges to prosecutors than to limit this discretion substantially. The guidelines might yield certainty in sentencing only for the minority of offenders bold enough (or foolhardy enough) to exercise the right to trial.

The sentencing guidelines provide a 258-box sentencing grid. Locating a case within the appropriate box in this grid (as well as resolving such additional issues as whether multiple sentences should run concurrently or consecutively) would require courts to resolve innumerable issues of guidelines interpretation, many of them far from clear. Appellate review of the resolution of these issues would be likely to increase substantially the already heavy workloads of the United States Courts of Appeals. Moreover, the guidelines might also promote complex trials as some prosecutors attempted to maximize sentences by charging offenses that would trigger consecutive sentences, by establishing the aggregate dollar amount of the bribes that a corrupt judge had taken, and the like. In light of the substantial freedom of judges to depart from the guidelines and in light of the Commission's failure to restrain plea bargaining, the cumbersome mechanism created by the guidelines would seem unlikely to yield a gain in certainty that would warrant its obvious costs.

The guidelines submitted by the United States Sentencing Commission are a backward rather than a forward step in the search for just, certain, and effective criminal punishments. Congress should prevent their implementation.

Some members of the Commission were plainly offended by my statement and by my response to questions before the subcommittee. Most notably, I had answered one question during the House hearings by saying:

In fact, the process that the Commission used in constructing its guidelines might have led to an increase in sentence length almost by inadvertance. Without any decision to change current practice, there may have been an incomplete awareness of this practice. I have heard rumors, and there are members of the Commission here who can either refute these rumors or confirm them, that when the Commission constructed its data on past sentences, it disregarded nonincarcerative sentences. It used as its statistical baseline only cases in which people had been sentenced to imprisonment. To be sure, the Commission knew what proportion of offenders had received nonincarcerative sentences; and when that proportion was high in a particular offense category, it was likely to make the guidelines sentence less severe than the average time spent by offenders who had been imprisoned.

In other words, the Commission did not construct its statistical baseline by looking to all federal offenders and by counting a sentence to something other than imprisonment as a sentence of "zero imprisonment." Now, as I say, I do not know whether that description is true or false. But if the description is accurate, the Commission's methodology would have seemed likely to yield sentences more severe than current practice.

A moment later, when I concluded my testimony, the following exchange occurred between Congressman John Conyers, the Chairman of the House subcommitte, and Judge Stephen Breyer, a member of the Commission:

> Mr. Conyers: All right, we want to thank you very much, and we will now adjourn the meeting.
> Judge Breyer: Would you like us to answer the rumors?
> Mr. Conyers: Sure, absolutely, Judge Breyer.
> Judge Breyer: As long as there are rumors, I would like the chance to respond and I think I will show you exactly—I would say, it is difficult for you, I think it is difficult for many of your witnesses, because they are being forced, for the first time, to deal with a very complex system that took us 18 months to develop, and therefore, my impression is that many of the things you have heard, are simply not so. The easiest way, I think, for me to deal with that from the judges is I would like to submit, for the record, not to discuss now, but I will just submit for the record, some things that I have written to Judge Merritt in the Sixth Circult and the ABA, to try to pinpoint the genuine differences.
> I would like to say the rumors are false and the easiest way, and you will see my reaction, if you understand how we did deal with this. I think Counsel is quite correct. I found Professor Alschuler's testimony misleading. I do not think it is a correct characterization of what we did and I found it much easier to deal with the Department of Justice and others, who might disagree with him, various academics, because it is difficult to focus specifically on the issue, on this particular issue.
> The way it was written is the following. Take an example like arson. If you will turn to the page on arson, you will see, for example, that we discovered from our pre-sentence reports, that many people convicted of arson, were actually people who, through malicious mischief, were burning wastebaskets. Therefore, what we did was say the base penalty for arson is a level six.

That level six means that people will not go to prison. We then developed a set of specific offense characteristics that tried to get longer prison terms for those people whom our data showed tended to be sentenced to longer prison terms.

It did not work perfectly, because we do not have data that describes every offender in the Federal system. That is why we introduced the right to depart. But if Professor Alschuler or others think that we sat there and sort of made things up out of the whole cloth based on non-data, that is not so. I think I can speak for everyone saying that we tried to look at the data. We tried to find distinctions that were there, and by and large, though not entirely, you will discover that those distinctions are reflected in the numbers in the report.

In fact, I had erred only by referring to my description of the Commission's methodology as grounded on "rumor." I had forgotten the published source of this description—Commissioner Paul H. Robinson's "Dissenting View on the Promulgation of Sentencing Guidelines by the United States Sentencing Commission." Moreover, Chapter 4 of the Commission's *Supplementary Report*, which set forth statistical materials used by the Commission in constructing its guidelines, had confirmed Robinson's description. Judge Breyer had testified before the House subcommittee, "[M]ost of [the Guidelines'] categories, distinctions, and sentences reflect typical existing sentencing practices (as determined by analysis of 10,500 actual cases)," but the Commission had determined "typical sentencing practices" by compiling average sentences only in cases in which offenders had been sentenced to imprisonment. As I later wrote, "Under the guidelines, some offenders are likely to be sentenced more severely, not because the Commission or anyone else considered the facts of their cases and decided they deserved it, but only because the Commission and its statisticians decided to count one thing and not another in assessing prior practice. In implementing the Sentencing Reform Act of 1984, the Commission provided, not merely sentencing by computer, but something more Orwellian—methodologically flawed sentencing by computer" [see Endnote 6].

Commissioner Ilene H. Nagel wrote a letter objecting to one portion of my statement—the claim that the Commission apparently had "studied sentences rather than sentencing." I replied, "On reflection, I agree that the passage that you questioned was inappropriate. I certainly accept the representations of your letter concerning the efforts that the Commission made and the procedure that it followed." Less graciously, I added, "What I should have said, I suppose, was not that you had apparently failed to study 'sentencing' but that evidence of this study was largely absent from your product." I devoted most of a six-page letter to documenting this conclusion.

I had provided Commissioner Nagel with a list of the judges and academics to whom I had sent copies of my statement before the House subcommittee. I later learned that many of these people had received from Kenneth Feinberg, a Washington lawyer and former member of Senator Kennedy's staff, what Feinberg called "materials in opposition" to my remarks. Most of the materials in Feinberg's package were published statements supporting the guidelines, but one was a letter to Dean Paul Marcus signed by Commissioner Nagel and Commissioner Michael K. Block. Although I had sent copies of my letters and statements to the Commission and invited the correction of errors, Nagel and Block had not sent me a copy of their letter to Marcus. Similarly, Judge Breyer, the author of a somewhat more temperate response to my statement included in the Feinberg package, had not favored me with a copy of his letter. Mr. Feinberg also had omitted this courtesy when he mailed his cover letter and package (and I still do not know who received copies of the Feinberg package).

The Nagel-Block letter did not repeat the one objection that Commissioner Nagel had voiced in her letter to me. Instead, it declared, "Professor Alschuler's letter goes beyond honest disagreement [and] distorts and misrepresents the nature, effect, and operation of the sentencing guidelines," adding that I had offered "grossly distorted portrayals" of the guidelines. To support these allegations, the letter presented what I regarded as a series of serious misrepresentations of my position, of the guidelines themselves, and of the reactions of others to what I had said.

Shortly after I had learned of the Nagel-Block letter, Commissioner Nagel greeted me at a conference. I expressed my displeasure with her letter, telling her that although most of our audience might not be interested in further discussion of the guidelines, I would probably write a response simply to defend my scholarly honor [see Endnote 7]. Commissioner Nagel explained that the Nagel-Block letter had been written by a staff member, and after some discussion, she agreed that it was inaccurate. She further agreed to write a letter recognizing the inaccuracy of the letter and asking recipients to disregard it. Commissioner Nagel later reported that Commissioner Block would join her in sending this letter, and I expressed my gratitude.

Commissioner Nagel failed to write the promised letter. She explained that she had not had time to draft it. Ultimately, she forwarded a draft that expressed only regret about the tone of the earlier letter while suggesting that my own "intemperate, strident language" had prompted this unfortunate tone. I responded that this draft fell short of the acknowledgement of error that she had promised. Commissioner Nagel then reported that, before sending the letter that she and Commissioner Block had agreed to write, Commissioner Block wished me to list the inaccuracies of the Nagel-Block letter. Acting on the dubious assumption that two Commissioners were acting in good faith and not simply procrastinating until the deadline for Congressional action had passed, I wrote Commissioner Block a letter noting seven inaccuracies of the Nagel-Block letter and offering him $100 if he could discover in my statement any of various remarks that he and Commissioner Nagel had attributed to me.

This letter was our last correspondence on the subject. Commissioner Block did not reply, and he and Commissioner Nagel never wrote the promised letter. I believe that the game that these Commissioners played is called "hardball."

Throughout this period, I also corresponded with members of the Commission's research staff. Various statements of the Commission and its staff had revealed that the Commission had determined the amount of "real" time that 10,500 past federal offenders had served and then had calculated the amount of time that these offenders would have served if they had been sentenced under the guidelines. The Commission, however, had not published the results of this resentencing study; it merely had used its calculations in preparing some complicated projections of future prison populations. When I telephoned William Rhodes, the Commission's Research Director, he agreed to send me the results of the Commission's resentencing study. I later sent the following letter to Mr. Rhodes:

July 9, 1987

William H. Rhodes
Research Director, United States Sentencing Commission
1331 Pennsylvania Ave., N. W.
Washington, DC 20004

Dear Bill:

Just a reminder that you promised two weeks ago to send me some figures not included in the Commission's *Supplementary Report*: What was the aggregate amount of time served (in "person-years" or whatever) by all of the offenders included in your 10,500 past-case sample? What would this aggregate amount have been had the same offenders been sentenced under the Guidelines? Because your research staff has calculated the appropriate sentence under the Guidelines for every case in the sample, I don't imagine that it would be very difficult to coax these figures

out of your computer. If you could give me the aggregate comparative figures with drug cases "in" and then with drug cases
"out," that would be so much the better.

I hope that I haven't messed up any of the Commission's data
in the enclosed letter to Senator Biden and Congressman Rodino.
If I have, please let me know. Many thanks.

Sincerely yours,

Albert W. Alschuler
Professor of Law

The reply that I received from the Commission contained data that
the Commission later acknowledged were erroneous. I present this
reply only because it is part of the story and not because the figures
that it offers indicate the probable effects of the guidelines:

July 21, 1987

Professor Alschuler
University of Chicago
The Law School
1111 East 60th St.
Chicago, IL 60637

Professor Alschuler:

I am writing in response to your query of Bill Rhodes. You
asked Bill for some figures regarding aggregate time served over
our entire data base.

As you are aware, the Anti-Drug Abuse Act of 1986 and the
Career Offender provision of the Crime Control Act of 1984
increased sentences for certain classes of offenders. The new drug
law and the career criminal provision constrained the Commission when drafting guidelines. Consequently, we report the
prison demands separately for these new laws, computing time
served under four conditions: current, under the new drug law,
under the drug law and the career criminal provisions, and under
the guidelines. The tables below reflect those aggregate calculations; they need some explanation.

First of all, the numbers are in "thousands of person-years."
The column under "prison" indicates time served in prison for
those whose sentences are straight prison terms. The column
under "split" indicates prison time for those who currently re-

ceive split sentences, and, for the guidelines, the prison time for those who receive intermittent sentences. The column under "Cond." indicates prison time for those who receive conditional probation.

We did not compute split or intermittent sentences under the drug law and career criminal conditions, so we really can't provide a comparable "total time" under those scenarios.

All Cases	Total	Prison	Split	Cond.
Current	21.5	20.1	1.4	
Drug law		24.7		
Car. crim.		46.4		
Guidelines	52.4	48.5	2.5	1.4
Without Drug Cases				
Current	11.1	10.1	1.0	
Car. crim.		16.3		
Guidelines	22.4	19.0	2.1	1.3

I hope the previous tables answer your questions. Please feel free to contact me or Bill if you have any other questions.

Sincerely,

Eric Simon
U. S. Sentencing Commission

The information that I received from the Commission prompted me to send the following letter to Congressman Conyers. Again I emphasize that, because this letter rests on erroneous data supplied by the Commission, its portrayal of the effect of the guidelines is inaccurate:

July 24, 1987

Hon. John Conyers, Chairman
Subcommittee on Criminal Justice
Committee on the Judiciary
United States House of Representatives
Washington, DC 20515

Dear Representative Conyers:

When I returned to my office after testifying before your Subcommittee, I found the enclosed letter from Eric Simon of the Sentencing Commission. Mr. Simon sent this letter in response to a request that I had made to William Rhodes, a copy of which is also enclosed.

Mr. Simon's letter provides some interesting information about the impact of the Sentencing Guidelines, information that the Commission has not previously reported. The Commission's projections of prison impact rest on a sample of 10,500 offenders who were sentenced in the federal courts in 1985, and Mr. Simon's letter offers further information about this sample.

Specifically, Mr. Simon reports that these defendants have served or will serve an aggregate 21,500 "person years" of imprisonment. Had these same defendants been sentenced (a) under the Guidelines (including the "career offenders" provisions) and (b) with the Anti-Drug Abuse Act in place, the aggregate number of "person years" of imprisonment would have been 52,400.

In other words, the aggregate number of years that these offenders would have served would have doubled *and more* had the post-1985 sentencing provisions been in effect. Indeed, the aggregate amount of imprisonment would have increased approximately 140 percent. This would have happened, moreover, even on the assumption that offenders who pleaded guilty would have received a "discount" of 30 percent from the sentences apparently prescribed by the guidelines and by the Anti-Drug Abuse Act.

Note that this figure does not rest on any assumption of increased prosecutions in the federal courts, nor does it project the likely increase in the current federal prison population. The same group of offenders would simply have been "put away" for substantially more than twice as long had the post-1985 provisions been in effect. Basically, the average federal offender would have served five years rather than two.

Mr. Simon's letter suggests that 4,600 of the additional "person years" of imprisonment would have been attributable to the drug law; 21,700 to the career offenders provision [Footnote 1: This number seems surprising. It suggests that an extraordinary number of career offenders are convicted each year in the federal courts and that judges regularly sentence these offenders to terms far below the statutory maximums. (Career offenders are defined as people over 18 who have previously been convicted of two serious drug offenses or violent felonies and who now have been convicted of similar drug offenses or violent felonies again.) What explains the Commission's figures? Are federal judges truly the "softies" that their critics think they are? Or are "career offender" cases less serious than the imposing statutory language seems to suggest on first reading? Or are the maximum sentences provided by the federal criminal code truly Draconian? The dramatic changes that the career offenders provisions will bring require some explanation that I cannot provide.]; and 4,600 to the guidelines alone [Footnote 2: 2,100 years in "prison" cases, 1,100 years in "split sentence" cases, and 1,300 years in "conditional probation" cases.] In other words, if the Guidelines *alone* had been in effect (without the Anti-Drug Abuse Act *or* the career criminals provisions), the number of "person years" of imprisonment would have gone from 21,500 to 26,100. Thus the Guidelines alone would have produced a 21 percent increase in the aggregate amount of imprisonment.

Obviously this increase would not immediately have produced a 21 percent increase in the federal prison population. Equally obviously, however, a 21 percent increase in the aggregate "person years" that each year's "crop" of offenders must serve *ultimately* would increase the federal prison population by about the same percentage. This analysis underscores the extent to which the Commission's low projections of "prison impact" depend on using as a "base," *not* the recent practices of the federal courts, but projected practices *after* both the career offenders provisions and the Anti-Drug Abuse Act have been implemented.

The Commission's 10,500-defendant sample represents about 27 percent of the 38,530 defendants convicted in the federal courts in fiscal 1985. Assuming the representativeness of this sample, implementation of the guidelines *alone* (without the Anti-Drug Abuse Act or the career offenders provision) would have produced an increase of 17,037 "person years" of imprisonment for all defendants convicted in 1985. On the assumption that every "person year" of imprisonment costs the federal government $17,500 (simply in operating expenses—capital expenditures for prison construction obviously are not included), the increased correctional expenditure attributable to the guidelines would have been about $300 million per year [Footnote 3: The annual correctional expenditure triggered by the 144,444 additional "person years" imposed by the combined action of the guidelines, the career offenders provision and the Anti-Drug Abuse Act would have been ($2,002,770,000.00). I cannot resist a comment. The Congress and the Sentencing Commission in their combined actions apparently are prepared to increase the sentence of the average federal offender from two to five years and to pay the more than $2 billion annual price that this "severity revolution" will carry. When one suggests that America could afford to give the average offender *a trial*, however, both Congress and the Sentencing Commission apparently regard the suggestion as unrealistic; they fear that any restriction of plea bargaining would "swamp the courts." Their motto seems to be: Billions for imprisonment but not an extra cent for due process. As we celebrate the

200th anniversary of our Constitution, we are likely to reveal our priorities more through our actions than through our rhetoric]. Of course, that amount would be higher today because the number of federal prosecutions has increased, and of course the Commission expects further increases in the volume of federal prosecutions.

Moreover, the statistical analysis becomes more interesting when drug cases are excluded from the 10,500-case sample. In the remaining cases, Mr. Simon's letter reports that offenders were required to serve ll,100 "person years." That figure would have risen to 22,400 "person years" under the Guidelines (including the career offenders provisions). In other words, the aggregate amount of imprisonment that one year's "crop" of *non*-drug offenders would have served would have doubled had the guidelines been in effect. Mr. Simon attributes 5,100 of the additional "person years" in non-drug cases to the guidelines alone, and 6,200 to the career offenders provisions. In other words, had the guidelines been in effect *without* the career offenders provision, the aggregate amount of imprisonment for non-drug offenders would have grown from ll,100 "person years" to 16,200 "person years," a 46 percent increase. It is only because the Anti-Drug Abuse Act "took the heat" for a large part of the sentence increase in the full sample that the portion of the increase attributable to the guidelines alone appeared to be just under 25 percent rather than just under 50 percent. The 46 percent figure probably offers a better approximation of how much more imprisonment the guidelines would require in the *absence* of the career offenders provision and the Anti-Drug Abuse Act [Footnote 4: In fact, I failed to ask the right question of Mr. Rhodes. The best way to determine the effect of the guidelines *alone* on sentence severity might be to exclude both cases in which the Anti-Drug Abuse Act applies and cases in which the career offenders provision applies, then to determine the aggregate number of "person years" that offenders would serve "before" and "after" the guidelines in the remaining cases. I'm sorry that I did not make this request].

In light of this analysis, it seems idle to suggest that, with relatively rare exceptions, the guidelines merely smooth out disparities and do not greatly increase the severity of federal sentences. It also seems idle to suggest that the guidelines are likely to have only a minimal impact on federal prison populations.

Sincerely,

Albert W. Alschuler
Professor of Law

After sending this letter, I received two letters acknowledging error in the data that the Commission's research staff had sent me. The first letter, written by Eric Simon, offered a relatively minor correction in these data; the second, written by William Rhodes, revealed that the data were much more seriously flawed. Although Mr. Rhodes' letter criticized my use of the defective data that his staff had supplied, Rhodes was apparently even more critical in a letter that he sent to several people along with his letter to me. In accordance with the standards of etiquette that prevail at the Commission [see Endnote 8], Rhodes did not send me a copy of this letter. The letters that I received from Mr. Simon and Mr. Rhodes follow:

July 28, 1987

Professor Alschuler
University of Chicago
The Law School
1111 East 60th St.
Chicago, IL 60637

Professor Alschuler:

It has come to my attention that there was an error in the tables I sent to you in my letter of July 21. The correct tables appear below. The error was the reported drug-law prison time. The erroneous number, 24.7, is actually the total thousands of prison years that drug law offenders serve under the new drug law. The correct number for the table, 36.2, is the total thousands of prison years served by everyone, after the application of the new drug law.

All Cases	Total	Prison	Split	Cond.
Current	21.5	20.1	1.4	
Drug law		36.2		
Car. crim.		46.4		
Guidelines	52.4	48.5	2.5	1.4
Without Drug Cases				
Current	11.1	10.1	11.0	
Car. Crim.		16.3		
Guidelines	22.4	19.0	2.1	1.3

Again, I hope the previous tables answer your questions. Please feel free to contact me if you have any other questions. I apologize for any inconvenience I may have caused.

Sincerely,

Eric Simon
U. S. Sentencing Commission

* * *

August—, 1987

Professor Albert W. Alschuler
The University of Chicago
The Law School
1111 East 60th Street
Chicago, IL 60637

Dear Professor Alschuler:

Having read your recent letter to Representative Conyers, I am perplexed. Your letter asserts that the portion of the increase in prison populations attributable to the guidelines greatly exceeds the Sentencing Commission/Bureau of Prisons projections. Your estimates and those of the Commission are based on the same data. What surprises me, then, is that the inconsistencies in results did not prompt you to make further inquiries before writing to Congress.

Had you and I consulted, you would have discovered that Mr. Simon's results, upon which you based your conclusions, were inappropriate for your purposes [Footnote 1: Given the press of business at the Commission, and given that yours was a special request for tabulations not provided routinely by our prison impact model, I did not adequately review the numbers reported in Mr. Simon's letter. Thus, I am responsible ultimately for providing you with the wrong numbers. The correct numbers (rounded):

	With Drugs	*Without Drugs*
Current (1985	37,000 years	19,000 years
After drug law	51,000 years	
After career offender	61,000 years	24,000 years
After guidelines	64,000 years	27,000 years

We received your special request for data at the same time that we were preparing testimony for Congress and assembling materials for GAO. You indicated some urgency in receiving a reply. Had we had more time to respond, I would have had Mr. Gaes, who has been responsible for the analysis that interested you, prepare a report. Unfortunately, Mr. Gaes was not available, and Mr. Simon—who received the assignment in his absence—was not aware of an important part of Mr. Gaes' computer program. The result was that Mr. Simon erred; because of the apparent urgency of your request and the press of business, I failed to provide Mr. Simon with the review that is otherwise standard for material provided by the research group.

Had you done further analysis, however, it would have been apparent that the figures reported by Mr. Simon were inconsistent with other data that were at your disposal. In fact, data for sentences from 1985 account for 37,000 years of prison time, not the 22,000 reported by Mr. Simon. On reflection, you might have concluded that Mr. Simon's original figures could not have been correct, because the current prison population is somewhat more than 40,000. [Footnote 2: Our data represent defendants who were sentenced in 1985. If the 1985 defendants were similar in numbers and mix of cases to defendants prior to 1985 and after 1985, then the 37,000 man-years of prison time generated by these defendants would imply a 1987 prison population of 37,000. In fact, the Bureau of Prisons reports a population of about 43,000 currently. The differences between the numbers is partly attributable to parole violators, unsentenced detainees, state boarders, and different accounting practices for community corrections confinement.]

Your letter to Congress is inaccurate and misleading. Mr. Simon's figures (when corrected) imply a 5 percent (about 3,100 man-years) marginal impact of the guidelines for all defendants sentenced during 1985. His figures imply a 11 percent (about 2,600 man-years) marginal impact of the guidelines after excluding drug offenses. Projections from the impact model, which used a more sophisticated method to distribute sentences over time, are consistent.

Even if the numbers provided you by Mr. Simon had been appropriate, your analysis of them was wrong. As explained in the Supplemental Report to Congress, the research staff sampled about 25 percent of all criminal cases reported in the FPSSIS data file. This sample was selected purposefully to overrepresent serious cases and offenders with extensive criminal histories. When we report impact results, we naturally adjust those results (using standard statistical techniques) to account for this over-repre-sentation.

Your simple correction was to multiply prison time by 4. This correction assumed that the sample was representative, when actually it was weighted more heavily toward serious crimes and repeat criminals. Furthermore, the results had already been adjusted, so no further correction was necessary. For example, by multiplying the 22,000 by 4, you would have estimated a current prison population of 88,000. Again, this should have appeared odd to you and prompted an inquiry, because the current prison population is less than half that amount. Nevertheless, you did not seek confirmatory checking, and consequently, you based your estimates of future impact on incorrect adjustment.

Putting the sampling issue aside, and ignoring the data problems, your results still would have been incorrect. When the Commission reported projected prison populations, we expressed confidence in the accuracy of the 5-year projections, less confidence in the 10-year projections, and scant confidence in the 15-year projections. One reason for caution about projections beyond 10 years is uncertainty about the very long terms required by the drug law, the career offender provision, and some parts of the guidelines. Accuracy of a 5-year prison projection requires only that sentence estimates be correct up to 5 years. Making an exact 10-year projection is more demanding, requiring that sentence estimates be accurate up to 10 years. Making precise estimates for 15 years and beyond is the most demanding, requiring that we accurately estimate the longest terms under the new drug law, the career criminal provision, and the guidelines for violent crimes. Because there are no close historical parallels for such long federal sentences, estimates are necessarily speculative, and consequently, we chose an impact methodology that does not require precise estimates for these long terms.

Your "steady-state" method for projecting prison impact, however, requires the sentence estimates to be accurate well beyond 10 years. This is a needless requirement, and one that is difficult to satisfy given the radical changes expected from the drug law, the career offender provision, and parts of the guidelines dealing with violent crimes.

Beyond issues involving methodology, the tone of your letter implies that the Commission attempted to mislead Congress about the guidelines' impact. This is baseless and false. Frankly, I am piqued. I would not certify findings from the research staff that I knew to be incorrect or misleading. No Commissioner has asked me to take an alternative position.

Instead, the Commission asked the research group to assess prison impact as accurately as possible given current technology. To do so, we worked closely with the Bureau of Prisons, and the projections are a joint product of the Bureau and the Commission. The Bureau, obviously, had no incentive to understate prison impact.

Furthermore, others (including experts formally trained in data analysis and modeling) have reviewed our work. First, we contracted for consulting services with Professor Arnold Barnett of MIT, in part because of his technical qualifications and experience with prison impact projections, but also because we wanted someone from outside the Commission to evaluate the ongoing impact estimation. Professor Barnett has not expressed to me any serious reservations about the quality of the work or our conclusions. Second, we have made all work products available to GAO. Based on their own review, GAO has testified that, subject to the uncertainty that necessarily surrounds prison projections, there is no reason to doubt the results. Third, researchers from the Federal Judicial Center have replicated many of our calculations and have reported that our calculations appear sound. Finally, we have distributed written reports, and we have hosted public discussions, laying out in excruciating detail the method by which those analyses were derived and the results produced. We have yet to receive a serious challenge to our basic conclusions: the guidelines will have a marginal effect on the prisons, but prison demands will increase greatly because of current trends in prosecutions, the Anti-Drug Abuse Act of 1986, and the career offender provision of the 1984 Crime Control Act.

I regret that, due to the press of work at the Commission and the apparent urgency of your request, we provided you with incorrect information about current and projected sentencing practices. In other similar situations, I have discussed conclusions drawn by outsiders from the Commission's data with those outsiders. Such discussion is invaluable for reducing misunderstandings and misuse of the data. It is regrettable that you and I did not consult about your findings, as consulting would have spared me the embarrassment of correcting an error made by the research staff and would have spared you the inconvenience of amending your earlier conclusions. Now that you have received the correct information, I am sure you will want to provide Congressman Conyers with your new assessment of the guidelines' impact. I have sent a copy of this letter to everyone who received your letter to Congressman Conyers, so that these people will know my position on the Commission's prison projections.

Sincerely,

William M. Rhodes
Research Director

Mr. Rhodes' letter prompted the following reply:

August 21, 1987

William M. Rhodes
Research Director
The United States Sentencing Commission
1331 Pennsylvania Avenue, NW
Suite 1400
Washington, DC 20004

Dear Mr. Rhodes:

You have an odd way of apologizing for the fact that a member of your staff sent inaccurate information in response to my simple request. Indeed, your letter has given me a new understanding of what criminal defense lawyers mean when they speak of the BLAME THE VICTIM strategy.

As you know, I sent copies of my letter concerning the data that Mr. Simon had supplied to a number of people who I thought would be interested in it. I doubt that these people will be as interested in the allegations of your letter. Nevertheless, because you were not content simply to send these bystanders a correction of Mr. Simon's error, I will, with regret, burden them with a copy of this letter as well.

This letter has four parts—first, some puzzled comments concerning your defense of your unchallenged scholarly honor; second, an explanation of why I considered the information I requested important, along with a response to your assertions that I used this information improperly; third, a response to your claims that I rushed you into error, should have recognized the error, and should have consulted you before using Mr. Simon's data as I did; and fourth, a request for some additional information that may further our understanding of the guidelines.

* * *

You report that you are "piqued" and that you found in the "tone" of my letter an "implication" that the Sentencing Commission had "attempted to mislead Congress about the guidelines' impact." Your letter protests that you "would not certify findings from the research staff that [you] knew to be incorrect or misleading." Finally, you talk at length about the knowledgeable people who have reviewed your conclusions and found them sound.

Man, it weren't me! I have no idea what language carried the tone that prompted your comments. I didn't suggest or imply (or even believe) that you had made any error, let alone that you had perpetrated some deliberate falsehood.

Indeed, I saw no incompatibility whatever between your *Supplementary Report* and the information that Mr. Simon had supplied or my comments about it. Your report and my letter had focused on very different issues. In response to the Sentencing Commission's statutory mandate, you had attempted to predict the federal prison population at various points in time and the contribution of the guidelines to that population. I had focused on past sentences and how the guidelines would have changed them. Indeed, after noting the apparent increase in the number of "person years" that past offenders would have been required to serve had the guidelines and the Anti-Drug Abuse been in effect, I declared expressly, "Note that this figure does not ... project the likely increase in the current federal prison population." You and I were calculating percentages from very different "bases." It didn't surprise me at all that our percentages differed. [Footnote 1: Indeed, even with your corrected figures, these percentages differ greatly. There is no reason why percentages measured from a base of "real" sentences imposed in 1985 should equal those measured from a base of the current federal prison population *plus* the inmates added by future prosecution at a higher rate *plus* the inmates added by the sentencing provisions of the Anti-Drug Abuse Act *plus* the inmates added by the career offenders provisions.] It astonished me to discover that you had interpreted my effort to look at the guidelines in a different way as an attack on your integrity and, perhaps, on that of the Sentencing Commission as well.

As you may recall, I have commented favorably on your scholarship both in print and in one pre-publication manuscript review for INSLAW. Your work for the Sentencing Commission has seemed to me to be of the same high caliber. Before receiving Mr. Simon's letter, I had suggested in a letter to Senator Biden and Representative Rodino that the low "percentage impact" attributed to the guidelines depended on calculating percentages from an artificially high base. But I was able to make that observation only because you had revealed your assumptions clearly. The criticism did not imply any derogation of your scholarship. My request for further information and my subsequent letter to Representative Conyers, insofar as they concerned prison impact, were designed to demonstrate the sensitivity of your analysis to the selection of a "base," something that surely is within the bounds of legitimate scholarly discussion.

Moreover, I know that it is not your responsibility to answer every bothersome request for information. That you were willing to supply further data at my request, knowing that I had urged Congress not to allow the guidelines to go into effect, was a mark of admirable scholarly openness. Scholarship should work that way, and government in a democracy should work that way too. Responding to a request for information in the manner that you and Mr. Simon did should be routine, but your response was nevertheless reassuring. (And that's so even though all of us occasionally make mistakes when we're trying to be cooperative.) I very much appreciate your assistance. Moreover, I wouldn't have requested information from you unless I had confidence in your ability and integrity.

* * *

Perhaps I should explain more fully the reasons for my request and at the same time respond to your claim that I misused the data that Mr. Simon supplied. Because you have devoted so much energy to studying "prison impact," you apparently assume that everyone else must be primarily interested in this question too. In fact, because any estimate of future prison populations must rest on extraordinary guesswork, I am not greatly interested in pursuing the fine points of how these populations should be calculated.

I am much more interested in the simpler information that I requested: How would application of the guidelines have affected past sentences? This information is of interest in itself, and it also bears on how much the guidelines are likely to increase the bargaining power of prosecutors. Determining how much more imprisonment the guidelines and the Anti-Drug Abuse Act would produce *if* the "guilty-plea discount" were to remain the same offers a basis for estimating whether the size of the "discount" *will* remain the same.

Because Congress and the Sentencing Commission have left the plea bargaining loophole wide open, I imagine that plea bargaining practices will nullify the guidelines and the Anti-Drug Abuse Act to a considerable extent. The "prison impact" of these measures probably will be *less* than your research group has anticipated [Footnote 2: At the same time, I believe that there is likely to be a significant prison impact for two reasons. First, some defendants—most likely those with plausible defenses—will insist on trial and, if they lose, are likely to be sentenced in accordance with the guidelines and the Anti-Drug Abuse Act. More importantly, to the extent that prosecutors have the leverage to "set sentences," they are likely to set higher sentences than when they must share sentencing discretion with judges.

For example, when a prosecutor and defense attorney sense that a judge is likely to award probation after a trial, the prosecutor cannot very well insist on a one-year term as part of a plea agreement. When, however, the guidelines or the Anti-Drug Abuse Act encourage the judge to impose a five-year term following a trial, the prosecutor may obtain one year on a plea, or, perhaps, two years, three or four. Under the guidelines and the Anti-Drug Abuse Act, sentences will increase at least to some extent when prosecutors wish them to increase.

Let me mention two other probable effects. First, in light of the prosecutor's increased bargaining power, the guilty-plea rate is likely to increase—but only slightly. When plea bargaining offers, explicit or implicit, already are calculated to overbalance nearly every defendant's chances of acquittal, increasing the prosecutor's bargaining power (even greatly) will affect the guilty plea rate only marginally. Second, the "sentence differential" between defendants convicted at trial and those who plead guilty is likely to grow, perhaps very substantially. (Moreover, "sentence recommendation bargaining" may become a substantially more common practice than it currently is in the federal courts.)

To what extent prosecutors will press for tough sentences and to what extent they will adhere to their current sentencing practices in guilty plea cases (and therefore nullify the guidelines and allow the sentence differential to grow) is anyone's guess. Both effects are likely to materialize; but to the extent that one does, the other won't. When one seeks a "handle" on the likely magnitude of these combined effects, however, it is useful to see how much more imprisonment the guidelines would require for a representative group of defendants, adhering initially to the assumption that the "sentence differential" will not in fact change.] In making my request, I was much more concerned about prosecutorial bargaining power than about actual prison impact.

At the same time, I believe that the information that I requested does provide a useful way of thinking about prison impact—a clearer and simpler way, in fact, than the more elaborate techniques that you have employed to present seemingly more precise estimates. [Footnote 3: With both techniques, it is necessary to proceed on the artificial assumption that the "guilty plea discount" or "sentence differential" will remain constant. Although this discount is likely to increase, any estimate of the magnitude of the increase would be arbitrary.] Plugging every factor needed to make a precise estimate of future prison populations into a "prison impact" formula is unlikely to yield real precision when the values attributed to many factors are little more than blind stabs. The attempt to be comprehensive may in fact compound error and lead observers astray (though I recognize that you were required to approach the task in the manner that you did and to make your best guess). The form of analysis that I used examines the effect of the guidelines in a far more reliable manner than direct, long-range estimates of prison impact; and as I will explain, it takes account of potentially significant sentencing effects that your form of analysis ignores.

Your claim that I had failed to recognize the inaccuracy of long-range projections of prison impact was baffling. I do indeed realize that fifteen-year projections of future prison populations are extremely problematic and, unlike you, that five-year projections are extremely problematic as well. *All* projections require guesses about the future rate of federal crimes, the future "mix" of these crimes, the percentage of future crimes that will lead to prosecution, changes in plea bargaining practices and the like. Unlike your research group, however, I did not *offer* long-range projections of prison impact; I spoke only of how much more imprisonment offenders *already convicted and sentenced* would have incurred had the guidelines and other post-1985 provisions been in effect.

This sort of analysis avoids most of the difficulties associated with long-range predictions of prison impact. It requires only accurate calculations of the "real time" sentences that the guidelines would have yielded in past cases (something that is essential to your mode of analysis as well). Perhaps you are correct that estimates of long sentences are more problematic than estimates of short sentences, but these estimates should be only marginally more problematic. After all, under the guidelines, "life" means "life," "30 years" means "30 years minus good time," "5 years" means "5 years minus good time," and so forth. The principal reason why estimates of the imprisonment required by long

sentences may be less accurate than estimates of the imprisonment required by short sentences is simply that offenders imprisoned for long terms are more likely to *die* before their terms are
completed (and one could correct for the "death effect" if one
wished to carry statistical precision to extremes).

The analysis that I employed involves a form of "accrual accounting" in which "real" sentences are "counted" in the year in
which they are imposed (and in which taxpayers assume the
practical obligation to pay for them) rather than the year in which
they are served (and in which the taxpayers pay for them in fact).
This analysis thus takes into account *every* significant change in
"real" sentencing practices.

Your "prison impact" analysis, by contrast, may neglect important changes. Suppose, for example, that some career offenders
currently serve 15 years but that they will be required to serve 30
years under the career offenders provisions. This change will
have *no* effect on the federal prison population during the first 15
years that the guidelines are in effect; it will be only during the
sixteenth year that this group of offenders will serve the first year
of imprisonment that they would not have served under former
practices. Thus even your dubious 15-year projection would miss
the effect of the change entirely, treating it as a nullity. But a
doubling of the career offenders' sentences should not be treated
as a nullity; as Americans have learned with the social security
system, someone is likely to pay the price sooner or later. For that
reason, simply recalculating past sentences under the guidelines
may provide a better sense of long-range prison impact than your
much fancier analysis.

Of course this example is extreme, and you may think it foolish
to take account of effects that are not anticipated for another
fifteen years. Nevertheless, the problem exists with every estimate of "prison impact" based on a projection of the actual prison
population at a future point in time. A five-year projection, for
example, affords *no* effect to increases in the sentences of offenders who would serve five years under current practice (however
dramatic these increases might be). Similarly, a five-year projection cannot attribute more than a one-year effect to increases in
the sentences of offenders who would serve four years under
current practices (again however dramatic these increases might
be). "Accrual" accounting provides a better and much simpler
way of viewing the problem. Although this technique is "rough"
in the sense that it offers no precise estimate of future prison
populations, it is far more accurate in accomplishing what it sets
out to do. At least this technique offers an alternative, legitimate

way of looking at the problem—one not deserving of your vituperation.

* * *

Your efforts to "blame the victim" for Mr. Simon's error seem woefully unpersuasive. First, your letter suggests that I rushed you into a departure from "standard" procedures; it expresses confidence that the error would not have occurred "had we had more time to respond"; and it indicates that Mr. Simon's error occurred only because I had "indicated some urgency in receiving a reply." Had I? Where and how?

I had seen a printer's proof of part of your *Supplementary Report* at a meeting on June 18 and 19. This document revealed that your research group had determined the amount of "real" time that 10,500 federal offenders convicted in 1985 would serve. Then your staff had calculated the amount of time that each of these offenders would have served had the Anti-Drug Abuse Act and the guidelines (including the career offenders provisions) been in place [Footnote 4: That work, apparently based on examination of the presentence reports in the 10,500 cases, must have required prodigious effort. How many "person years" did it consume? How many people do you have working for you anyway? Might some "standard statistical techniques" beyond my ken have simplified the task?]

Although your staff had done this impressive work, the amount of "extra" imprisonment that the Anti-Drug Abuse Act and the guidelines would have produced in the 10,500-case sample was not reported. For the reasons explained above, I was much more interested in this basic unreported data than in your more elaborate (and more questionable) prison population projections. I therefore telephoned you and asked whether you could give me this information. You agreed to do so. After two weeks had passed (actually it was closer to three, but I said two in my letter because I didn't want to seem pushy), it occurred to me that the conversation might have slipped your mind and, in any event, that it would be desirable to make my request in writing. I therefore wrote you "just a reminder." I fail to see any pressure to depart from "standard" procedures in these actions. [Footnote 5: Moreover, I thought I had merely asked you to add "before" and "after" sentences that your staff had previously calculated. If your computer had the capacity to add numbers, the task shouldn't have required more than a moment or two. It never occurred to me that the addition would be difficult or complicated, a task whose performance would be prone to error and require extensive review. (Indeed, you had told me on the telephone that compiling the requested figures would not be difficult. I am still uncertain how the error occurred and what, if anything, the numbers initially reported by Mr. Simon represented.)

Second, you suggest that I should have noticed Mr. Simon's error because the number of "person years" that he had reported offenders sentenced in 1985 would serve did not correspond to the current federal prison population. Surely, however, there is no reason to expect the number of "person years" of imprisonment *imposed* in a given year to equal the number of people *already imprisoned* in that year. If a universe of 100 offenders are sentenced to "real" terms of 10 years each, the aggregate number of "person years" of imprisonment required by their combined sentences will be 1,000. During the year that these sentences are imposed, however, they will add to the existing prison population only 100 people minus the number who are released.

To be sure, if the same number of offenders are sentenced to the same terms of imprisonment year after year, the number of "person years" of imprisonment imposed in one year ultimately will equal the number of "person years" served in that year. And because every occupied prison bed produces one "person year" of imprisonment, the number of years of imprisonment served in a year will equal the prison population. No one imagines, however, that anything like this "steady state situation" has obtained recently in the federal courts or the federal prisons. To the contrary, as you have reported (*Supplementary Report*, Figure 1, page 67), the number of federal convictions has increased enormously—from fewer than 30,000 in 1981 to more than 40,000 in 1986. [Footnote 6: See also note 99, page 58, suggesting that "the growth in criminal cases has been greater than that reflected in Figure 1."] Moreover, as you also have reported (*id.* at note 96, page 56), "federal sentences have been increasing." The average federal sentence (*n.b.*, not the "real time" sentence) has in fact grown from 49 months in 1979 to 64.6 months in 1986 (see Bureau of Justice Statistics, *Federal Offenses and Offenders: Sentencing and Time Served*, 1987).

In this situation, one would expect the number of "person years of imprisonment" imposed in any recent year to have exceeded— and perhaps to have exceeded greatly—the number of "person years" served in that year. I had assumed that Mr. Simon's figures referred only to your 10,500-case sample and that this sample was representative (of which assumptions I will say more later). The figures thus suggested that the number of "person years" of imprisonment imposed in 1985 were a bit less than twice the number served in that year. Had I thought about it (and I didn't), this number might have seemed high—though had I known that serious cases were overrepresented in your sample, the contrast would have been less surprising.

What seems much more surprising, however, are the new and supposedly correct figures that you report—figures that show *fewer* years of imprisonment imposed in 1985 than were served in 1985 (but that you may be able to bring up to the mark by correcting for unsentenced detainees, state boarders, and the like). How can these figures be reconciled with a great increase in the number of convictions and with greatly increased average sentences? If we have been at or below the "steady state" mark, why has the federal prison population grown to the point that our federal prisons are now 50 percent over capacity?

Moreover, I am at a loss to reconcile the corrected figures that you have supplied with those offered by the Bureau of Justice Statistics in its recent report, *Federal Offenses and Offenders: Sentencing and Time Served*, a copy of which is enclosed. This document reports at page 5, Table 4 that the average time served by all "Federal offenders convicted of Federal offenses" is 43.3 months. (Despite the heading of the table, the reference is only to offenders sentenced to imprisonment for longer than one year— the offenders subject to Parole Commission jurisdiction. See page 8.) According to the BJS (page 1), offenders sentenced to imprisonment constituted 51 percent of the 40,740 offenders (page 2) convicted and sentenced in fiscal 1985. Thus 20,777 offenders were sentenced to imprisonment. The BJS says (page 3) that sixteen percent of these offenders (3,324 offenders) were sentenced to terms of one year or less. Nevertheless, the remaining 17,453 offenders would have served 755,715 months or 62,976 "person years" of "real" time.

This figure obviously differs enormously from your much lower figure—37,000 "person years"—and the figure does not include everyone (the offenders sentenced to one year or less). The figure is in fact closer to the one that I would erroneously have projected from Mr. Simon's mistaken data. Can you explain it? Of course, if there is any error, I cannot know whether it is yours or the BJS's, but the BJS does seem to have worked from "real" numbers rather than "weighted samples" and "projections." Might you have missed another "important part of Mr. Gaes' computer program"? Sadly, despite my hope for the "law and social science" enterprise, I am beginning to doubt that lawyers can gain very much by listening to you seemingly knowledgeable statistics buffs. Whenever two of you talk about the same phenomenon, you appear to be miles apart. I hope that I have missed something.

In any event, as I say, it never occurred to me to compare the "real" sentences imposed in 1985 with the federal prison population in that year. I gather that it did not occur to you either for a considerable period. You note that you "did not adequately review the numbers reported in Mr. Simon's letter," but apparently you did review them. Mr. Simon reports that he had shown you his letter before mailing it. Moreover, on July 28 (which I suppose was after you had received my letter to Representative Conyers), Mr. Simon wrote to correct an error in one of his figures (a serious but not a critical error). Again he reports that he had shown you his letter (with both of his tables corrected and repeated) before mailing it. I gather that even at this point his central error did not "leap out" at you. To berate a lawyer who has never had a statistics course for failing to catch an error that two full-time statistics mavins missed repeatedly is remarkable, especially when the berator is himself one of the numbers-crunchers.

Third, I did err in assuming that Mr. Simon's figures referred to your 10,000-case sample rather than to all federal offenders convicted in 1985. That is to say, I erred in assuming that Mr. Simon had answered the question I had asked: "What was the aggregate amount of time served (in 'person-years' or whatever) by all of the offenders included in your 10,500 past-case sample?" When Mr. Simon referred to your "entire data base," I assumed that he *was* answering my question and that he meant this sample—the cases concerning which you had data—rather than the universe of 1985 cases, reconstituted like orange juice through "weighting" and "projection." (Of course, if the BJS is correct, you may still need another can of water.)

Moreover, I erroneously assumed that the 10,500-case sample was representative (noting explicitly that my analysis depended on this assumption). I think, however, that you should forgive this error, for the Sentencing Commission has made it too. See the January 1987 *Revised Draft Sentencing Guidelines* at 8–9 ("A representative sample of 10,000 cases was drawn from all offenders sentenced during fiscal year 1985."). Were there perhaps two samples?

Fourth, you express surprise that "inconsistencies in results did not prompt [me] to make further inquiries before writing to Congress." [Footnote 7: It would in fact have been difficult for me to do so. I was planning to (and did) leave the country for an extended period on Saturday, July 25. The previous Tuesday, I was invited to testify about the guidelines before the House Criminal Justice Subcommittee (or, more precisely, funding for my travel was unexpectedly approved). I flew to Washington the next day, testified on Thursday, and returned to my office to find Mr. Simon's letter on Friday. (I had, however, had an advance peek at the letter when Mr. Conyers, Mr. Yellen and I spent 10 minutes or so reviewing and discussing Mr. Yellen's copy on Thursday afternoon. Please note that I was not the first person to, in your words, "write to Congress" with your research staff's erroneous data.)

Once I had Mr. Simon's letter in hand, there did seem to be a need to hurry. I was leaving for London the next day (where, incidentally, I recounted some of Mr. Simon's erroneous data to an international conference); and the House Subcommittee had scheduled its hearings on prison impact for the following week. Although I had many other things to do, I thought that the information contained in Mr. Simon's letter was important, and I spent most of my last day at home writing to Representative Conyers. It would have been difficult to involve you in the process—though, as explained above, I doubt that I would have seen the need if I'd had more time.] What "inconsistencies in results?" As I have noted, I didn't see any then, and I don't see any now. Indeed, I explained in my letter to Representative Conyers why the percentages that I derived from Mr. Simon's figures did not seem to me incompatible with those that you had earlier presented in the Commission's *Supplementary Report*: "This analysis underscores the extent to which the Commission's low projections of 'prison impact' depend on using as a 'base,' *not* the recent practices of the federal courts, but projected practices *after* both the career offenders provisions and the Anti-Drug Abuse Act have been implemented." [Footnote 8: Your letter, when it refers to "a 5 percent marginal impact" and "an ll percent marginal impact" of the guidelines, again seems to calculate the guidelines' effects from the largest possible "base." Why, in calculating these percentages, have you "plugged in" the guidelines last—*after* the career offenders provisions and the Anti-Drug Abuse Act? If you had done it the other way around, you would have concluded, "In non-drug cases, the guidelines alone (without the career offenders provisions) would have increased the amount of imprisonment imposed in 1985 from 19,000 years to 22,000 years—an increase of 16 (not 11) percent." As I will indicate, even this 16 percent figure probably understates the guidelines' effect on imprisonment, for it includes in the "base" the career offenders cases, cases in which the guidelines alone could *not* have affected imprisonment. That is, although the 16 percent figure excludes the *effect* of the career offenders provisions, it leaves the prior sentences imposed in career offenders cases as part of the base from which the guidelines' effect is calculated.]

In my letter to Representative Conyers, a copy of which I mailed to you, I said:

"In fact, I failed to ask the right question of Mr. Rhodes. The best way to determine the effect of the guidelines *alone* on sentence severity might be to exclude both cases in which the Anti-Drug Abuse Act applies and cases in which the career offenders provision applies, then to determine the aggregate number of 'person years' that offenders would serve 'before' and 'after' the guidelines in the remaining cases. I'm sorry that I did not make this request."

In a handwritten note to Mr. Simon, I asked whether it would be difficult to supply the information that I failed to request earlier. Neither you nor Mr. Simon responded. I probably should have requested this information more directly.

Please, if you will, take the cases in which you have attributed sentencing effects to the Anti-Drug Abuse Act and the career offenders provisions and exclude them from your analysis. Then let me know the aggregate number of "person years" that offenders will serve in all of the remaining cases in which sentences were imposed in 1985. Finally, calculate how many "person years" these offenders would have been required to serve had the guidelines been in effect.

The logic of this request should be clear. Essentially, the Commission has said, "It's not our fault that sentences will increase dramatically in Anti-Drug Abuse Act cases and career offenders cases. We take responsibility only for the other cases." Nevertheless, the Commission has left the Anti-Drug Abuse Act cases and the career offenders cases in its base when calculating the effects of its guidelines. At least when one is concerned with "sentencing effects" rather than "prison impact," this approach seems unsound.

If the Commission will "take the heat" only for some cases, those cases merit separate analysis. Drug cases and career offenders appear to constitute a very large proportion of all federal cases—a significant majority I would guess—and their presence in the database is likely to dwarf the guidelines' impact. Obviously the "percentage impact" of the guidelines would appear even smaller if one were to gauge their impact from a "base" that included still other cases in which the guidelines have no effect—state court cases, for example, or Japanese cases. The inclusion of state court cases plainly would be misleading, however; and in discussing such issues as whether the guidelines merely even out disparities, it is also misleading to measure the guidelines' sentencing effects from a base that includes the Anti-Drug Abuse Act and career offenders cases.

Once I receive the requested information, I will be happy to write again to Representative Conyers to discuss the probable effects of the guidelines.

* * *

Finally, a little preaching. The greatest quantitative analysts doing law-related work—for example, Zeisel, Zimring, Lempert, and Blumstein—usually look for simple approaches to complex problems. Their first impulse is not to "model the universe." They usually follow a line of statistical reasoning that even I can understand.

I recognize that, in light of the Commission's statutory mandate, you had little alternative to the comprehensive approach that you took to the problem of assessing "prison impact." I imply no criticism. Nevertheless, one danger of the ambitious techniques that seem to be the norm in your profession is that so much depends on the vigilance and competency of researchers who may prove as fallible as the rest of us. A well-trained and seemingly capable analyst may miss "an important part of Mr. Gaes' computer program" and therefore generate wildly inaccurate figures signifying nothing. Then no one—certainly no lay "consumer" of the information that the analyst has generated—may catch the error for an extended period. When one is dealing with numbers that matter, elaborate statistical techniques can be scary.

Of course, in requesting further information about the effect of the guidelines in non-drug, non-career-offenders cases, I am again manifesting my faith in your integrity and competency—a faith that has never been in doubt.

But please! Don't let me rush you.

Sincerely yours,

Albert W. Alschuler
Professor of Law

Mr. Rhodes was not rushed by my letter into revealing the extent to which the guidelines would have increased past sentences even in non-drug, non-career-offenders cases. One can know from figures that Mr. Rhodes supplied that this increase would have been at least 16 percent, and it probably would have been substantially more. Perhaps the figure that Mr. Rhodes did not provide would have embarrassed commissioners who were "selling" the guidelines on the representation that they largely incorporated past sentencing practices.

When Mr. Rhodes did not respond to my request for information, Representative Conyers, the Chairman of the House Criminal Justice Subcommittee, wrote to request the same information. Mr. Rhodes did not respond to Representative Conyers' request either.

I ultimately reached Mr. Rhodes to ask whether he intended to supply the information that Representative Conyers and I had sought. He replied that he would not have time to compile this information before the deadline for Congressional action had passed. I asked Mr. Rhodes whether he would send the information after the deadline had passed, and he said that he would. It has now been 16 months since the Congress permitted the guidelines to become effective. I am still waiting.

* * *

For practical purposes, the most significant issue that Congress considered following the Commission's submission of its guidelines was whether to delay their implementation. Delay would have permitted field testing of the guidelines, training in their use, and (perhaps) some revision of the guidelines. The American Bar Association, the Judicial Conference of the United States, several Circuit Conferences, and the Federal Judges Association favored delay. Moreover, the Commission itself submitted a statement favoring a nine-month delay—a statement that it never withdrew. Nevertheless, the Executive Director of the Commission informed Congress that three unnamed members of the Commission had authorized her to report that they no longer favored delay. Why these Commissioners chose to remain anonymous is unclear.

After some negotiation and compromise, the Democrats and Republicans on the House Criminal Justice Subcommittee approved a bill providing for a nine-month delay; and because this bill was not expected to prove controversial, they agreed to a procedure that would require the House to vote on the bill without debate. During a period of unrestricted debate, however, one Congressman objected, "Mr. Speaker, the leftwing loonies who control the agenda of this Congress sometimes give the Members a pretty good idea about who they really are and what they really believe. We are learning at this moment how soft on crime they have really become" [see Endnote 9]. Another, apparently wise enough to be unpersuaded by the Commission's claim that the guidelines embodied past sentencing practices, declared that any delay of the "tougher sentences" provided by the guidelines would provide "a window of opportunity for those who are convicted criminals" [see Endnote 10].

Attorney General Meese was probably more influential in defeating the delay bill than these Congressmen. He wrote a letter opposing any delay, declaring that delay "could be inconsistent with effective law enforcement," and threatening a Presidential veto. Meese's letter maintained, "Since no hearings have been held on H.R. 3307, we have not had an opportunity to make our case against delay." In fact, the House subcommittee had conducted extensive hearings on the guidelines, and whether to delay their implementation was an often discussed topic of these hearings. The subcommittee had drafted its delay bill following the hearings so that technically it had not conducted hearings "on H.R. 3307." Nevertheless, the Department of Justice had not been denied an opportunity to "make [its] case against delay."

Meese's letter also declared, "The Sentencing Reform Act had been in force for hardly a year before opponents of reform were back in Congress urging a one-year delay in the effective date; from November 1, 1986 to November 1, 1987. There were sound arguments for that delay proposal and we did not object to it. The time for delay, however, is past" [see Endnote 11]. Meese did not mention that the initial delay had occurred prior to the drafting of the guidelines because the Administration had failed for nearly a year to appoint the members of the U. S. Sentencing Commission. The purpose of the earlier delay had been simply to afford the Commission the time to prepare the guidelines that the Sentencing Reform Act had contemplated [see Endnote 12].

By a vote of 231 to 183, the House rejected the Criminal Justice Subcommittee's proposal for a nine-month delay. Although the Senate Judiciary Committee belatedly conducted a one-day hearing on the guidelines, this Committee was preoccupied with the nomination of Robert Bork to be an Associate Justice of the United States Supreme Court throughout the period that it might have considered the guidelines. It gave the guidelines almost no attention. I had done my share, I suppose, to ensure that Congress received what guidance the academic community could provide on the difficult issues posed by the guidelines. I would not do it again.

ENDNOTES

1. See 28 U.S.C. Sec. 994(g). As I write this chapter 16 months after the implementation of the sentencing guidelines, the Commission has not submitted to Congress any recommendation to increase the capacity of federal prisons. Nevertheless, when the Commission first submitted its guidelines to Congress, it predicted that their implementation would significantly increase the population of a prison system already 50 percent over capacity. The Commission attributed most of the projected increase in the federal prison

population to recent sentencing legislation rather than to decisions made by the Commission itself. Congress, for example, had directed the Commission to set sentences at or near the statutory maximums in cases involving career offenders. The Sentencing Reform Act requires the Commission to recommend prison expansion only when this expansion "might become necessary as a result of the guidelines." Nevertheless, prison expansion may become "necessary as a result of the guidelines" when the Commission has responded to Congressional mandates in drafting its guidelines, just as it may when the Commission has had greater discretion. The fact that the Commission's discretion was limited in some respects offers no justification for its default on its statutory obligation.

2 See 18 U.S.C. Sec. 3553(b).

3. See 18 U.S.C. Sec. 3582(c).

4. Guilty plea rates are currently so high that even substantial increases in prosecutorial bargaining power cannot yield great increases in these rates. Moreover, because sentence severity and guilty plea rates are inversely correlated, an increase in the bargaining power of prosecutors coupled with an increase in sentence severity might not yield any increase in guilty pleas; enhanced prosecutorial power might merely permit prosecutors to continue to secure guilty pleas in a higher-stakes system in which a larger number of cases otherwise would have gone to trial. Indeed, the fact that prosecutors have enhanced bargaining power does not ensure that they will use it; recent Department of Justice policy statements, although they contain ambiguous language and substantial loopholes, generally direct prosecutors to seek guidelines sentences without compromise. If prosecutors do not stretch and take advantage of the loopholes, guilty plea rates may decline.

5. See P. L. 98–473, Sec. 235, *reprinted* at 18 U.S.C. Sec. 3551. During the year preceding submission of the guidelines, I had testified before the U. S. Sentencing Commission twice, discussed the proposed guidelines with members of the Commission and its Executive Director, and written a number of letters to the Commission. Although a supporter of sentencing guidelines in principle, I had been critical of the Commission's early drafts. The draft submitted to Congress seemed much better. I was initially uncertain whether this draft would, on balance, improve the pre-guidelines sentencing system (although, as this chapter will reveal, I later came to the conclusion that the Commission's draft would do substantially more harm than good).

6. Albert W. Alschuler, *Departures and Plea Agreements Under the Sentencing Guidelines*, 117 F.R.D. 459, 468 (1988).

7. I assumed that, with persistence, I could obtain a copy of Mr. Feinberg's mailing list.

8. Lest I paint with too broad a brush, I should note that the "etiquette" of some members of the Commission is not in doubt. Most notably, although the Commission's chairman, Judge William W. Wilkins, Jr., and I disagree about the merits of the guidelines and about a great many other sentencing issues, Judge Wilkins' conduct has always been courteous, open, and fair. In performing his duties, Judge Wilkins has (at some possible personal cost)

exhibited independence from the Department of Justice and from influential political figures. I admire his professionalism.

9. *Congressional Record*, October 6, 1987, at H 8145 (remarks of Mr. Walker).

10. *Congressional Record*, October 5, 1987, at H 8109 (remarks of Mr. Lungren).

11. Meese's letter appears in the *Congressional Record*, October 5, 1987, at H 8109.

12. See *Congressional Record*, December 16, 1985 (remarks of Mr. Rodino).

5

Prosecutorial and Judicial Discretion

Ellen Hochstedler Steury

INTRODUCTION

The long-awaited federal sentencing guidelines from the U. S. Sentencing Commission have been the center of much controversy and discussion, since years before they appeared. There is some belief that the very establishment of the Sentencing Commission violates the non-delegation principle of legislative responsibilities, and that the composition of the Commission—appointment by the executive of members of the judiciary—violates the separation of powers doctrine (Liman, 1987). More common is the concern over the practical effect of severely restricting judicial sentencing discretion (Alschuler, 1978, 1988; Coffee and Tonry, 1983; Rhodes and Conly, 1981; Schulhofer, 1980) or of specific component parts of the proposed guidelines (e.g., establishing a penalty discount for waiving trial and real-offense sentencing, Schulhofer, 1980).

There is in fact, much in these guidelines to fuel a controversy. Part of the controversy stems merely from the fact that determining the appropriate narrow range of sentences for particular offenses is a difficult task of making "hard choices" (Coffee and Tonry, 1983) based on conflicting or competing aims and values (Blumstein, 1987; Robinson, 1987; Stier, 1987; von Hirsch, 1987; Zimring, 1987). Any criminal code revision involving specification of penalties stimulates controversy. After all, what is a robbery worth, and what is it worth compared to embezzlement or assault? (For criticism of the designated relative worth of such offenses, see Alschuler, 1988.) The Commission declined to identify a single guiding justification or goal of punishment that would provide a consistent explanation for the structure of penalties. Instead, and consistent with most bodies charged with formulating sentencing guidelines (Wilkins, 1981), they settled, as has been typical of bodies charged with formulating sentencing guidelines (Wilkins, 1981), for "an empirical approach that uses data estimating the existing sentencing system as a starting point" (U. S. Sentencing Commission, 1987:1A3).

In addition, however, the Commission ventured past the typical boundaries of existing penal codes, and specified which factors should be considered relevant to the sentencing decision and which should not. Furthermore, the guidelines specify exactly **how much** each of the relevant factors is worth in a simple calculation whereby one arrives at "the" appropriate sentence. Some experts have argued that to attempt to identify such factors is a hopelessly complex endeavor and should not be undertaken (Zimring, 1981), while others have suggested that the guidelines as presented do not anticipate enough relevant factors (Alschuler, 1988). Of course, there will be unending debate (and rightly so) about whether the amount taken in a robbery should incur the same penalty enhancement as that incurred through embezzlement or larceny, and whether the enhancement incurred from brandishing a weapon or threatening victims should be cancelled out by a demonstration of "accepting responsibility" for the crime. Despite the controversy over the issues of "comparable worth" of various features of the crime, criminal, victim, and context, I suspect that the real test of the details of the guidelines will be whether the assumption that the whole is the sum of the parts is in fact a correct assumption. I happen to doubt that it is.

The controversy and doomsaying notwithstanding, the U. S. Sentencing Guidelines likely will enjoy widespread compliance and will have a noticeable impact on the adjudication and punishment of offenders. The guidelines were commissioned and then approved by Congress, their use is mandated by law, they may be enforced through a system of appellate review, and compliance will be monitored by the Commission itself, all features which engender compliance (Blumstein et al., 1983:29). In this chapter, I consider the likely effect of the reform on the practices of the prosecutor and judge in adjudicating felony defendants, and I discuss some of the anticipated concomitant problems these changes will create.

THE MECHANICS OF THE GUIDELINES

Under the new guidelines, any particular felony, committed in any particular context, by any particular offender has a corresponding range of months of incarceration established by the Commission. The judge, except in unusual circumstances, is mandated to select a sentence from within that relatively narrow range of sentence lengths, the maximum of which is no more than 25 percent greater than the minimum. Terms of probation are not available as alternatives for most offenses. The offense of which the offender is convicted has an associated "base level" score, to which points are added by the court for established aggravating factors such as degree of bodily injury inflicted, value of property taken or damaged, the type of victim selected, and the degree of planning involved. The information supporting these aggravating factors is provided the court through a presentence report, independent of the information offered by the prosecutor or stipulated in a plea agreement. In a case where a defendant demonstrates "acceptance of responsibility for the crime" (U. S. Sentencing Commission, 1987:3E1.1), 2 points might be subtracted from the offense score.

Offenders also have criminal history scores, which are based on the number, length, and recency of prior sentences. The criminal history scores are cross-tabulated with offense level scores to yield the proper sentencing range. Even when a sentence within the prescribed range is imposed, it must be justified by a statement made in open court as to its appropriateness in that particular case. If judges impose sentences outside the prescribed range, this action must be justified by a statement made in open court, transcribed, and forwarded to correctional officials (18 U.S.C., Sec. 3353(c)).

A hypothetical offense situation might be helpful in portraying the mechanics of the guidelines. Consider the case of a defendant convicted of armed robbery, where the facts are as follows: (1) the robbery offense; (2) was carefully planned; (3) $23,000 was stolen; (4) the robber pointed a gun at the teller; (5) no injuries occurred; (6) the offender had three previous felony convictions, of which two carried terms of imprisonment longer than 13 months and one carried a term of probation; (7) the offender had been out of prison six months at the time of committing the instant offense, but was not under legal sentence at the time of the offense; (8) had no other currently pending charges; (9) confessed to the crime, wholly cooperated with law enforcement authorities, and offered restitution. In the ordinary case, this fact situation would require the court to sentence the offender to a term of imprisonment between 57 months (4 years, 9 months) and 71 months (5 years, 11 months). In the hypothetical situation detailed above, each of the items would carry the following values:

1. The robbery itself carries a base level score of 18.
2. The "more than minimal planning" does not affect the sentence in the case of robbery, but it does (inexplicably) in other offenses such as burglary, property damage or destruction, embezzlement, and aggravated assault.
3. The amount of money taken increases the base level by two points.

4. Brandishing a firearm increases the base level by another three points.
5. The fact that no victim injuries occurred avoids other possible level increases, which would otherwise be calculated on the basis of the degree of the injury.
6. The criminal history score totals nine points, comprised of three points for each sentence of imprisonment longer than thirteen months, and one point for the sentence of probation; while the recency of the latest imprisonment incurs two additional points.
7. The absence of other pending charges avoids a possible score increase.
8. The confession, coupled with the cooperation and the volunteered restitution might persuade the court to conclude that the offender had "accepted responsibility" for the crime, which could result in decreasing the offense level score by two points.

In the above example, the offense points sum to 21, and the criminal history points sum to 9. The sentencing range associated with offense level 21 and the criminal history score of 9 (Category IV) is 57 to 71 months. Defendants so sentenced, or the government, could appeal by claiming that the guidelines had been incorrectly applied (18 U.S.C., Sec. 3742(a)(2) and Sec. 3742(b)(2), 1988). An appellate court would review the case.

If the sentencing court in its wisdom believed that the offender deserved less than 51 months or more than 63 months, a departure from the guidelines would be allowable, provided a written justification from the judge accompanied the departure. In such cases, defendants (if the sentence were longer than the maximum specified by the guidelines) or the government (if the sentence were shorter than the minimum specified by the guidelines) could appeal for a review of the stated reasons given by the judge for the departure (18 U.S.C., Sec. 3742(a)(3)(A) and Sec. 3742(b)(3)(A), 1988).

PROSECUTORIAL DISCRETION

The literature reflects a fair amount of concern that limiting judicial discretion will increase the bargaining power of prosecutors in fixing sentences through charge reduction or selection [see Endnote 1]. Given the increased certainty of sentence associated with particular charges, the argument is that the prosecutor would be in a stronger position to negotiate guilty pleas (Alschuler, 1978, 1988; Coffee and Tonry, 1983; Rhodes and Conly, 1981; Schulhofer, 1980). The concern over the possible abuse of discretion encompasses both the fear of excessive leniency and excessive severity, and how each of these positions relate to the prosecutor's leverage in negotiating guilty pleas.

Excessive Severity

The Commission has formulated counting rules for the manner in which multiple counts of the same kind of offense will affect the base level score. For example, if the armed robber in our example above had gone from teller to teller, pointing the gun at each of them and taking money from each, he could conceivably be charged with multiple counts of armed robbery arising out of the same event. The guidelines state quite clearly that such behavior should not be treated as separate offenses, and that prosecutors should not attempt to increase their bargaining leverage by threatening to charge several counts. (Of course, the advantage in doing so exists in large part because of the rigidity of the guidelines themselves. In a system of wide judicial sentencing discretion, multiple counts would carry no more importance than a single count, given knowledge of the entire criminal transaction.)

Likewise, if our example had included bodily injury to a teller, the guidelines would direct that the injury be counted as an aggravating factor and not treated as the separate crime of aggravated assault. In situations where charging multiple counts is appropriate, the guidelines specify counting rules which allow for penalty increases to the main offense only in small increments, and they totally discount those offenses that are dramatically less serious than the most serious offense. These policies effectively neutralize much of a prosecutor's discretion to be excessively punitive, or to employ the threat of such punitiveness as a lever in plea negotiations.

Degrees of Leniency

The prosecutor's discretion to be lenient under the guidelines, that "most important weapon in the prosecutor's arsenal" (Blumberg, 1967:58), can be explored more easily by returning to the hypothetical example posed above as a point of departure. Suppose that our defendant did not act alone but in concert with an accomplice. Further suppose that the cooperation he offers the government includes testimony that will convict his robbery partner of not only the offense in question, but several other bank "heists," of which he has knowledge, but in which he took no part. For this, of course, he wants leniency. In fact, he wants more than the reduction of two points (about a 20 percent reduction in the length of the term and measly in his mind) from the offense level score allowed for "acceptance of responsibility." Suppose the government badly needs and wants his testimony. Suppose that to the prosecutor, this information is worth reducing the robbery charge to theft.

In defense of the prosecutor's action, it must be explained that the charge reduction of such magnitude is necessitated by the structure of the guidelines. Under the guidelines, there is no base offense of armed robbery which might be easily reduced to robbery. The guidelines include only a base offense of robbery, and the armed part of it works as an aggravating factor to add points to the basic offense score. It appears that under these new rules, a prosecutor will not have the option to negotiate over "factual nuances" of a particular crime because that information will be independently forwarded to the court and the court is instructed to base the sentence on all relevant information or justify the departure.

A. If an indictment or information for robbery has already been filed, then the terms of the negotiation would have to include the dismissal of the robbery charge and a plea of guilty to the crime of theft, and a promise by the defendant to provide testimony against his partner. If this plea agreement were accepted by the court (a matter to be discussed in a later section of this chapter), the court would calculate the appropriate sentence based on the same fact situation and the same criminal history, adding all the relevant factors, as was done in the previous hypothetical calculation of penalty, but using the lesser offense as the base charge. The result would be a prison term of between 15 and 21 months (assuming the court would not be disposed to give the two-point penalty discount for "acceptance of responsibility," given that the base offense charge has been reduced for this reason).

It is worth noting that one fact situation results in very different calculations for aggravating factors for the two different crimes of theft and robbery. More than minimal planning, which did not add anything to the robbery score, adds two points to the theft score. The amount of money taken in the robbery added two points to the robbery score, while the same amount taken in a theft adds six points to the base theft score of 4. The use of a firearm is not anticipated by the guidelines for theft, and so no provision is made for a score increase.

B. If an indictment for robbery has not already been returned, then there is no need to base a plea agreement upon a dismissal. The prosecutor who is quick to show leniency will be in a position initially to file the charge to which the defendant is willing to plead guilty. This course would result in the same sentence as imposed in the scenario described immediately above, but the terms of the agreement would not include the dismissal of the robbery charge, there would be no need to make a promise about pursuing or not pursuing other potential charges, and therefore, if the guidelines and commentary are to be interpreted literally, and presumably the court acknowledges the possibility of a guilty plea that is *not* part of a "plea agreement," then the judge would have less discretion to reject the plea agreement than otherwise (but see Alschuler, 1988:474, n.57) [see Endnote 2].

C. Alternatively, the prosecutor and defendant might enter into an agreement that included a plea of guilty to the robbery charge, but specified a particularly lenient sentence as a part of the plea negotiations. If the court accepted such an agreement, it would be obligated to impose the specified sentence or justify in writing any term falling outside the guidelines for this factual crime situation and criminal history.

D. It is only the very lucky defendant who has information to trade for leniency, however. Suppose that our defendant has no information, but only a guilty plea to trade. Suppose the prosecutor wishes to avoid a trial. The prosecutor and defendant enter into a plea agreement to the charge of theft, with stipulations of fact that prove the robbery. This sort of agreement operates to allow the court to sentence according to the robbery guidelines, but it also ensures that the defendant will not receive a sentence longer than the statutory (not guidelines) maximum allowed for theft. In this case, the defendant would be sentenced to a term no greater than five years' incarceration and fined $5,000, as provided by the applicable federal criminal statute (18 U.S.C., Sec. 661, 1988).

A five-year sentence is not substantially less than the midpoint of the guideline range for robbery with these attendant factors and credit for "accepting responsibility" (5 years, 4 months), yet it is substantially more than the midpoint of the guideline range for theft with these attendant factors (2 years). This example portrays, then, how plea agreements and stipulations might provide the equivalent of the "hollow promise," a gesture of leniency that requires only the slightest actual yield from the state. Such has been the goal of prosecutors for decades, a goal often routinely realized.

Stipulations

Stipulations are not requirements of plea agreements, but if used, they must "set forth the relevant facts and circumstances of the actual offense conduct and offender characteristics" (U. S. Sentencing Commission, 1987:6B1.4). Commentary accompanying this section makes clear that **all** relevant facts must be disclosed, obviating the possibility that the adversaries might bargain over which "relevant" facts should be included. Facts in dispute are to be included, and identified as such.

At first glance, a stipulation which provides more serious conduct than is charged may hold little attraction for the defendant, but it may find acceptance if it is the only deal offered. Further, if the resulting sentence is substantially less than the defendant might receive were the case tried, it might enjoy some popularity. A stipulation also has the advantage of demonstrating cooperation through full disclosure and admission. Finally, it provides the opportunity for the defendant, in concert with the prosecution, to note positive factors in the justification of the lenient sentence anticipated without contesting the facts, much like what is accomplished in a "slow plea" to the bench (Eisenstein and Jacob, 1977).

Courts will find the stipulated agreements convenient if they speed the disposition of cases and can be trusted for reliable and complete information. A stipulated agreement may be more helpful for determining an appropriate penalty than a presentence investigation report which is the result of a rudimentary investigation and subject to frequent error (see *Wisconsin Law Review*, 1986). Because the judge is not bound by the stipulation, and because the presentence investigation report will serve as a check on the stipulation's reliability, it is likely that stipulations will become reliable and a primary component of negotiated plea agreements. Finally, stipulated agreements require adversaries (rather than the court) to justify out-of-range penalties, and provide certainty that sentences will not be appealed.

Despite vociferous claims to the contrary (e.g., Fine, 1986), the best empirical evidence we have suggests that plea negotiations are not fast, loose, and wild deals that result in the "escape of the guilty" (Nardulli et al., 1985; Feeley, 1979; Heumann, 1978; Rosett and Cressey, 1976; Maynard, 1984; Miethe, 1987). Excessive leniency in plea negotiations certainly is not the goal of most prosecutors, although surely sometimes it is a by-product of inadequate resources, incompetence, or sheer laziness (Alschuler, 1968; 1981). The prevailing opinion among practitioners and scholars is that plea negotiations are "essential" and "should be encouraged" (*Santobello v. New York*, 1971), and the guidelines seem to reflect that perspective. This novel notion of the stipulated plea agreement seems particularly designed to support the practice of plea negotiation, while at the same time establish a record of admission of the actual facts involved.

The various hypothetical courses of action that a prosecutor might take, reviewed above, portray the kinds of problems feared by those who express concern about prosecutorial power over sentencing under the guidelines. It is clear that disparate results can be achieved. It is also clear that the charge makes a significant difference in the calculation of the sentence, and that negotiations can make substantial differences in resulting sentences as well. Nonetheless, I predict that experience will show that the prosecutor's discretion will be restricted, not expanded, under the provisions of these guidelines. It will be restricted through a change in judicial supervision of plea agreements mandated by the guidelines (discussed below). It will also be limited by the fact that leniency through charge selection in some cases can be granted only in huge allotments, not in small increments, as the hypothetical examples portrayed. I think it is probable that agreements specifying the sentence will grow in popularity, in contrast to previous practice which favored charge negotiations (Rhodes and Conly, 1981), and that plea agreements with stipulations will become the common method of settling cases. As portrayed above, these forms of negotiation offer a compromise between the extremes of no leniency and leniency that may well be unacceptable to the court and repugnant to the prosecutor. These changes may not be totally unwelcome to prosecutors. It is possible that prosecutors working under these guidelines will not resent their diminished discretion to reward guilty pleaders and may be glad to pass the pressure on to the next decision-maker (Church, 1976). Certainly, if prosecutors and judges alike wish to limit the plea discount to a maximum of two points, the opportunity need only be seized.

JUDICIAL DISCRETION

Sentencing

It seems apparent enough that these guidelines do restrict judicial discretion in the selection of sentences. Not only has the range of length of imprisonment been narrowly specified, but the "in/out" decision has been limited. Probation is unavailable for many offenses, and probation without some kind of jail term is rare. Despite these restrictions, the Commission has issued a very broad and explicit invitation for judges to depart from the guidelines, provided they offer adequate written justification. The guidelines urge consideration of departure under some specified circumstances, and there is a guarantee by the Commission that at least for the present, the only departures prohibited *a priori* are those based on reasons of race, sex, national origin, creed, religion, socioeconomic status, economic hardship, or in most cases, physical condition or drug dependence. "With those few exceptions, however, the Commission does not intend to limit the kinds of factors (whether mentioned anywhere else in the guidelines) that could constitute grounds for departure in an unusual case" (U. S. Sentencing Commission, 1987:1A4.b). If judges are willing to use this discretion frequently, it is possible that the impact of the guidelines will prove minimal, depending, of course, upon the results of the appellate review.

Plea Discounts

Implicit rewards to guilty pleaders will be more difficult to grant under the new guidelines. Even for within-range sentences, judges are required to provide a verbal explanation of the appropriateness of the particular sentence (18 U.S.C., Sec. 3553(c)(1), 1988). It is likely that these routine justifications quickly will become comprised of standard catchwords and phrases devoid of any meaningful or telling information. Nonetheless, the fact that some reason unrelated to pleading must be explicitly stated, together with the fact that the narrowed ranges limit the size of the potential plea discount, will make it more difficult for judges to encourage guilty pleas through implicit rewards. Such implicit rewards might persist, but at the very least, the message could not be so clear or so dramatic.

The Commission attempted to capture, control, and standardize the judicial inclination to reward guilty pleaders by providing a discount for those whose post-offense deeds support an inference that they have "accepted responsibility" for their crimes. For such offenders, the guidelines specify that courts may (not "must") subtract two points from a pleader's offense level score. Applied to prison terms of at least two years, this discount amounts to a 20 percent reduction, and it is greater (a 25 to 33 percent reduction) for less serious offenses within shorter prescribed ranges. To avoid the appearance of approving a reward for the waiver of constitutional rights, however, the Commission was careful to state very clearly that neither merely pleading guilty nor requesting a trial on the facts is dispositive of the matter of "accepting responsibility" (U. S. Sentencing Commission, 1987:3E1.1(b),(c)). Despite the Commission's statements in this regard, it is perhaps naive to expect that the "responsibility" discount will operate as anything other than a pleader's discount (see Alschuler, 1988:466).

Plea Supervision

Proper judicial oversight of plea negotiations is outlined in the Federal Rules of Criminal Procedure. One provision in the new guidelines appears to have increased judicial discretion in accepting pleas pursuant to plea negotiations, at least in tone, although practice may prove no effect. The extent of this expansion will not be left entirely up to the judges, but it will depend in large part on the opportunities provided by the antecedent actions of the prosecutors.

For several years, federal judges have been required to document the terms of plea agreements for the record, to ensure that the defendant's guilty plea is entered knowingly, understandingly, and voluntarily, and to ascertain that the defendant comprehends the certain and potential consequences of entering a guilty plea (Fed. R. Crim. P. ll(c), (d), 1988). In addition, judges are required, before accepting a guilty plea, to determine that the evidence provides a "factual basis" for a conviction on the charges (Fed. R. Crim. P. ll(f), 1988). This fact-finding could be an important check on the prosecutor's selection of charge. Clearly, this rule prohibits the kind of unrelated charging described decades ago by Sudnow (1965). On the other hand, there seems to be nothing to discourage accepting pleas to lesser-included-offenses; on the contrary, this is explicitly anticipated (Fed. R. Crim. P. ll(e)(l), 1988). Obviously, a fact situation describing a robbery provides a "factual basis" for pleading guilty to a theft. The current operationalization of the term "factual basis" implies a criterion of minimal sufficiency of evidence, without a concern for a surfeit. In other words, the judicial check on pleas operated as a check for government error, as well as protection for defendants.

The innovation in the guidelines directs the judge, when presented with a plea pursuant to an agreement based on dismissal of charges or promises not to pursue other potential charges, to reject a guilty plea unless the court "determines, for reasons stated on the record, that the remaining charges adequately reflect the seriousness of the actual offense behavior..." (U. S. Sentencing Commission, 1987:6Bl.2a). This instruction represents an important change in the balance between the judiciary and the executive in the adjudication of criminals, and it is unnecessary and ill-advised. Furthermore, the desired end—regulation of prosecutorial leniency in plea negotiations and preservation of the sentencing function for judges—could be accomplished through other means which would do less damage to the separation of powers.

Under the guideline 6B1.2a, the nature of the judicial check on the charge in a plea agreement is no longer a matter of ensuring sufficiency of evidence, but of ensuring some rough equivalency between the evidence and charge [see Endnote 3]. In fact, one commentator concluded that "under the guidelines, a judge should not accept any agreement that permits a defendant to plead guilty to an offense less serious than the one that he or she apparently committed" (Alschuler, 1988:474).

This is clearly an encroachment on the prosecutor's discretion to be lenient, despite the Commission's dubious attempt to first deny it and then to justify it:

> This requirement does not authorize judges to intrude upon the charging discretion of the prosecutor. If the government's motion to dismiss charges or statement that potential charges will not be pursued is not contingent on the disposition of the remaining charges, the judge should defer to the government's position except under extraordinary circumstances (Rule 48(a), Fed. R. Crim. P., 1988). However, when the dismissal of charges or agreement not to pursue potential charges is contingent on acceptance of a plea agreement, the court's authority to adjudicate guilt and impose sentence is implicated, and the court is to determine whether or not dismissal of charges will undermine the sentencing guidelines (U. S. Sentencing Commission, 1987:6B1.2).

The requirement in 6B1.2a does too little and too much at the same time. It does too little in that it can be easily circumvented. Neither the prosecutor who wishes to show leniency, nor the defendant who wishes to benefit thereby, has anything to gain by including in the terms of the agreement either dismissals or promises not to pursue other potential charges. This invitation for judges to reject guilty pleas based on reduced charges is something that the two adversaries could easily cooperate to avoid, and it is naive to think that such terms cannot be avoided. Perhaps more negotiating will occur prior to the filing of charges, avoiding the need to later seek dismissals and judicial approval. And surely, an unspoken agreement to decline pursuit of other potential charges could be arranged. In fact, if one adopts a broad meaning of "other potential charges," such an agreement is implicit in all plea negotiations [see Endnote 4].

It does too much in that it is clearly an encroachment on prosecutorial discretion to *nol pros* or dismiss charges—either outright or as a path to a reduced charge—in a gesture of leniency. That such leniency is in exchange for a guilty plea does not make it any more a matter for judicial correction than if it were in exchange for nothing, at least not as long as our judiciary approves of and encourages plea negotiations. The justification offered by the Commission is unsatisfactory. Every choice the prosecutor makes has "implications" for subsequent judicial choices. The court's authority to adjudicate guilt or impose a sentence is equally "implicated" by the prosecutor's selection of charge, whether it is a part of a plea negotiation or not a part of it. The Commission has designed a provision that essentially requires the judge to determine the extent of the **enforcement** of the law, a prerogative of the executive. Although the courts have been reluctant to limit their own discretion in this respect, and the matter of the balance between judicial oversight of plea negotiations and the prosecutor's discretion in the selection of charges is not well-settled case law (*United States v. Bean*, 1977), where the line **should** be drawn to keep the executive and the judiciary in balance and operating as checks on each other is not difficult to discern. The opinion in *United States v. Ammidown* (1973), taking into consideration the implications of plea bargaining for the judge's sentencing discretion, states clearly the position that protects the separation of powers and duties between the judiciary and the executive:

> . . .trial judges are not free to withhold approval of guilty pleas . . . merely because their conception of the public interest differs from that of the prosecuting attorney. The question is not what the judge would do if he were the prosecuting attorney, but whether he can say that the action of the prosecuting attorney is such a departure from sound prosecutorial principle as to mark it an abuse of prosecutorial discretion (at 622).

Of course, rules have to be operationalized, and experience may prove the equivalency of these two different-sounding rules. Perhaps we will find that when the charges in a plea negotiation do not "adequately reflect the seriousness of the actual offense behavior," we would all agree that there has been "abuse of prosecutorial discretion," but I doubt it. I think guideline 6B1.2a encourages and even requires the court to substitute its judgment for the prosecutor's in the selection of charges in negotiated pleas [and only in negotiated pleas—see Endnote 5], and that it does not limit it to those situations where there is clear abuse of discretion.

The requirement in 6B1.2a does too much because it is unnecessary, as well. The judge is free to depart from the prescribed sentencing range associated with any particular charge, provided adequate written justification is offered. Truly excessive leniency (or an abuse of prosecutorial discretion) must surely be an adequate justification for departure from the guidelines. When the prosecutor has charged too leniently, the judge may balance that decision wholly within the normal bounds of the judicial function—the sentencing decision. If this solution is inadequate because the range of sentence available is limited by the statutory maximum for the lesser offense charged, then rather than redefine the role of the judiciary, the better course would be for the legislature to alter penalty maximums [see Endnote 6].

Use of the Presentence Investigation Report

To assist in imposing a sentence that adversely reflects the seriousness of the offense, the guidelines provide the judge with an investigative agent that might significantly alter the nature of the adjudicatory process in this country. Guideline 6Al.l requires that a presentence investigation report be filed with the court before any sentence is imposed on the convicted offender. This practice is of long standing, except that the new guidelines have effectively deleted that part of the rule which allowed defendants to waive the investigation and preparation of the report (Fed. R. Crim. P. 32, 1988). The guidelines further mandate that in the case of plea agreements, the plea may not be accepted and judgment entered until after the presentence investigation report has been filed and considered. This guideline is consistent with current practice as well, where judges consult the presentence investigation report to assist in determining that a "factual basis" (minimally sufficient evidence to establish an offender's guilt beyond a reasonable doubt) exists for the plea and that the charge is not an erroneous one. The important change in the role of the presentence investigation report has to do with how it will be used in conjunction with guideline 6Bl.2a, requiring charge-evidence equivalency.

Presentence investigation reports have been used by the court for two purposes: (1) to individualize the sentence in each case and (2) to guard against possible errors against the defendant in cases where guilty pleas are negotiated. Use of presentence investigation reports for justifying punitive sentences has enjoyed a long tradition of acceptance, despite the fact that the information does not meet trial-admissible standards (*Williams v. New York*, 1949), may include wild speculation and wholly unsubstantiated claims (for examples, see Remington et al., 1968), and is often erroneous (*Wisconsin Law Review*, 1986). Evidence suggests that presentence investigation reports do have an appreciable influence on judges' selection of penalties (Rush and Robertson, 1987; but see Rosecrance, 1988).

In negotiated cases, presentence investigation reports have been used as a check on the factual basis for guilty pleas. In these cases, the presentence information is in many ways a substitute for facts that would otherwise be presented at a trial (Fennell and Hall, 1980:1627). But a proffered guilty plea is clearly a different matter than a trial, because the plea constitutes an admission to the elements of the charged offense and a waiver of rights attendant to trial. Problems of accuracy in the presentence investigation report are not of the same magnitude in negotiated plea cases, because the facts are not in dispute with respect to the charged offense. In this instance, the presentence investigation report is used as a shield for the defendant, not as a sword for the punitive forces of the state.

Now under the guidelines, the presentence investigation report may be used to assess the adequacy of the charge. A judge is required to reject a plea agreement involving a dismissal of charges or a promise not to pursue other potential charges if the remaining charge does not adequately reflect the seriousnesss of the actual offense behavior (U. S. Sentencing Commission, 1987:6B1.2a). Now, an agent of the judiciary will conduct an investigation to gather information to assess guilt in relation to the charge. The information will be used as a sword of the state not only at sentencing, a judicial function, but in second-guessing the charge selection, not a judicial function heretofore. With respect to finding a factual basis for negotiated pleas, this information of questionable reliability will no longer be used only as a shield, but as a sword as well. Furthermore, reliability of the information will not necessarily be ensured by disclosure to the defense. The guidelines do not explicitly require disclosure of the presentence investigation report before the court relies on that information for rejecting a guilty plea. The guidelines and the Federal Rules of Criminal Procedure (1988) merely require timely disclosure before sentencing. And, despite that explicit requirement, investigation of judicial practice indicates that a substantial minority of judges have not honored the spirit of this mandate (Fennel and Hall, 1980). When the defense has inadequate opportunity to check and counter the claims contained in presentence investigation reports, inaccuracies are even more likely to persist.

Traditionally in our system of adjudication, the adversaries controlled exclusively the evidence considered by the fact-finder, a passive entity forbidden to direct any investigation or independently gather evidence. Using presentence investigation information to assess the charge-evidence equivalency makes the presentence investigation more like an independent judicial investigation. This change is a marked departure from the traditional manner of presenting evidence in our adversarial system, even in our adversarial-turned-negotiating system, and a move toward the inquisitorial system's powerful figure of investigative magistrate (Ploscowe, 1935). Might this subtle but very important change be yet another step in abandoning our adversarial system of adjudication? This change requires the judiciary to become involved in the investigation of crime in order to shape enforcement of the law, which are duties of the executive branch.

SUMMARY AND CONCLUSIONS

The expressed goal of the Commission was to curtail judicial sentencing discretion. To reach this end, the Commission devised a set of narrow sentence ranges, one of which would apply to any particular offense and offender, to be imposed by the court unless a departure from the range was explicitly justified. At the same time, the Commission heeded fears expressed by many that the result of restricting judicial sentencing discretion would be to allow the prosecutor, through the selection of charges, to determine in large part the resulting sentence. In an effort to control what must have been viewed as excessive prosecutorial leniency in plea negotiations (despite evidence that excessive leniency is not a hallmark of prosecutorial policy), the Commission strengthened the role of judges in overseeing plea negotiations, requiring them to reject guilty pleas in cases where the charge does not "adequately reflect the seriousness of the actual offense behavior," or in other words, to regulate the selection of charges. To provide judges with the information needed to make the charge-evidence equivalency check, the Commission has directed that an agent of the judiciary conduct an independent investigation (called the presentence investigation, but used now for purposes other than for which it was designed), and to file a report with the court prior to the acceptance of a plea based on an agreement.

I have pointed out that this new judicial role in plea supervision seems to be an encroachment on the discretionary powers of prosecutors. And I have suggested that to use the presentence investigation report for assessing an equivalency between charge and evidence changes the very nature of our adversarial system of adjudication and furthers the encroachment of the judiciary on the legitimate function of the executive. The delicate balance of powers between the executive and the judiciary that has served our system well thus far is threatened by these changes.

How, then, does one control prosecutorial discretion, particularly that associated with plea negotiations, when judicial discretion, which might otherwise be used to compensate for prosecutorial discretion, has been so severely restricted? If the aim is to control prosecutorial discretion, it should be accomplished directly. If Congress has the authority to restrict judicial sentencing discretion through mandatory guidelines, it has the power to curb prosecutorial discretion as well. And if the aim is not really to control prosecutorial discretion generally, but only that which is used in plea negotiations, then mandatory guidelines can accomplish that. If the discretion available to each of the primary decision-makers in the system—prosecutors and judges—were equally restricted by the legislature, then the balance within the criminal justice system would remain intact. It is risky business first to create an imbalance of influence by restricting the discretion of judges, and riskier still then to attempt to correct that imbalance by blurring the distinction between the function of the judiciary and the function of the executive.

ENDNOTES

1. Conventional wisdom has long held that discretion in the criminal justice system is a fixed sum and that if it is restricted at one point, it will merely be increased at another point. There is neither compelling logic nor empirical support (Miethe, 1987) for this adage, and it is advisable to clarify the terms here. First, there is no reason to assume that discretion is a fixed sum. When the range of choices is broadened, there is more discretion in the system than when they are narrowed. Second, when the discretion of one decision-maker is restricted, it does not necessarily follow that the range of choices available to another decision-maker has changed at all. What is likely, all else being equal, is that when the discretion of one functionary is limited, the **effects** of the discretion of another functionary may be more direct or more pronounced, but that is something different than the discretion being increased.

2. Although in many jurisdictions guilty pleas are not seen as necessarily pursuant to negotiations or an "agreement," this may not be the case in the federal jurisdiction. Some practitioners report that virtually all guilty pleas in their district are treated as "plea agreements."

3. It is interesting to note that what is required by 6B12.a could have been accomplished easily years ago under the "factual basis" requirement of Rule ll(f) of the Fed. R. Crim. Proc. Judges could have, but did not, interpret "factual basis" to mean evidence-charge equivalency rather than evidence sufficiency.

4. It is intriguing to speculate on the repercussions of the following scenario: A prosecutor presents to the court a plea negotiation involving a charge reduction acceptable to the defendant, but the court finds it unacceptable because the charge does not adequately reflect the seriousness of the actual offense behavior. The defendant withdraws his plea, and the prosecutor persists in bringing only the lesser charge. There is a "trial" to the bench in which no defense is offered other than the not guilty plea. In this case, the

court would have exactly the same options for sentencing that would have resulted from accepting the new guideline 6B1.2a plea. Consider this possibility where there is more at stake than the plea itself, such as information the prosecutor desires. While conflict between prosecutor and judge is a possibility invited by the increased judicial supervision, it is more likely that cooperation will prove the primary model. Prosecutors will justify their leniency, and judges will concur. To do otherwise would create more work and workplace tension.

5. It is ironic that judges are to superimpose their judgment of the appropriate charge only in the case of negotiated guilty pleas, but necessary because of the justification offered for the usurpation of power. For the prosecutor who does the negotiating before filing charges and who thereby avoids having to seek a dismissal, there is no supervisory judicial check explicitly provided by these guidelines. Furthermore, there is no check if there is a "trial" rather than a "plea agreement."

6. It is understandable that Congress did not undertake a broadening of statutory limits on penalties at a time when they were imposing on judges narrow sentencing guidelines. On the face of it, such a move would seem contrary to the larger effort. However, the manner in which the guidelines were established created this very problem of the lack of charge reductions in small increments. Expanding the statutory maxima would allow sentencing judges to compensate for charge reductions that entail too great a penalty reduction. Such a scheme, however, would require that judges depart from the guidelines with some frequency, and it would raise the problems involved in being convicted of one offense but sentenced for another. This latter problem, of course, is not unique to a system of sentencing under the guidelines.

6

Case Processing and the Federal Sentencing Guidelines

Lynne Goodstein   John H. Kramer

INTRODUCTION

Case processing can be viewed as the movement of cases through the various stages of the criminal justice system from arrest through sentencing. The recent implementation of sentencing guidelines mandated by the Congress in the Comprehensive Crime Control Act of 1984 has significant implications for case processing.

The guidelines system developed under this mandate consists of 43 offense levels (measuring severity of offense), six criminal history categories, and numerous enhancements such as degree of bodily injury and weapon use. The base offense level for a particular crime is set by the conviction offense, but it can be adjusted upwards for elements such as the vulnerability of the victim or downwards for such issues as defendant's acceptance of responsibility for the offense. These 43 offense levels combine with the six criminal history categories to establish a 258-cell matrix. Within each matrix category a range of months of prison time is indicated which is the guideline recommendation for judges to follow in sentencing. By statute, judicial departures from the guidelines are limited to whenever "an aggravating or mitigating circumstance . . . was not adequately taken into consideration by the Sentencing Commission" (18 U.S.C. Sec. 3553(b),1989).

The sentencing guidelines have initiated sweeping changes that reverberate through the various stages in the process from arrest to conviction. This chapter will focus upon the guidelines' impact on the following parts of the process: (1) the decision to charge; (2) the decision as to the level of the charge and "adjustments" to the charge; (3) setting of bail and pretrial detention; (4) decisions regarding trial, guilty pleas and dispositional findings; (5) sentencing decisions; and (6) appellate review. Although case processing would generally include discussions of correctional and parole processing, we will leave that to other authors.

One objective of the Commission as set forth in the legislative mandate is that it [should] "provide certainty and fairness in meeting the purposes of sentencing, avoiding unwarranted sentencing disparities among defendants with similar records who have been found guilty of similar criminal conduct" (28 U.S.C. Sec. 99(1)(a), (1)(b), 1989). However, there are many opportunities in the chain of case processing for similar offenders not to be processed similarly. Will prosecutors charge crimes in the same manner across diverse jurisdictions? Will prosecutors unilaterally remove all or some of the aggravators or mitigators and will this vary depending upon the aspects of the defendant, the offense, region of the country, predilections of the judiciary or other factors that may result in the appearance of fairness and disparity in reality?

Questions arise also as to the role of the probation officer in the application of the guidelines and whether any shift in the probation officer's role will affect the processing of cases. For example, if probation officers are key individuals in preparing presentence investigation reports upon which guidelines decisions are based, they may be required to make significant decisions regarding enhancements, credits, and perhaps reasons for departures.

Guidelines may not only be changing sentencing; they may also influence role relationships among the judges, defense attorneys, U. S. Attorneys, and probation officers. Some research has indicated the significance of the courtroom work group and its implications for sentencing (Eisenstein, 1977). In this chapter we will also explore the roles of the various actors, their interrelationships in the courtroom work group, and how they may be changing as a result of the guidelines and their impact on case processing.

METHODOLOGY

To obtain some preliminary observations from individuals involved in the implementation of the guidelines, we interviewed a commissioner of the U. S. Sentencing Commission, several Commission staff members, several U. S. Attorneys, and several federal probation officers, as well as reviewing relevant literature. Interviewees provided us with accounts of their limited experience with the guidelines as well as their speculations about future directions [see Endnote 1]. Although the guidelines apply to all offenses committed after November 1, 1987, the normal lag time necessary to process cases, coupled with the debate as to the guidelines' constitutionality, has meant that relatively few guidelines cases have been processed to date. With the U. S. Supreme Court's opinion in *Mistretta v. United States* (1989), holding that the U. S. Sentencing Commission is constitutional, the full processing of cases will move forward.

ORGANIZATIONAL CONTEXT

The U. S. Attorneys are appointed by the President, with the advice and consent of Congress, and serve as chief prosecutors in 95 district offices geographically scattered throughout the United States. The Attorney General's office sets administrative guidelines for these U. S. Attorneys to follow and the office has established an Executive Committee to act as a liaison between the Attorney General's office and the U. S. Attorneys' offices.

While researchers have investigated the reactions of state prosecutors to these guidelines (Miethe, 1987; Lubitz and Kempinen, 1987; Casper and Brereton, 1984), there are reasons to believe that U. S. Attorneys may respond differently to sentencing reforms at the federal level. Available research on the responses of district attorneys to guidelines focuses on local elected officials who are dependent upon fulfilling the mandate of the local electorate and are not a part of an organizational network that provides administrative leadership and direction.

The coordination of the U. S. Attorneys' offices by the Attorney General's Office may be of major importance to the implementation of sentencing guidelines. Compared with decentralized state offices, there is greater likelihood that consistent policies will be adopted across the U. S. Attorneys' offices in the application of guidelines case processing. However, Eisenstein's (1977) research of U. S. Attorneys suggests that this coordination may be more form than substance. For example, Eisenstein found that certain U. S. Attorneys' offices have historically functioned independently of the Attorney General's office and thus would be unlikely to respond to pronouncements from the central office about processing of cases under the new guidelines.

An additional issue in attempting to distinguish between the federal level and the state prosecutions is that of backlog and case processing pressures. Because of a better resource to case ratio, the federal system does not suffer from the same backlog as the state courts. Hence, U. S. Attorneys' offices have greater discretion in deciding whether to risk trial or to bargain for guilty pleas. Thus, the discussion of the federal implementation of guidelines is not hampered by caseload backlog typical of sentencing reform implementation in state courts.

APPLICATION OF THE GUIDELINES: A SAMPLE CASE

In order to demonstrate both the application of the guidelines as well as to serve as a departure point for systematically raising questions regarding case processing, we will begin our discussion with a sample case: Assume a defendant has been arrested for selling heroin to undercover agents on three separate occasions. In the first transaction, the sale involved five grams. The other sales, were eight and fifteen grams respectively. The defendant has used a 15-year-old high school student as the courier for the third sale, which occurred 700 feet from a high school. When arrested, the defendant had a loaded pistol in her purse.

There is much that is still unknown about the case. Many facts are missing which are likely to influence the sentence received by the defendant if she is convicted. The best estimate that may be made at the time of arrest involves an analysis of the facts of the offenses themselves. Considering the fact that our defendant proffered heroin to undercover agents on three separate occasions in exchange for money, we could predict that this woman will be convicted of drug trafficking (U. S. Sentencing Commission, Sec. 2D1.1, 1987). Computation of the defendant's likely sentence would be made as follows. First, in the case of multiple drug offenses, the Commission has specified that the total quantities of all drugs in the three transactions be added together (Sec. 2D1.1, Commentary). In addition, the drug quantity is doubled if the transaction involves the use of a juvenile between 14 and 18 years of age in the trafficking (Sec. 2D1.2). Since the third offense involved a 15-year old courier, the quantity for the third offense is doubled. In addition, since the transaction occurred within 1,000 feet of a school yard (Sec. 2D1.3), the amount of drugs is again doubled. Furthermore, the loaded firearm in the defendant's possession at the time of the third offense further increases the base offense level by 2 points.

To calculate the offense level, using the best information available at the time of the arrest, the total quantity of drugs on which to base the sentence would be computed as follows:

1st sale—5 gr. heroin
2nd sale—8 gr. heroin

3rd sale—15 gr. heroin x 2 (youth enhancement) = 30 gr. heroin x
2 (1,000 ft. from school) = 60 gr. heroin
Total = 73 grams of heroin

By consulting the Drug Quantity Table (Sec. 2D1.1), we see that the
distribution of 60–79 grams of heroin results in a base offense level of
22, increased by two levels to 24 due to the defendant's possession of
the firearm during the commission of the third offense. If this defendant has no prior criminal history, if no other facts relevant to the case
become apparent after the arrest, and if this defendant is convicted
of the offenses as described above, the guidelines provide that she
should be sentenced to prison for a term of between 41 and 51 months.
    What will be revealed through the probation officer's search of our
defendant's criminal history is that she was on probation at the time
of her arrest and had previous convictions for drug possession and for
burglary. For the drug possession charge, she received a 90-day jail
sentence and for the burglary, she received a 1–2 year sentence. The
Commission's guidelines specify that points are accrued based upon
prior sentences received by the defendant. The defendant received
three points for each sentence with a maximum exceeding one year,
one month, two points for each prior prison sentence of at least 60
days, and one point for other sentences not counted up to a maximum
of four points. Therefore, our defendant's criminal history score
would be computed as follows:

90-day sentence = 2 points
2-year sentence = 3 points
Parole supervision = 2 points
Total = 7 points

With an offense score of 24 and a criminal history score of 7, which
places the defendant in Category IV (See Appendix B), the suggested
guidelines range is 77–96 months.
    This example illustrates how guidelines may be applied whenever
information concerning the most critical elements in the sentencing
system, current offense and criminal history, are known. By applying
the guidelines as we have above, discretion has been limited, but it
clearly has not been eliminated. There remains a significant range of
time from the minimum to maximum guidelines sentence allowable
for this defendant. Additional latitude in sentencing results from the
impact of special guidelines considerations, such as the defendant's
level of involvement in the offense (major, minor, minimal) or the
defendant's willingness to accept responsibility for the offense. Finally, other mechanisms, not necessarily consistent with the spirit of

the guidelines but employed nevertheless, may also effect a sentence adjustment. In the remaining chapter sections, we discuss the various stages of case processing under the guidelines, focusing upon how implementation of the federal sentencing guidelines has influenced the manner in which cases are handled.

DECISION TO RELEASE ON BAIL

One major impact of the guidelines on case processing concerns the degree of certainty about the likely sentence available to a defendant immediately after arrest. As was the case with our triple heroin dealer, defendants can be informed early in the process of their likely sentences, based at least on the seriousness of the offense and information concerning their criminal history known to prosecutors.

Given that there has been virtually no discussion of the impact of the guidelines on the pretrial detention process, it might be assumed that the decision to grant bail would change little as the result of guidelines. However, when defendants such as our drug trafficker confront a prison term of 6 ½–8 years in prison, they would have a different equation to balance than the one they would have faced prior to the guidelines. Under the former system, any defendant could anticipate that the sentence might be heavy, light, or non-existent, depending on factors such as the strength of the state's case, opportunities provided for cooperation, or the particular sentencing judge assigned to hear the case. Under the guidelines, it is still possible that a particularly weak case could result in charges being dropped, or that the guidelines sentence would not be imposed if the defendant engaged in substantial cooperation. However, the intent of the sentencing guidelines is to make the sentencing decision both more uniform and *more predictable* (Albonetti, 1987). Therefore, defendants would be able to estimate with relative accuracy the length of prison time they are likely to serve upon conviction.

There may be a significant difference in a defendant's assessment of the value of appearing for trial when one *knows* that one will spend five years in prison, as opposed to one perceiving that the sentence *could* be that long. Therefore, it is reasonable to expect that under guidelines, those criminally experienced defendants arrested for offenses with high base offense level scores would seriously consider "jumping bail" [Endnote 2].

To our knowledge, no studies have investigated the impact of sentencing guidelines on the rates of non-appearance at trial. However, even if there were no impact, decisions of court officials to grant pretrial release at arraignment hearings may be influenced by the guidelines. Should the court perceive an increased likelihood that defendants will not appear for trial after having been granted bail under the guidelines, it is possible that the guidelines will result in pretrial detention of proportionately more defendants.

In turn, this possibility would likely have serious adverse consequences for defendants. In comparing the dispositions of defendants who made bail with those who spent their pretrial period in jail, researchers have found that detained defendants are more likely to be convicted and given prison terms than those who have been permitted bail (Rankin, 1964; Single, 1982). While a third study utilizing a more sophisticated methodology and more extensive statistical controls reported that pretrial custody appears unrelated to decisions dealing with dismissal, diversion, and adjudication, it was found to increase the likelihood that convicted defendants will receive sentences of incarceration (Goldkamp, 1979). Although guidelines are intended to eliminate such disparities, it is possible that judges would use the restricted discretion they retain under the guidelines to sentence defendants in pretrial custody more severely than similarly situated bailed defendants.

THE CHARGING DECISION AND PLEA NEGOTIATIONS

Much has already been written on the probable impact of the guidelines on decisions to charge and plea negotiations (Alschuler, 1988; Miethe, 1987). The guidelines require the prosecutor to charge the offense or offenses that can be proven which will yield the most severe criminal penalties. If the prosecutor routinely follows this prescription, the charging process would be fairly straightforward and predictable.

For the most part, prosecutors report that they are following the prescriptions of the Commission and charging the offense for which the most serious sentence could be imposed. However, there are several factors which influence the degree to which U. S. Attorneys completely conform to the Commission's prescription.

Mathematics of the Guidelines

The first factor is the relative newness and complexity of the guidelines themselves. The application of the sentencing guidelines can be a tedious, complex, and cumbersome process. In many ways, it is similar to learning a new language, requiring not only that the person acquire knowledge concerning the guidelines but also that the person become familiar with them through repeated application. For many Assistant U. S. Attorneys the mathematical aspects of the guidelines applications are both intimidating and aversive. As one Assistant U. S. Attorney said, "The guidelines are not fun to deal with. Most people who become attorneys didn't do so to perform calculations."

Many writers have argued that the prosecutor may be the most powerful criminal justice actor in the system (Gottfredson and Gottfredson, 1980) [see also Chapter 1]. Cases will not be initiated without the encouragement of the prosecutor and without the prosecutor's decision to charge. In addition, the prosecutor will determine the level of the charge, the decision to reduce the charge, the decision to *nolle prosequi*, and the decision to move for enhancements and one or more credits. Gottfredson and Gottfredson (1980:145) state that "the discretionary power to initiate formal criminal charges against a suspect places the prosecutor in a position of influence perhaps unparalleled in the entire system of criminal justice."

However, others view prosecutors as functioning within a bureaucratic framework which severely limits their ability to exert unregulated discretion. Rather, the process of obtaining guilty pleas is governed by "rules . . . embedded in the social and cultural experience of the courtroom" (Mather, 1979) and is actually quite orderly (Feeley, 1979; Nardulli, Fleming, and Eisenstein, 1985). Indeed, Maynard (1984) reports in his study of plea negotiations that most guilty pleas are obtained by one party simply offering a disposition to the other, with few cases resolved by compromises. In many cases, the prosecutor has clear evidence to convict the defendant and the defendant knows it; hence, there may be little reason for defendants to prolong their uncertainty concerning the outcome of the case by going to trial. Nevertheless, the potential for the prosecutor to influence case processing in so many ways indicates the need to examine the U. S. Attorney as a key actor in the application of the guidelines.

In speculating about the impacts of determinate sentencing, many critics have posited that the reduction of judicial discretion in the sentencing decision may result in increased discretion at earlier stages, most notably at the time of charging (Alschuler, 1978; Casper and Brereton, 1984; Coffee and Tonry, 1983). Speculations concerning the impact of the federal sentencing guidelines generally have focused upon the retention of prosecutorial authority to obtain plea agreements as vesting greater power in that office. Opponents of the guidelines contend that the provisions relating to plea bargaining are "cast in vague and ambiguous language" and that even the Commission expects plea bargaining to remain "essentially unregulated" (Alschuler, 1988).

What traditional methods of plea bargaining have been retained and which ones have been dropped? What new methods of bargaining have evolved as the result of guidelines implementation? Analyzing non-guidelines forms of case processing, Padgett (1985) proposes four types of plea bargaining: (1) **implicit plea bargaining,** where defendants plead guilty to the original charge with the expectation that a more lenient sentence will be imposed; (2) **charge reduction plea bargaining,** where prosecutors downgrade or eliminate multiple charges in exchange for guilty pleas to lesser offenses; (3) **judicial plea bargaining,** where judges, after consulting with prosecutors and defense counsels, offer defendants specific sentences in exchange for guilty pleas; and (4) **sentence recommendation bargaining,** where prosecutors recommend specific sentences to judges in exchange for guilty pleas from defendants.

The adoption of the relatively narrow sentencing ranges within the cells of the guidelines matrix mandated by the 25 percent rule (28 U.S.C. Sec. 994, 1989) suggests that judicial discretion in sentencing determination is substantially restricted once the guidelines have been calculated. Hence, any plea bargaining arrangement which rests upon the expectation that judges will award reduced sentences in exchange for guilty pleas from defendants will be altered significantly by the adoption of a guidelines model. Guidelines, by their structure, will restrict all types of plea bargaining which rely upon the judge to agree to awarding a lesser sentence [Endnote 3].

Charge Bargaining

Opportunities for charge reduction bargaining continue to exist under the guidelines. As one interviewee stated, "Prosecutors may not be able to go 'judge shopping,' but they can still go 'guidelines shopping.'" Let us return to the case of our three-time heroin seller. Assuming adequate supportive evidence, the offense behavior on which the charge should be based is covered under Sec. 2D1.1 of the guidelines (i.e., the unlawful manufacturing, importing, exporting, or trafficking of drugs). However, should the prosecutor wish to clear this case quickly, or if the prosecutor feels that the defendant may provide additional information to police about other criminal activity involving drugs, the prosecutor may be willing to charge the defendant under Sec. 2D2.1 (unlawful possession). For possession of drugs, quantities are not considered and there are no enhancements for proximity to a school or the involvement of minors. Hence, rather than receiving a base offense score of 24, as she would have received for the distribution charge, our defendant would receive a base offense score of 8 and a substantially shorter incarcerative term [Endnote 4].

Fact Bargaining

Another new type of bargaining which did not exist under the former sentencing model is "fact bargaining," in which the prosecutor allows the defendant to stipulate to certain facts related to the offense as a part of the guilty plea. Generally the facts stipulated by the defendant involve less serious criminal conduct than the prosecutor has evidence to support, thereby reducing the severity of the sentence. To illustrate, suppose our heroin seller agreed to plead guilty to drug trafficking (Sec. 2D1.1), but she stipulated that the quantity of heroin for the third arrest was not 15 grams (for which the prosecutor has definite proof), but rather, 9 grams. Considering the fact that the drug quantity for this last offense was quadrupled (due to the proximity of the drug exchanges to the school yard and the involvement of a minor as a courier), the number of grams involved in this offense would be computed to be 36 rather than 73, thus resulting in a reduction of the base offense level from 22 to 18.

Guidelines Bargaining

Finally, there is guidelines bargaining which involves negotiation not over the "facts" of the case *per se*, but over so-called "guidelines factors." This type of bargaining becomes possible because of the many ways in which a sentence can be enhanced or reduced due to factors which formerly only loosely contributed to the judge's ultimate sentencing decision. Under guidelines, however, such issues as the presence of a vulnerable victim, the defendant taking a leadership role in the commission of the crime, and the defendant willfully impeding the prosecution can all have significant bearing on the eventual sentence imposed.

Conversely, defendants with "minor" involvement would have their base offense levels reduced by two levels while having a "minimal" role in the crime would call for a reduction of four levels. "Acceptance of responsibility" can also be a valuable behavior; defendants who "clearly demonstrate a recognition and affirmative acceptance of personal responsibility for [their] criminal conduct" (U. S. Sentencing Guidelines, 1987: Sec. 3E1.1) can also have their offense levels reduced by two levels.

To illustrate the importance of the guidelines factors in influencing the sentence, let us return to our drug seller. Suppose that this person is a relatively small actor in a larger drug operation and that she possesses valuable information about other drug sellers who play major roles in the heroin marketing scheme. Suppose further that in the transactions for which she was arrested and charged, the investigation discloses that she merely sold the drugs to the undercover agent; other unknown actors had been responsible for arranging the buys and instructing her to be at certain places at certain times.

This information may turn out to be quite beneficial to the defendant. However, how small was her role? Was it minimal? Was it minor? The answer to these and other questions is obviously a discretionary one; we are dealing less with facts than with interpretations of guidelines factors. Obviously, this is an element of the case which would allow for some negotiating by the prosecutor, defense attorney, and the defendant herself. If she pleads guilty, for example, perhaps the prosecutor might be more inclined to hold that her behavior was minimal rather than minor, resulting in a reduction of an additional two levels in her offense score.

The guidelines factor of "acceptance of responsibility" also allows for considerable "wiggle room" by prosecutors. While the guidelines explicitly state under Sec. 3E1.1(c) that "a defendant who enters a guilty plea is not entitled to a sentencing reduction under this section as a matter of right," the decision as to whether the defendants have accepted their responsibility for the crime is clearly one which allows for wide latitude in interpretation. For example, it would be understandable and difficult to contest if the prosecutor argued that our defendant "accepted responsibility," on the evidence that she acknowledged her guilt through a guilty plea. The vagueness in the language surrounding the acceptance of responsibility guidelines factor is likely to make it, perhaps more than any other aspect of the guidelines, misused for the purpose of negotiations.

Indeed, in interviews with Commission personnel as well as with probation officers and U. S. Attorneys, we were told that the acceptance of responsibility factor is being used extensively as an incentive for defendants to plead guilty. One large and busy federal district was alleged to award this guideline factor to virtually every defendant who pleads guilty despite statements from the Attorney General's office that this is an inappropriate practice. This may be reflect Eisenstein's (1978) conclusion that field officers vary considerably in their degree of autonomy and conformity to central office mandates. Other districts appear to use the clause more prudently. However, it is generally regarded as one of the few remaining mechanisms the prosecutor may use with impunity to encourage defendants to plead guilty or cooperate with their investigation.

Defendants who offer "substantial assistance to authorities" by providing important information to the U. S. Attorney about other important criminal prosecutions have the potential to be sentenced without consideration of the guidelines, as "departure" cases. Considering our defendant again, if she agreed to cooperate with the Assistant U. S. Attorney's investigation of the larger drug distribution by providing information which could be used to convict more significant actors, then there might be justification for the sentence to be a departure entirely from that prescribed by the guidelines. However, we must again ask the question about how "significant" and "useful" is the defendant's assistance? The answer is that this is clearly a judgment call, open to individual interpretation and discretion by both prosecutors and the court.

PLEA BARGAINING UNDER GUIDELINES—A CRITIQUE

The forms of plea bargaining which continue to be used under the guidelines were not intended by the Commission and are clearly outside of the limits of their guidelines policy. The Commission and the Congress are extremely clear about their disapproval of the practice of manipulating the charging offense as a mechanism for extracting guilty pleas from defendants. The Commission states that "Congress indicated that it expects judges to examine plea agreements to make certain that prosecutors have not used plea bargaining to undermine the sentencing guidelines" (28 U.S.C. Sec. 994(a)(2)(E), 1989).

Strong language opposing charge dropping can also be found in the U. S. Sentencing Guidelines Manual (1987). The Commission (Sec. 6B1.2, Commentary) states that "When the dismissal of charges or agreement not to pursue potential charges is contingent upon acceptance of a plea agreement, the court's authority to adjudicate guilt and impose sentence is implicated, and the court is to determine whether or not dismissal of charges will undermine the sentencing guidelines." Thus, the Commission emphasizes the illegitimacy of dropping or lessening charges as a part of plea agreements unless the ultimate sentence reflects the criminal acts on which the original dropped charges were based.

Finally, the Commission also specifies the invalidity of the third type of plea bargaining, "fact bargaining." In its discussion of stipulations used in guilty pleas, the Commission states, "It is not appropriate for the parties to stipulate to misleading or nonexistent 'facts' for purposes of litigation. Rather, the parties should fully disclose the actual facts and then explain to the court the reasons why the disposition of the case should differ from that which such facts ordinarily would require under the guidelines" (Sec. 6B1.4, Commentary).

Given the long history of plea bargaining, it is unrealistic to anticipate that the adoption of the guidelines will eradicate it (Sanborn, 1986). Indeed, the Commission appears to accept the fact that plea bargaining will continue and it is prepared to develop further standards geared to restricting its use. To quote the Commission, "The Commission shall study plea agreement practice under the guidelines and ultimately develop standards for judges to use in determining whether to accept plea agreements" (U. S. Sentencing Commission, 1987, Part B, Introductory Commentary).

It is difficult to estimate the extent to which the types of plea bargaining described above are being used. To our knowledge, there have been no published systematic studies to date of the plea bargaining process under the guidelines. Nevertheless, given the fact that virtually all of our interviewees could cite specific cases in which one or more types of bargaining described above have occurred, this situation is one which the Commission will have to contend with in the future. On the other hand, our interviewees argued that in most districts and in most cases, prosecutors are adhering to guidelines provisions regarding plea agreements. While plea negotiations under the guidelines continue, for the most part they are proceeding without compromising the spirit of the guidelines. Assistant U. S. Attorneys employ two "legitimate" incentives for the guilty plea: the recommendation of a sentence at the bottom of the guidelines range, and, when a defendant merits it, the reduction of the base offense score by two levels for the defendant's acceptance of responsibility. Our extremely preliminary and tentative conclusions about plea bargaining under guidelines support the findings of other researchers who have not uncovered unbridled discretion and abuse of power by prosecutors in other jurisdictions with sentencing guidelines (Miethe, 1987) and in general (Maynard, 1984; Nardulli, Fleming, and Eisenstein, 1985).

SENTENCING GUIDELINES AND JURY TRIALS

Traditionally, plea bargaining has been used as a mechanism for avoiding costly jury trials and to facilitate the smooth and rapid processing of cases to obtain convictions. Although the adoption of sentencing guidelines was viewed initially by some critics as an invitation to defendants to seek jury trials, an event which would place considerable strain on federal district courts, research in Minnesota

(Knapp, 1984) and Pennsylvania (Lubitz and Kempinen, 1987) has found no significant increase in jury trials.

THE SENTENCING PROCESS UNDER THE GUIDELINES

The most dramatic impact of guidelines on case processing occurs after the defendant has been convicted. Obviously, the introduction of explicitly detailed formulae for computing sentences, specifying what the sentencing agent may and may not take into account, amounts to a radical departure from the former sentencing system. By Commission design, these changes are not anticipated to influence the *average* sentences for most offenses, as the guidelines sentences for most offenses were based upon past sentencing practices. Given the wide interjudge and interdistrict variations in sentencing practices which existed under the former model, significant changes in sentence length are likely to occur where practices resulted in sentences which were relatively discrepant from the mean.

While the guidelines may not alter actual sentences for most offenses, the post-conviction sentencing process has changed markedly. Formerly, judges had few constraints on their discretion. The statutory minima and maxima afforded them broad choices for sentence setting. The **presentence investigation (PSI) report** provided judges with ample information about the defendant's personal, social, and criminal history to consider or ignore, at their discretion. The adoption of the sentencing guidelines has altered the manner in which information is prepared and used in the sentencing process. Under guidelines, the number of months one must spend in prison is inextricably tied to specific elements of the offense and the defendant's criminal history; hence, information documenting these elements carries significant weight. As an example, our heroin seller would serve additional months in prison for "brandishing" a weapon, as opposed to simply "possessing" it. Therefore, it is crucial that the information concerning these elements of the case and which could dramatically influence the defendant's sentence be presented accurately and completely.

Probation officers, traditionally responsible for preparing the materials to be used by the court in sentencing, play critical roles in case processing under the guidelines. While the officer's authority in the area of individualized sentencing no longer holds sway under guidelines, this has been replaced by the officer's control over the information presented in the PSI report, information which has direct and strong bearing on the guidelines sentence [Endnote 5]. This authority over the PSI extends to providing the necessary documentation and information to substantiate departures. Unlike before, the PSI report now has the status of a quasi-legal document in the sentencing process (Grunin and Watkins, 1987); hence, under guidelines, probation officers are responsible for insuring the veracity of information such as the exact amount of drugs or specific value of stolen property. Probation officers are also responsible for interpreting information concerning guidelines facts and factors. For example, these officers are forced to interpret guidelines facts, such as whether the offense occurred within 1,000 feet of a school, and factors such as whether the defendant played a minor or minimal role in the offense, and to calculate guidelines sentences based upon the information presented in the PSI report.

Probation officers become even more significant because, of all the actors other than the judge, they are the only ones with no vested interest in the sentencing outcome. At times, this position demands that officers attempt to resolve disputes between opposing counsels who may argue for divergent interpretations of a guidelines fact or factor (Grunin and Watkins, 1987). Other times, probation officers may find themselves in conflict with both the defense and prosecution. For instance, to provide our heroin seller with an incentive to enter a guilty plea, both counsels may have to agree that she played a minimal role in the third transaction. However, the probation officer may analyze our defendant's behavior as actually playing a minor role, thus increasing the base offense level by 2 points.

Probation officers have considerable responsibility in the current sentencing process. From all indications, they are generally producing complete and accurate PSI reports and are applying the guidelines appropriately in their recommendations. The effectiveness of these key actors in their function as "defenders of the guidelines" is one of the most crucial elements contributing to successful guidelines implementation.

To some extent, the independence shown by probation officers in applying the guidelines during this relatively early phase of implementation may erode over time. Thus far, probation officers have been considered as experts on the guidelines within the courtroom work group, having received the most extensive training on guidelines application. However, as other actors become more skilled in the use of these guidelines, probation officers, who are relatively low status members of the courtroom work group (Eisenstein, 1988), may choose to rely upon their judgments on more complex legal issues. Indeed, in one district, there are already indications that probation officers who are reluctant to exercise much discretion in interpreting ambiguous information are turning to prosecutors to aid them in making relevant guidelines determinations. This arrangement, if it continues and expands, will seriously compromise the effectiveness of the guidelines process.

THE JUDGE AND THE GUIDELINES

The judge is the actor formally charged with the application of sentencing guidelines. However, it appears that since the guidelines have gone into effect, the degree of commitment and conformity to the guidelines varies greatly among federal district judges. To some degree, judges have been faced with the same dilemma as attorneys: given the complexity of the guidelines and the difficulties in their application, the investment in mastering them was not worthwhile until the guidelines passed their many constitutional challenges.

Nevertheless, the information we received concerning judges' use of the guidelines is that many do not know the guidelines well. Rather, most judges rely on the probation officer's expertise in developing the most appropriate guidelines sentence. To some extent, it appears that judges have taken the guidelines too literally, preferring to view the guidelines' facts and factors, once they are documented in the PSI report, as immutable and not open to alternative interpretations. This reliance on the probation officer's interpretation of a case is not consistent with the intent of the guidelines, which was to allow for limited judicial discretion, both through accepting the appropriateness of departures and by including certain guidelines factors which virtually demand discretionary judgments. According to several interviewees, there also appears to be a reluctance on the part of some judges to depart from the guidelines, a phenomenon supported by other jurisdictions with guidelines (Knapp, 1984; Kramer and Lubitz, 1985).

Since the U. S. Supreme Court's opinion upholding the constitutionality of the guidelines in *Mistretta*, it is now likely that judges will become more active in making discretionary decisions regarding guidelines application. As judges become more intimately familiar with the guidelines, we should expect to view their roles changing from accepting the suggestions of probation officers to evaluating and exercising appropriate discretion in processing the facts contained in PSI reports. We would expect an increased use of departures, as has been the case in Minnesota (von Hirsch, Knapp, and Tonry, 1987). These departures would not necessarily be an indication of a lack of conformity to the guidelines, but rather a recognition of their limitations in dealing with the wide variations of human behavior found in federal district courtrooms.

For guidelines to be implemented successfully, it will also be necessary for judges to play significant roles in creating a climate of conformity to the guidelines. From their central and powerful position in the courtroom work group, it will be important for judges to demand that sentences accurately reflect the most serious offense of conviction as well as all relevant information contained in the PSI report. As long as judges allow sentences which do not embody the spirit of the guidelines, those who stand to benefit from manipulations of the guidelines will continue to attempt to do so.

APPEAL OF SENTENCE

With the implementation of the sentencing guidelines the right to and basis of an appellate review of sentences was expanded to allow appeals by both the defense and prosecution. In effect, this is the enforcement mechanism that will be crucial to the ability of the guidelines to elicit compliance. Appeal of sentence is crucial in at least two respects. First, defense attorneys and prosecutors must appeal sentences which they think are inappropriate. Second, the appellate court must take seriously the restriction of judicial discretion and must carefully review the accuracy of the guidelines and the appropriateness of the court's interpretation of guidelines facts and factors.

The first of these issues is technical in nature and somewhat complicated. For example, the guidelines case that was presented earlier raises numerous issues that may be subject to appellate challenges such as whether the court should have added two offense levels for the possession of the dangerous weapon "during the commission of the offense" (Sec. 201.2(b)(1), 1987). The appellate court must review such enhancements to determine whether they are interpreting the guidelines correctly, and whether the fact that the defendant was in possession of the firearm when arrested is sufficient to substantiate that she possessed the firearm during the commission of the offense. This is a technical issue but one of many which, as we have indicated earlier, will influence how cases are processed. In addition, to reduce sentencing disparity, the basic goal of the guidelines, it is essential that all courts process cases equitably. In order to process cases equitably, it is necessary that the appellate courts resolve ambiguities in the guidelines.

With the implementation of guidelines in Minnesota and Pennsylvania, the right of appeal was extended similarly to both the defendant and the government. Subsequently, both states have evolved a significant history of appellate review of sentencing (McCloskey, 1985). Although the direction of the appellate courts in each state is somewhat different, both states' appellate courts have taken sentencing review seriously and have begun the important development of a common law of sentencing. In both states, appellate review has had important implications for case processing. For example, in Pennsylvania the appellate courts have wrestled with when a prior conviction becomes a prior conviction for the purpose of being tabulated in the prior record score (comparable to the criminal history score in the federal sentencing guidelines). The appellate court determined in *Commonwealth v. Mourar* (1986) that in order for the court to consider an offense a prior conviction, the offense, the conviction, and the resulting sentence must all have occurred prior to the commission of the current offense. In a Minnesota case, *State v. Hernandez* (1989), the Minnesota Supreme Court reached a very different conclusion and established the rule that the only limitation on the use of prior convictions was that the "defendant must have been convicted prior to the current sentence." The appellate courts in both states undertook the responsibility of clarifying issues of law that historically have been concealed in the general language of sentencing but that now have a direct impact on the sentence and therefore come under the careful scrutiny of appellate review.

What will the impact be of such scrutiny on the processing of federal cases? The anticipated impact will be the careful review by both the U. S. Attorney's office and the defense counsel of the definition of guidelines factors. As the courts continue to articulate, for example, the differences between such terms as "brandished" versus "used" a dangerous weapon, case processing will result in greater clarity for defendants as to the probable guidelines sentences they will receive; and the U. S. Attorney will be able to assess more adequately the punishment for which defendants are vulnerable. This will clarify for both the impact of any charge bargain or bargains regarding sentencing enhancements or credits.

A second major issue relates to the standard under appeal. The enabling legislation establishes that the standard for departures from the guidelines is whether the sentence is "unreasonable" (18 U.S.C. Sec. 3742(e)(2), 1989). Appeals challenging the reasonableness of the sentence may be taken by the defendant "if the sentence is greater than (1) the sentence specified in the applicable guideline, (2) the sentence specified in plea agreements, if any (18 U.S.C. Sec. 3742(a)(3), 1989), or (3) by the government if the sentence is less than the guidelines sentence or the sentence recommended in the plea agreement (18 U.S.C. Sec. 3742(b)(3), 1989)." The issue is whether the appellate courts will use the "unreasonableness" standard to enforce the guidelines or to reinforce judicial discretion.

If the appellate courts take the approach of strongly enforcing the guidelines, they will be prone to scrutinize the basis for departures and to place the burden on sentencing judges to substantiate clearly, on the record, the court's reasoning for these departures. In Minnesota, the standard is "substantial" and "compelling" circumstances which must be explained by the judge in writing (Knapp, 1984). Minnesota's appellate court opinions enforced the guidelines by finding that the sentence be based on the offense of conviction and not on unproven behavior and be proportional to the seriousness of the offense in comparison to other offenses (Parent, 1988).

For example, the Minnesota Supreme Court ruled in *State v. Schantzen* (1981) that proportionality was not served with excessive departures and established a general policy that upward departures be limited to double the guidelines sentence. The court has maintained this position in numerous subsequent opinions. In Pennsylvania the appellate review of sentences, while more procedural in focus than Minnesota, has, according to Judge John Dowling (1988:927), led to a "common law of punishment" which he says governs sentencing more than the guidelines. Thus, in both states with a track record of appellate review, the appeal of sentence provision has resulted in strong enforcement of the guidelines. The important issue is whether such review will occur under the federal guidelines, and if so, what will be the impact on case processing? The expectation is that the appellate review will occur and that the court of appeals will, as in the Minnesota and Pennsylvania cases, carefully review the procedural application of the guidelines.

Through clarifying areas of ambiguity which remain in the guidelines, the appellate review process should result in greater uniformity in the application of the guidelines. With greater uniformity in application will come greater equity in case processing.

The appellate review process is more than a means of clarifying ambiguities, however; it is also a potential enforcement mechanism. The appellate court will ultimately set boundaries for guidelines departures by ruling on the appropriateness of the factors used by the courts both in decisions to depart from the guidelines and the extent of such departures. If the appellate process enforces the guidelines, then the guidelines will probably have their intended effects. On the other hand, if the appellate courts reinforce judicial discretion to individualize sentencing, guidelines' impacts on case processing will be minimized.

The power of the appellate court to enforce guidelines as intended by the Commission depends upon the filing of appeals by both the defendant and the government whenever the guidelines appear to have been incorrectly applied and interpreted. If the appellate courts evolve a common standard for reviewing sentences and appropriately balancing concerns for judicial discretion and guideline constraints, the guidelines will become an effective tool for federal sentencing policy.

SENTENCING ALTERNATIVES

The Commission has been subject to considerable criticism for its apparent dismissal of alternatives to prison as viable criminal sanctions (Alschuler, 1988). The Commissions' projections (*U. S. Sentencing Commission Supplementary Report to Congress*, 1988) indicated that proportionately fewer defendants will be given probation sentences. For some offenses, the projected proportion of defendants receiving probation is reduced dramatically, from 18 to 3 percent for robbery; 20.8 to 5.1 percent for drugs; and 57 to 3 percent for income tax offenses. These reductions reflect explicit decisions by the Commission to impose prison sentences for offenses which previously rarely received them, such as income tax or fraud offenses, and to impose harsher sentences for violent crimes. Nevertheless, these decisions have helped to create a guidelines structure which appears strongly weighted in favor of incarcerative sanctions.

This inference is also supported by reviewing the guidelines matrix. Judges are authorized to impose probation sentences only to offenders who fall within the lowest 21 cells of the 258-cell matrix, with offenders in the next lowest 21 cells being eligible for combinations of probation and conditions of intermittent or community confinement. This leaves incarceration as the guidelines sentence for all offenders whose offense level and criminal history place them in the remaining 216 cells. The guidelines have also been accused of neglecting the use of fines, in that fines are authorized as a supplement to other punishments rather than as an alternative (Alschuler, 1988). Moreover, while other sentencing alternatives such as home detention, community service, and occupational restrictions are discussed by the guidelines, they, too, cannot be employed exclusively as the criminal sanction.

In defense of the Commission, it is important to recognize that the proportion of criminal defendants projected to be eligible for probation or probation coupled with other conditions is not small. A substantial proportion of offenders sentenced under the guidelines are likely to be sentenced in the 42 guidelines cells for which probation can be imposed. Even if probation or other conditions such as home confinement or placement in community-based correctional facilities were emphasized more strongly in the guidelines, there would still be logistical limitations to their use. With the increased weight given the PSI report and the additional probation officer time required for consultations with attorneys and the court, many districts have reallocated resources to enable more probation officers to work exclusively on these documents. Ultimately, this shift will effect the probation department's ability to perform its other major function, offender supervision.

Other sentencing alternatives also suffer from resource limitations. Facilities and structures for intermittent confinement are scarce, as are community residential programs (Petersilia, 1987a). Electronic surveillance, a promising development in community corrections not discussed explicitly in the guidelines, is itself costly, not only to purchase and install the necessary hardware but also to train staff to monitor such programs approriately (Petersilia, 1987a). Therefore, for such sentencing alternatives to be realistic, more attention will have to be directed to the development of such programs for federal offenders.

Nevertheless, the need for rethinking the position of sentencing alternatives in the guidelines may be exacerbated by the rapid increases in the federal prison population projected to occur (Block and Rhodes, 1987). While these increases are not fully attributable to the guidelines themselves but rather to the passage of a stringent new law against drug offenses (Block and Rhodes, 1987), the ability of the Commission to modify the guidelines may be an effective mechanism for dealing with this problem.

At the state level, over the past several years there has been a dramatic rise in interest regarding sentencing alternatives (Petersilia, 1987a). Although these programs are generally less than three years old, the limited research conducted to date indicates that some programs may be cost-effective (Pearson, 1987; Pearson and Bibel, 1986; Petersilia, 1987a) compared with imprisonment costs, especially when the costs of building new prisons is considered. Additionally, while available research suffers from the lack of appropriate controls, it is generally found that these programs are doing quite well in protecting public safety. Recidivism rates for offenders on intensive supervised probation, for example, are about 30 percent, with most of the recidivism attributable to technical violations such as curfew, alcohol use, or nonpayment of program maintenance costs (Pearson, 1987; Cochran, Corbett, and Byrne, 1986). This contrasts favorably with the figure one would expect from released prisoners (Blumstein, Cohen, Roth, and Visher, 1986).

With its different "mix" of offenders in comparison with the various states, the federal system could implement a sentencing alternatives program to encompass significantly more offenders than would currently be eligible under the guidelines—without a threat to public safety. Proportionately more federal defendants are sentenced for property crimes compared with state defendants, and recidivism studies generally find these offenders to be better risks for community-based supervision (Blumstein et al., 1986).

SUMMARY AND CONCLUSIONS

The question raised in this chapter is whether the avowed purposes of the U. S. Sentencing Guidelines to "provide certainty and fairness in meeting the purposes of sentencing, avoiding unwarranted sentencing disparities among defendants with similar records who have been found guilty of similar criminal conduct" will be met. The cynical view of reform efforts referred to as the "hydraulic effect" is that guidelines' attempts to reduce discretion will merely press greater discretion into the hands of the prosecutor and the probation officer. The result of the "hydraulic effect" is the continuation of uncertainty, unfairness, and disparity through the different processing of cases. To date we know relatively little about the impact of sentencing guidelines on case processing. Miethe's (1987:175) work on the Minnesota sentencing guidelines concluded that ". . . the hydraulic displacement of discretion is not inevitable and does not necessarily dampen the success attributed to the primary reform effort."

Our analysis of the U. S. Sentencing Guidelines can be summarized by the following set of hypotheses:

1. In view of the increased severity of the guidelines and with the assumption of increased certainty of sentence, it is postulated that defendants are more likely to suffer pretrial detention.
2. In addition, it is hypothesized that defendants will be less likely to appear for trial if released due to the increased severity and certainty of sentences under the new guidelines.
3. The discretionary authority left within the guidelines ranges is sufficient to allow for maintaining judicial disparity between pretrial detainees and those permitted release on bail.
4. It is anticipated that charge bargaining and fact bargaining will increase under the guidelines.
5. It is further hypothesized that such bargaining will not totally undermine the guidelines' goal of reducing sentencing disparity.
6. There is no reason to expect that the proportion of jury trials will increase.
7. The role of the probation officer will change from social investigator to guidelines expert, fact-finder, and negotiator with the defense attorney and prosecutor as to the correct calculation of the guidelines.
8. Probation officers will become even more instrumental in the sentencing process to the degree that they will control the information and information flow.

9. Over time, it is anticipated that the judiciary will become more comfortable with the guidelines and with departures from the guidelines, as they become more cognizant of the limitations of the guidelines.

10. With appellate review of sentences available to both prosecutors and defense attorneys, it is anticipated that the number of appeals taken will increase significantly.

11. Based on the standard under appeal and the lack of a single overriding philosophical premise, it is anticipated that the courts of appeal will focus on clarifying procedural ambiguities in the review process.

12. It is hypothesized that appellate review will reduce procedural ambiguities and will therefore reduce disparity resulting from disparate application of the guidelines.

13. With the divergent philosophical premises of the guidelines, it is expected that the courts will reinforce judicial discretion regarding the purposes of sentencing and therefore will allow departures to use diverse and disparate philosophical premises to justify departures from the guidelines.

14. The guidelines will reduce the use of probation and other alternatives to incarceration although such alternatives will continue to be a major sentencing option.

15. As a result of the declining use of probation, it is anticipated that probation officers will spend more of their time in the preparation of guideline-related information and less time on supervisory responsibilities.

In effect, it is speculated that the guidelines will have major implications for the processing of cases in the federal court system. The roles of the prosecutor, the defense attorney, the judge, and the probation officer will change in various ways. The information required at sentencing will be more uniform both in terms of what information is available and how it is weighed. In addition, the surveillance of the courts by courts of appeal as well as by the media will be enhanced because of the structure and specificity of the guidelines.

Although the authors do not see that all disparities will disappear as a consequence of the guidelines, they do not portend the disaster that many critics have postulated would occur with the implementation of the guidelines. Jury trials will be continue to be few. Plea bargaining will continue, but it will probably be more predictable. Role relationships will change, although new relationships will emerge to adjust to changes the guidelines have generated. Despite these caveats, it is anticipated that sentencing will change as it has in Washington, Minnesota (Knapp, 1984; Miethe, 1987; Miethe and Moore, 1985) and Pennsylvania (Kramer and Lubitz, 1985), and that the change will be toward greater fairness, certainty, and less disparity.

ENDNOTES

1. Our interviews were not intended to represent a scientifically drawn sample but were merely a means to understand better the Federal processing of cases and to develop some "grounded" perspectives on the impact of the guidelines. We interviewed individuals in relatively close proximity with whom arrangements could be made on short notice. All but one of the interviews was in person with the other being a telephone interview. Each interview lasted approximately one hour.
2. Defendants may be less likely to appear at trial if released due to the increased severity and certainty of the sentence. This hypothesis would also apply to mandatory minimum provisions.
3. It is important to note, however, that while judicial discretion in selecting sentences will be reduced, it will not be eliminated. Especially at the higher ends of the guidelines table, significant variation remains between the lowest and highest sentence which can be imposed within any given cell. Therefore, bargaining will occur to obtain the lowest legitimate sentence within a cell.
4. While charge reduction bargaining existed prior to the implementation of the guidelines, the existence of so-called "date bargaining" is the result of the change to a new system and is transitional in nature. Date bargaining involves negotiation between the prosecution and defense over whether a particular case should be sentenced as a "guidelines" case or under the former sentencing system. Given that the guidelines were designed to impose longer prison sentences for certain offenses (e.g., drugs and violent crimes) and to impose shorter incarcerative sentences for offenses which rarely received them in the pre-guidelines period (e.g., fraud, income tax evasion), it would be in the interest of some defendants to be processed under the former sentencing system rather than under the new guidelines.

   For those who committed their offenses either before or after the effective guidelines date, there is no chance of attempting to date bargain. However, many prosecutors have been confronted with defendants who have committed multiple criminal acts, where some occurred prior to the effective date and some occurred afterward. In these cases, the Assistant U. S. Attorney has significant discretion in decisions to process the case as a guidelines case or an "old law" case.

   Date bargaining involves the prosecutor's willingness to drop the charge for the offense or offenses which occurred after the guidelines effective date in exchange for cooperation or the defendant's entry of a guilty plea to offenses committed during the pre-guidelines period. This practice is directly related to the period of transition between the old and new federal sentencing systems. Thus, it is only temporary. To our knowledge, while date bargaining is not particularly prevalent currently, within a few years it will cease to exist as a bargaining alternative.

5. Some researchers contend that probation officers never had much influence in this area anyway, and that the roles in researching the defendant's social history and amenability to treatment were more symbolic than substantive (Rosecrance, 1985, 1988).

7

Critical Perspectives on Selective Incapacitation and the Prediction of Dangerousness

James G. Fox

HISTORICAL OVERVIEW

The efforts of American society to rid itself of dangerous, persistent, and predatory criminals has a history of reflective changing societal definitions of dangerousness and extremely varied social control responses (Walker, 1980). Since the birth of the penitentiary system, American society has sought to isolate, control, and incapacitate those deemed as being "dangerous" (McKelvey, 1977). While there have been a wide range of civil and criminal mechanisms employed, the criminal law (and the criminal justice system) has been the primary tool of social control over a wide range of offenders (Chambliss, 1969). In this context, changes in sentencing practices and parole policies have been widely used to insure lengthy prison terms for dangerous and persistent offenders. For example, statutes authorizing enhanced sentence lengths for persistent or habitual felons have been a part of the criminal justice system since the 1920s (Sleffel, 1977). More recently, state legislatures have increasingly enacted mandatory and/or lengthy determinate sentences for a growing number of serious criminal offenses (Bureau of Justice Statistics, 1985).

One of the most salient features of criminal justice in the United States has been the influence of ideology in determining both the targets and the methods of social control (Michalowski, 1981, 1985; Platt, 1982; Reiman, 1979). Specifically, the dominant ideological perspective, as represented by the incumbent presidential administration, has served to persuade lawmakers and criminal justice policy-makers to establish goals, priorities, and strategies consistent with dominant perspectives on crime and crime control. While there have been brief periods during which liberal reform has received popular support (Walker, 1980; Barak, 1980), the major picture that emerges is the use of repressive powers to control and regulate crime (Rusche, 1978; Reiman and Headlee, 1981; Michalowski, 1981). However, ideological perspectives influencing criminal justice policy have not been limited to a singular political party or perspective. Liberal and conservative ideology have both influenced criminal justice priorities and policies. For example, the "Rehabilitation Era" of the 1960s is frequently associated with liberal ideology. More recently, conservative political campaigns, emphasizing "law and order," have moved criminal justice policy and practice more directly into the political arena (Davis, 1983; Fox, 1983). Consequently, public attention has been focused on the dangers of street crime, its control, and toward the utilization of imprisonment and incapacitation as primary crime control strategies, spawning a neo-conservative movement which has traditionally ignored the etiology of crime and social dysfunction.

This movement, fueled by media distortions of the relative harm and danger to the public, has encompassed large sectors of the voting population as well as criminal justice professionals (Reiman, 1979). State and federal criminal justice policies and priorities have subsequently shifted according to the prevailing political and ideological perspectives. Under conservative influence, deterrence, retribution, and incapacitation have emerged as central concepts in the "war on crime." Little or no significance has been given to structural inequality or racism as factors in the production of "criminal" or antinormative social behavior. At the same time, little attention has been directed to the impacts and costs attributed to "suite" crimes or to the activities of "elite" criminal actors (Simon and Eitzen, 1986; Cullen, Maakestad, and Cavender, 1987). In this context, the advocacy of lengthy prison sentences has been accepted as an expensive but necessary solution to regulating underclass dysfunction (Fox, 1983).

In the current political mainstream, there appears to be a blending of liberal and conservative interests in formulating criminal justice responses to persistent and dangerous offenders. That is, prison expansion programs and sentencing revision at the state and federal levels have been accomplished with liberal and conservative ideological interests apparently being fulfilled (Greenburg and Humphries, 1980; Paternoster and Bynum, 1982; Goodstein and Hepburn, 1985). This has been most apparent in state sentencing reforms which have sought the "middle ground" between indeterminate and determinate sentencing. In this context, sentencing guidelines such as those adopted in the states of Minnesota and Washington reflect political compromises which allow both liberal and conservative lawmakers to claim loyalty to their respective constituencies. This has also been apparent in prison construction and expansion programs which require a relatively broad base of political and public support (Jacobs, 1984; Fox, 1986).

Consequently, prison populations have soared to record levels during the past decade (Bureau of Justice Statistics, 1988a), and indications are that they will continue to grow under current policies and priorities. For example, at yearend 1987 there were 581,609 inmates in state and federal prisons (Bureau of Justice Statistics, 1988a). These same data reveal that the annual rate of increase for federal prisoners (8.2 percent) was greater compared with state prisoners (6.5 percent). One of the most startling aspects of both prison bedspace expansion and prison population increases has been the disproportionate representation of racial and ethnic minorities, particularly black males (Christianson, 1981). A 1986 survey of state prisoners indicated that while blacks comprise approximately 13 percent of the U. S. population, they make up 47 percent of all state prison inmates (Bureau of Justice Statistics, 1988b). While this figure has remained fairly constant during the 1980s, a proportionately greater number of black males are being incarcerated than white males. When age and gender are taken into account, black male overrepresentation in state prisons is even more striking. Christianson (1981) reports that black males represented only 5.4 percent of the U. S. population during the late 1970s, but they accounted for 45.7 percent of the prison population.

Despite the commonly argued position that rising prison populations reflect an increase in crime among an enlarged age-risk cohort, record prison population increases appear to be more directly linked with a relatively small number of factors. These include shifting public attitudes toward lawbreakers, ideology, and declining socioeconomic conditions for those who have traditionally made up society's "offending classes."

CHANGES IN SENTENCING AND THE PUNISHMENT OF OFFENDERS

In response to the public perception of the dangers from predatory street criminals, state legislators have freely advocated crime control strategies associated primarily with the goals of retribution and incapacitation. Similar changes have occurred within the federal criminal justice system. Enhanced crime control methods such as **Repeat Offender Programs (ROPs)** and **Prosecution Management Information**

Systems (PROMIS) have gained in popularity among the public and appear to have increased the effectiveness and efficiency of law enforcement in dealing with chronic offenders. Most of the criminal justice policies implemented since the mid-1970s have followed the tenets of retribution. Simultaneously, these policies have rejected the value and potential for offender rehabilitation and the restructuring of social institutions to have a long-range impact on crime and juvenile delinquency.

Sentencing practices in the United States have attracted the greatest interest and controversy (von Hirsch, 1976, 1981; Forst, 1982; Rothman, 1983). As stated earlier, sentences for criminal offenses have not only been substantially increased, but many states have enacted mandatory prison terms for second (and subsequent) felonies and/or for the possession of firearms or other dangerous weapons during the commission of felonies. These changes have been linked to increases in state prison populations, and they have spurred expansion of prison bedspace (Fox, 1986). However, changes in sentencing have focused primarily upon the shift from indeterminate to determinate sentencing. As indicated earlier, sentencing guidelines have been increasingly accepted as a compromise in some jurisdictions. During the 1960s, with criminal justice policies generally supportive of offender rehabilitation, most states had enacted some form of indeterminate sentencing structure. Within a period of ten years, presumptive or determinate sentences have either replaced or supplemented existing indeterminate sentencing schemes in about a third of all state jurisdictions (Shane-DuBow, Brown, and Olsen, 1985), particularly those with wide ranges in the minimum and maximum statutory sentence.

One of the most common rationales for sentencing revisions and reforms has been the standardization, or removal of disparity, among sentences for those offenders convicted of similar crimes. This reform was widely supported by liberal and conservative interests, and ironically by some prisoner advocates (Prisoners' Unions) who thought that sentences would be reduced and that prisoners would benefit by knowing precisely their scheduled release dates. However, several states have revised their penal codes primarily to increase sentence lengths rather than reduce them (e.g., California). Other jurisdictions have enacted new sentencing procedures in an attempt to standardize sentencing severity across similar offenses and to provide sentencing judges with a framework to weigh mitigating and aggravating circumstances of the offense and/or characteristics of the offender (e.g., Minnesota and Washington). The net result, however, has been that the availability of prison bedspace has not kept pace with these changing sentencing practices, although at least one state has linked its use of sentencing guidelines with available bedspace.

Criticisms of the short-term and long-term costs of sentencing policies based on retribution and incapacitation have been abundant. The increased need to devise more effective utilization of existing limited bedspace has fostered several proposals and sentencing reforms. In turn, this has stimulated substantial debate over the empirical and methodological soundness of "just deserts" sentencing and reliance on retribution and incapacitation.

Retribution and (collective and selective) incapacitation are grounded in the notion that a small number of persistent offenders account for a disproportionate amount of crime and victimization. Given the politics of limited prison bedspace, a policy consistent with retribution and incapacitation, which targets limited criminal justice resources for those offenders who would account for the greatest proportion of predatory crime, would be hailed as a much needed weapon in the arsenal of crime control. It was within this context that the proposal for the selective incapacitation of chronic offenders emerged as an attractive crime control strategy (Greenwood, 1982; Cohen, 1983).

SELECTIVE INCAPACITATION AND RETRIBUTION STRATEGIES

Findings of a relatively small number of studies (e.g., Wolfgang, Figlio, and Sellin, 1972; Chaiken and Chaiken, 1982; Greenwood, 1982) suggesting that a small proportion of young, male offenders commit a disproportionately large number of serious felony offenses has added to the popularity of selective incapacitation and retribution among criminal justice policy-makers. Selective incapacitation is tied to the desirability of targeting dangerous or persistent offenders who would be given lengthy sentences. The popularity of selective incapacitation has emerged within the context of failing crime control policies, limitations of available prisoner bedspace, shifting public opinion concerning the strategies for addressing conventional or "street crime," and overcrowded local and state correctional facilities. Hence, selective incapacitation has been viewed as a panacea for addressing the shortage of expensive prison bedspace, the deterrence of future offenders, and the reduction of urban street crime.

While the concept of selective incapacitation has received substantial recognition among lawmakers and has, in part, been incorporated into the U. S. Sentencing Guidelines, it has been widely debated in the criminological literature (Tonry and Morris, 1983; Greenwood and von Hirsch, 1984; Blumstein, 1983; Forst, 1983, 1984). Much of the debate has centered on methodological and/or ethical issues (Cohen, 1983; Blumstein, 1983; von Hirsch, 1984; von Hirsch and Gottfredson, 1984; Gottfredson and Gottfredson, 1985; Janus, 1985) and policy concerns (Feinberg, 1984). Nevertheless, the use of selective incapacitation as a crime control strategy continues to have numerous advocates (e.g., Johnson, 1978; Wilson, 1983; Forst et al., 1983; Greenwood and von Hirsch, 1984; Feinberg, 1984; Wolfgang, 1985).

Among the most widely contested issues is the validity and utility of the prediction of future dangerousness and persistent criminal behavior. Central to the selective incapacitation objective of incapacitating persistent and dangerous offenders over the period of their active criminal careers is the ability to accurately identify and predict dangerous and persistent offenders. Such predictions are to be made at the front end of the system rather than by parole boards assessing risk factors associated with an inmate's early release from confinement. Generally, selective incapacitation advocates have drawn on two statistical approaches. The first relies on aggregated estimates of future criminal behavior using criminal history and current offense as predictive attributes. The other approach, sparking a greater debate on methodological and ethical grounds, utilizes a much wider range of variables and individual offender characteristics. Among the offender characteristics used in selective incapacitation research have been (1) prior (official and self-reported) criminal history, (2) incarceration during a recent period, (3) race, (4) age at first conviction, (5) drug use, and (6) employment history. It is equally important to observe that these approaches have relied almost exclusively on incarcerated adult offender populations, ignoring the variation in base rates that might be expected from random samples of arrestees, probationers, and adjudicated or non-adjudicated juvenile offenders.

The accurate prediction of future behavior has not been well-established in either the crimininological or clinical literature. Generally, prediction studies fall into either statistical or clinical categories. Parole and recidivism research (e.g., Wilkins, 1969; Waller, 1974), the federal experience with its parole matrix, together with several cohort studies, have been the basis for statistical studies asserting that the incapacitation of "high-risk" offenders would result in a reduction in the crime rate (e.g., Van Dine, Dinitz, and Conrad, 1977; Greenwood, 1982; Chaiken and Chaiken, 1982; Moore et al., 1984). However, criminologists are not in agreement about the claims made by selective incapacitation advocates. Gottfredson and Gottfredson (1985:142), for example, argue that it is uncommon to explain more than 20 or 30 percent of crime-related behavior by the use of prediction equations.

In a similar vein, Cohen (1983:49) asserts that a false positive rate of 55 percent may be expected for those classified as high-risk offenders. Likewise, Gottfredson and Gottfredson (1985) and von Hirsch and Gottfredson (1984) suggest that the false positives in predicting future criminal behavior may be unacceptably high on both methodological and ethical grounds. In an analysis of the research on selective incapacitation, Petersilia (1980) has said that current criminal career research does not provide the statistical confidence to identify career offenders accurately or to predict crime reduction impacts of their selective incapacitation.

The shortcomings of these studies has led some researchers and policy-makers to argue for the use of juvenile records in determining penalties for adult criminal behavior. This proposal is contradictory to the standing philosphy of the juvenile justice system, which is intended to protect against stigmatization and insure that the youth's best interests are considered. While recent legislation in several states has modified this social contract by balancing the protection of the community with the juveniles' best interests for serious offenses, there remains the guarantee of complete confidentiality for youths processed or adjudicated by the juvenile court. To use juvenile records in establishing sentence lengths for adult criminal offenses not only violates the principles of fundamental fairness and undermines the integrity of juvenile courts, but it also adds little, if anything, to the statistical validity of predictions of future dangerousness or criminal behavior.

The clinical literature, representing a wider range of behavior, also reveals substantial concern regarding the ability to accurately determine future dangerous behavior (e.g., Monahan, 1981; Steadman, 1972, 1977; Steadman and Cocozza, 1974; Thornberry and Jacoby, 1979). Kozol, Boucher, and Garofalo (1972), in one of the more rigorous multidisciplinary efforts, were able to predict future violent crimes among convicted offenders only a third of the time during a ten-year follow-up period. The complexity of predicting dangerous behavior is increased with the inclusion of individual and situational interaction factors such as previous use of violence or aggressive behavior, drug use, victim experiences (e.g., child abuse), duration and effect of institutionalization, differential tolerance levels of situational stress, socioeconomic status, education, lifestyle, and a host of other variables which may affect the social context of violence. Those who possess dangerous propensities may only be dangerous in certain situations (Steadman, 1982; Monahan, 1981), and socioeconomic conditions may be more predictive of dangerousness than one's social or mental history. Finally, violence or dangerousness has a relatively low base rate of occurrence, making accurate prediction inherently cumbersome and inclined toward overpredictions.

SELECTIVE INCAPACITATION AND DANGEROUSNESS

The concept of **dangerousness** also has lengthy social and legal history which, although related to similar sociopolitical dynamics, has produced a broader system of social control. In contrast to the social control of dangerousness, which has been focused upon mental illness (Kittrie, 1971) and sexual psychopathy (Sutherland, 1950), selective incapacitation is primarily aimed at persistent or dangerous criminal offenders. Legal and sociological interpretations of dangerousness have kindled sharp debate within the academic community as well as among policy advocates. Historically, behavior labeled as "dangerous" has included an extremely diverse range of conduct viewed as being socially, culturally, politically, and physically threatening. Consequently, "dangerousness" has elicited a wide range of societal reactions and social controls. Among those perceived as being dangerous have been heretics, witches, the poor (paupers), vagrants (tramps), the mentally ill, sexual psychopaths, those with contagious diseases (persons with AIDS, currently), and those who have committed a wide range of relatively minor offenses. These "offenses" often carried extreme civil or criminal sanctions with lengthy periods of social control. In contrast, interpersonal violence, while broadly accepted as falling within the scope of dangerous conduct, has not always been accompanied by severe sanctions. This has occurred differentially within American society because regional or subcultural social norms and values often prescribed violence as an acceptable or desirable method of resolving interpersonal or cultural disputes. For example, duelling, the western frontier gunfight, and self-defense (with wide-ranging statutory definitions) are illustrations of interpersonal violence that have received moderate social acceptance—often concurrently with the existence of legal sanctions which impose severe punishments for nonviolent, but socially offensive, conduct.

Dangerousness remains more as a socio-legal and political phenomenon rather than a form of conduct which has readily definable qualitative and quantitative dimensions of risk and threat (Kittrie, 1971). Historically, the social control of dangerousness has been largely the domain of civil law. As such, it has evolved legal standards emphasizing (or requiring) treatment rather than punishment. When a greater number of persons are defined as being "criminally dangerous," and when they are brought within the scope of criminal law, the opportunity for treating them decreases and the application of punishments becomes a symbolic gesture that has little bearing on public safety. Furthermore, social and physical harm, which should be the foundation of dangerousness, often plays only a secondary and insignificant role in the definition of dangerous conduct. For example, despite changing public opinion, systematic environmental devastation by legal and illegal toxic waste disposal plants, corporate illegality and improprieties, worker exposure to hazardous working conditions (through both management negligence and cost-savings from health and safety reductions), and governmental corruption and "sleaze" continue relatively unsanctioned in spite of producing extremely dangerous, costly, and socially harmful conditions (Coleman, 1985; Simon and Eitzen, 1986; Cullen, Maakestad, and Cavender, 1987). In this vein, "face-to-face" victimization which occurs on the street or in the home is defined as "crime" while victimization resulting from corporate profit-seeking is most often characterized as "bad judgment" at worst and "just business" at best.

In the detection, judicial processing, and punishment of violent street offenders, particularly those with drug involvement, the criminal justice system and the political context in which it operates has increasingly expanded the degree and extent of social control over marginal groups in American society. As stated earlier, official statistics continue to show that the nation's prison population increasingly discloses demographic characteristics representative of an underclass, and that the disproportionate representation of blacks and other racial or ethnic minorities continues to grow. Concern that the nation's prisons and jails currently hold a disproportionate number of young black males for lengthy periods is most frequently dismissed lightly or merely attributed to their alleged overrepresentation in violent street crime arrests.

Powerless and marginal groups in American society have historically been the target of repressive social control strategies. It is difficult to imagine similar attention being given to the prediction of dangerous behavior of corporate or elite actors, many of whom have been directly or indirectly responsible for equal or greater personal injury, loss of life, and social harm. It is impossible to escape the implications of criminal justice policies which rely on the use of predicted dangerousness and selective incapacitation of America's black male population. According to the prediction equations used by advocates of selective incapacitation, black males between the ages of 18 and 28, who may have used illegal drugs, and were unemployed for a six-month period prior to their conviction offense become the "dangerous class" of the 1990s.

CRITICAL PERSPECTIVES ON THE U. S. SENTENCING GUIDELINES

The previous chapters have raised several questions about the propriety, legality, and social impact of the U. S. Sentencing Guidelines. It is not the intention of the present chapter to restate these arguments, but rather, to focus attention on those aspects of the sentencing guidelines which correspond with the concepts of dangerousness and selective incapacitation.

As illustrated in Appendix C, the U. S. Sentencing Commission, composed of seven voting and two non-voting members appointed by former President Ronald Reagan, was established as an independent body of the judiciary by the Comprehensive Crime Control Act of 1984. Its charge was to establish sentencing guidelines for the federal criminal justice system that would fulfill the purposes of deterrence, punishment, incapacitation, and rehabilitation (although the latter does not appear to be an integral element of the resulting guidelines). The Commission was also charged by Congress to provide projections of the impact of the guidelines on the federal prison population. It should be noted that two additional influences that have the potential of having a significant impact on the size and composition of the federal prison population were passed during this time frame. Namely, the "career offender" provision of the 1984 act charged the Commission with adopting guidelines which would provide lengthy prison terms for adult repeat offenders convicted of violent or drug offenses, and the 1986 Anti-Drug Abuse Act expanded the scope and severity of penalties for drug and drug-related offenses.

While the Commission guidelines have been heralded by some as a much needed, innovative response to the multitude of problems in the federal penal code and have received broad bipartisan political support and general acceptance by members of the federal judiciary, several critical concerns remain unaddressed. To understand the implications of the broad-based political support, it is necessary to examine the goals of these federal sentencing reforms. Among the intended objectives were the standardization of sentence length, established release dates, reducing costs of supervision (through the abolition of parole), and targeting persistent and dangerous offenders. Some critics have suggested that the guidelines lack "rational unifying principles" and will not reduce sentencing severity (Robinson, 1987), and that they will produce unintended outcomes such as increased prison populations (leading to costly prison expansion) and the disengagement of therapeutic mechanisms—which have survived relatively longer in the federal correctional system than in many state systems.

Available research suggests that at least some of these arguments have merit. For example, Block and Rhodes (1987), using projection methods with approximately 10,000 recent federal cases, indicate that the average time served will increase from 15.8 months to 29.3 months under the guidelines, with most of this increase attributed to lengthening of sentences for robbery, drugs, and crimes against the person. However, they assert that the guidelines alone will not have a major impact on the federal prison population. Rather, they view the drug law as having the most significant influence on prison population growth, with the career offender provision having slightly less of an impact. In addition, Block and Rhodes (1987) indicate that probationary sentences will decrease from the current 41.4 percent of those convicted of crimes against the person to a projected 25.4 percent. Hence, it is anticipated that the guidelines will serve to reduce non-incarcerative alternatives and emphasize incapacitation as a crime control strategy. These projections, together with those indicating the average amount of time served, will likely have a greater impact on racial and ethnic minorities, especially blacks (Petersilia and Turner, 1985), who are already overrepresented in arrest and prison population statistics for crimes against the person. This leaves open the question of the impacts of racial discrimination during the criminal justice process from arrest to incarceration (Blumstein, 1982).

Furthermore, a greater concentration of "career," drug, and violent offenders, serving more lengthy prison sentences, will have a profound effect on the quality of life in correctional institutions. As greater concentrations of these offenders, many of whom are likely to represent the profile of the "typical" street offender, are confined in maximum-security institutions, substantial organizational and racial conflict may be expected (Carroll, 1974; Jacobs, 1977, 1979; Fox, 1982). In turn, greater use of (and reliance upon) coercive controls, enhanced custody measures, and escalation of conflict and turmoil may be anticipated.

Among the outspoken critics are former U. S. Sentencing Commission Commissioner Paul Robinson, who issued a dissenting view raising several objections about the guidelines (U. S. Sentencing Commission, 1987b). His criticisms include (1) the impropriety of basing guidelines on mathematical averages of past sentences, (2) the failure to rank offenses systematically according to seriousness, (3) requiring departures, and thus inviting disparity by adopting skeletal rather than comprehensive guidelines, (4) the failure to prevent plea bargaining from subverting the goals of the guidelines system, (5) the failure to permit adequate appellate review, and (6) the failure to provide an impact assessment. In response to these criticisms, six commissioners who formed the majority issued a rebuttal addressing each of

Robinson's points. They asserted that Robinson's approach was "excessively impractical, a kind of academic fantasy" which bore "little or no relation to the actual statutory elements of an offense" (U. S. Sentencing Commission, 1987c).

Other critics (e.g., Liman, 1987; Morrison, 1987) have raised legal questions, addressing the constitutionality of the guidelines and its approach to sentencing federal offenders. Liman (1987) and Morrison (1987), for example, question the constitutionality of the guidelines on the basis of violations of the separation of powers doctrine. Liman (1987) argues that the Sentencing Reform Act of 1984 first violates the nondelegation doctrine by locating the power to determine sentences in an administrative agency. Secondly, he asserts that the requirement that Article III judges sit on the Sentencing Commission (with presidential appointment powers) compromises judicial independence and impartiality. Liman (1987) suggests the alternatives of having the Commission serve as an advisory body in the judiciary or to have Congress enact the guidelines into law—thus avoiding the separation of powers conflict and insuring that the imposition of criminal sanctions is in accordance with a set of principles set into law rather than by an administrative process. While the U. S. Supreme Court has ruled on these and related issues in *Mistretta v. United States* (1989) and has upheld the constitutionality of the guidelines, several other unsettling issues remain.

Among the remaining concerns of this writer are the differential weighting of severity of harm, the use of elements of the offense to aggravate the sentence, and the use of offender characteristics and criminal history in computing the "base offense level." Even a cursory examination of the guidelines indicates that base offense levels are heavily weighted on Part A offenses (e.g., homicide, assault, criminal sexual abuse, and kidnapping). These offenses carry base offense levels ranging from 43 for first-degree murder, 33 for second-degree murder, 25 for voluntary manslaughter, 20 for assault with intent, to 15 for aggravated assault. In addition, the use (discharge or brandishment) of a firearm can add from 3 to 5 levels as does the infliction of varying degrees of bodily harm (2 to 6 levels). Similarly, Part B offenses such as robbery and residential burglary, which are typically committed by members of marginal socioeconomic groups, carry bases offense levels of 18 and 17 respectively, and they may be enhanced up to 6 levels according to the amount of monetary loss reported. In contrast, Part F offenses such as fraud, deceit, and insider trading carry base offense levels of 6 and 8 respectively. In this scheme, it is possible for an inside trader to realize a $5 million gain involving more than one victim and receive only a base offense level of 16, while an armed robber who nets only $11,000 receives a base offense level of 20. This is further complicated by the potential for substantial "adjustments" for the offender's role in the offense (Chapter 3) and criminal history (Chapter 4). In the latter instance, a criminal history score is determined by the use of several factors including 3 points for *each* prior record of imprisonment exceeding one year, 2 points for *each* prior sentence of six months or less, 2 points for commission of the current offense while under any form of criminal justice supervision, and 2 points for the commission of the current offense during a period of less than two years since release from a previous sentence. The combined base offense level is then cross-tabulated with the criminal history score (from I to VI) on the Sentencing Table [see Appendix B]. It is quite obvious that the "typical" street offender will suffer a substantial enhancement of sentence for prior criminal history. Offenders who commit street crimes will not only have a greater likelihood of having a criminal history but they will further suffer from not having the resources (and connections) to escape much of the severity of criminal sanctions through "effective assistance" of counsel. In addition to having a favorable social profile, elite or corporate offenders enjoy the advantage of being able to acquire the best legal talent with which to seek charge reductions through plea bargaining—despite the extent of monetary loss or, in some instances, the infliction of substantial social or physical harm.

CONCLUDING COMMENTS

It is important to understand the ideological underpinnings and the political processes which have influenced the development of the sentencing guidelines. One point that remains clear is that the Commission emerged from an organizational context which was heavily influenced by both political processes and *a priori* acceptance of the utility of retributive crime control policies. As stated earlier, liberal and conservative political interests and perspectives have found common ground in the establishment of the Commission. The Commission, in turn, was subject to the ideological influences and imperatives of the incumbent presidential administration, not only in terms of power of appointment, but also in terms of advancing ideology further into the federal criminal justice system. In this context, it is ludicrous to view the guidelines as being an "objective" approach intended to resolve widespread dissatisfaction with sentencing disparities, plea bargaining, and parole release and supervision.

Furthermore, the logic supporting the notion that specific reforms within the criminal justice system can reduce crime or produce a "safe society" is seriously flawed. Liberals and conservatives alike have pursued criminal justice reforms from a perspective that has been tainted with self-interests and political and ideological myopia. Ultimately, public safety and social justice can only emerge from major alterations in social structure and a criminal justice system that is truly responsive to a wide range of social harms that plague the daily lives of citizens. The reform efforts of Commission merely to serve to divert attention from these fundamental problems and focus attention on the micro-social levels of phenomena such as "dangerousness" and "career" criminal behavior. In this sense, structural racism and social dysfunction which contributes to drug abuse, violence, and property crime are systematically ignored as factors to be considered in the imposition of retributive justice.

Finally, the reforms of the Commission aggravate the long-term effects of incapacitation through increases in the degree of social control over conventional offenders while simultaneously ignoring the need for and desirability of developing non-incarcerative alternatives to achieve the objective of offender treatment and rehabilitation. At a minimum, there needs to be a better balance between incapacitation and the utilization of non-incarcerative alternatives, especially those alternatives which permit offenders to achieve economic empowerment and self-sufficiency. To continue along the path of retribution in our efforts to control conventional crime, while generally dismissing the degree of danger and social harm of corporate and white-collar offenses, will breed further hostility and perceptions of injustice among the marginal members of society. As the prison systems of the nation continue to incarcerate larger numbers of marginal members of society for more lengthy periods, the chances for achieving social, economic, and racial/ethic justice and the prevention of social dysfunction leading to predatory street crime will continue to elude us. In the end, the guidelines only address a more "systematic" manner of dispensing criminal sanctions while ignoring the social and political reality that new generations of future offenders will be entering the criminal justice system in predictably larger numbers.

Part IV

Corrections

8

Diversion and Probation

Franklin H. Marshall

INTRODUCTION

By the mid-1970s the American criminal justice system began show-ing the strains of the liberal thinking and activities of the preceding decade, particularly in the area of drug use. Conservatives were in power and the times were changing rapidly. Drug use and crime were on the rise in all social spheres. The common denominator was drugs, social use, addiction, and drugs-for-profit, with an emphasis on the latter. Many people were upset by these drug use trends. By the late 1970s the drug of choice was cocaine. It had spread to all parts of society. The desire for cocaine fueled crime, and the supply and demand cycle relating to cocaine escalated like wildfire while the price for these drugs declined appreciably. More than any other factor, the **drug problem** and its accompanying crime-related activities brought us to the point of seriously devising new federal sentencing guide-lines.

FEDERAL SENTENCING OPTIONS—1976

In 1976 I was appointed as a U. S. Probation Officer in Philadelphia, PA. My work area was the inner city known as "North Philly," a large, high-crime, impoverished, decaying area. When I began my work, the sentencing provisions followed by federal district courts were very different from those sentencing guidelines recently devised and im-plemented by the U. S. Sentencing Commission.

At that time, sentencing options available to federal judges were limited to a three-tiered system including (1) **juvenile provisions**, (2) **youth corrections provisions**, and (3) **adult provisions**. The juvenile statutes were designed to give the courts the authority to sanction those under age 18 at the time of their conviction. Much like state statutes, these federal juvenile provisions took into account the concept that the protection of minors was most important to the citizens of the United States. The law permitted juveniles to be processed through the criminal justice system and enter the adult world without a prior criminal record. These provisions gave federal district judges considerable discretion in dispensing justice. The concept of **judicial discretion** is one of the more prominent themes throughout the legal system that has been repeatedly challenged, and these challenges have been influential in the development of the new federal guidelines.

The second level was the **Youth and Young Adult** provisions, usually referred to as "YCA sentences." These provisions authorized federal courts to handle offenders between the ages of 18 and 25 at the time of their convictions. The overt purpose of these provisions was to give the court a means of adjudicating first-time offenders. These offenders were given the opportunity of having their convictions set aside after serving their time, regardless of the types of sentences imposed. Both incarcerative and nonincarcerative sentences under these provisions were eligible to have the conviction set aside. For probation officers, this law was an important and useful tool in the federal correctional system. A custody sentence under YCA was known as the "deep six," since it permitted a maximum four-year term of imprisonment with two years on parole, or a combination of the two not to exceed a total of six years. A straight probation sentence could be imposed up to the maximum of five years allowable by law.

Realistically, many youthful offenders with prior criminal adjudications or convictions got through various cracks in the system and would be granted YCA sentences by federal district judges. The beauty of this type of sentence was that (1) the setting aside of the conviction was not automatic, and (2) it had to be recommended to the court by probation officers handling each case. This "screening" usually caught those with prior criminal records and they did not benefit from these YCA provisions. Nevertheless, it was very important for young, first-offenders not to have federal convictions to report when seeking subsequent employment or applying for educational training.

The YCA sentencing provision was abolished by the Comprehensive Crime Control Act of 1984. This was unfortunate because the statute was useful for both serious federal offenses as well as for those not ordinarily considered serious crimes. For example, many U. S. highways are within federal jurisdiction. Suppose you are 20 years of age and returning to Philadelphia by automobile from an earlier trip to Washington, DC. It is a late time of night with foggy road conditions. You see an exit and believe it is the one you are seeking. You begin to exit and immediately realize that it is the wrong exit. You pull back on the highway quickly, causing other cars behind you to veer to avoid colliding with you. The police stop you and arrest you for reckless driving and recklessly endangering other people on the highway. To your misfortune and surprise, you are taken before a U. S. magistrate to answer the charges which have been filed against you. You plead guilty and the court orders a presentence investigation (PSI) report before imposing a sentence. The local U. S. Probation Office nearby becomes involved, just as though you had committed and been convicted of a major crime. You are now having your entire life under review. Eventually you are granted probation and successfully complete the term. However, you have a federal conviction on your record which must be reported to future employers and others. The YCA provisions functioned to remove these types of minor convictions when probation was successfully completed. Currently, this option is nonexistent.

The third and most widely used sentencing provisions are known as adult provisions. These options have provided judges with numerous alternatives and great discretion in determining the type of sentence to impose. Even for some of the most serious crimes, probation was sometimes granted as an option, if appropriate in the opinion of the presiding federal judge. In some instances, diversion in lieu of a formal prosecution would be granted, involving an agreement between defense counsels and the U. S. Attorney's office. The growing use of probation and diversion would emerge as critical and controversial issues for the 1980s.

THE DEVELOPMENT OF THE SENTENCING GUIDELINES

How could judges impose sentences of probation or diversion on those convicted of serious crimes? Furthermore, how could offenders convicted of identical crimes in different jurisdictions or even codefendants in the same jurisdictions be given widely different sentences by judges when federal criminal statutes prescribed specific penalties? The general public and interested politicians were mindful of these sentencing disparities. In effect, they believed that more sentencing consistency was needed among the federal judiciary with less personal sentencing discretion. Furthermore, an increasingly "just deserts"-oriented populace urged their representatives and other political leaders to promote greater severity in sentencing.

By the mid-1980s Congress and the Reagan Administration had worked out a bipartisan solution to the sentencing disparity problem. It was expressed partially in the form of the Comprehensive Crime Control Act of 1984. It provided for longer prison terms for offenders upon conviction. It also provided for larger fines accompanying longer prison terms for drug distributors and traffickers. These and other similar changes in federal sentencing patterns were to reverberate throughout the entire criminal justice system, drastically modifying existing conceptions of diversion, probation, and incarcerative sentences. Eventually abolished was the extensive use of straight probationary sentences, and "time off" or "good time" credits earned by incarcerated offenders were greatly reduced.

Congress did something else that it seldom does. It provided for the eventual abolition of a part of government. The part to be abolished is the U. S. Parole Commission which is administratively under the Department of Justice. It is responsible for determining when and under what conditions federal inmates will be released from confinement. As an administrative agency, the U. S. Parole Commission is not bound by the same legal constraints as the federal courts. They make their own rules and amend them as required by changes in the law or by judicial decisions. Parole or early-release decisions have been determined by certain statutory constraints, a review of inmate life experiences, the PSI report, and one's adjustment to incarceration. While the parole system has not been perfect, it has worked reasonably well for many decades.

The U. S. Parole Commission is scheduled for abolition in November 1992, five years after the implementation of the November 1987 U. S. Sentencing Guidelines. The replacement agency, the U. S. Sentencing Commission, exists under the judicial branch of government. It is designed to develop and implement the new sentencing guidelines. While these guidelines will themselves raise numerous issues and considerable debate, their most important function will be to introduce consistency in sentencing among federal district judges and to limit their discretion in sentencing decisions. Ideally, earlier discretionary abuses by the courts, prosecutors, and other criminal justice system actors, including probation officers will be remedied with the implementation of these guidelines.

Another major change in the new sentencing system is that it will provide only for **flat** or **real jail time** for a majority of convicted offenders. The theory seems to be that it is better for convicted offenders to know how much jail or prison time they actually face from the outset, rather than rely on opinions and judgments of paroling authorities. This knowledge should eliminate or at least reduce some inmate anxiety and function as a potential deterrent to further criminal behavior. "Good time" provisions have not been entirely eliminated. Under Chapter 229, Sec. 3624 of the new guidelines provisions, federal prisoners sentenced to terms of imprisonment of more than one year (other than life imprisonment) will receive credit of fifty-four (54) days at the end of each year of their imprisonment, provided that they comply with their institutional regulations and requirements (U. S. Sentencing Commission, 1987b). This has become known as "credit toward service of sentence for satisfactory behavior" (a rose by any other name . . .).

Another major change is that the new guidelines are weighted numerically in specific areas to aid in the elimination of judicial sentencing discretion. The result is a sentencing range within which the judge must conform. Any departures from the guidelines by federal judges have to be justified in writing, including the reasons for such departures. Thus, it is perhaps inevitable that the PSI report emerges as a most important and influential document in federal courtrooms as fodder upon which to justify occasional sentencing range departures.

During the interval between 1985 and November 1987, the tasks of assembling the U. S. Sentencing Commission and formulating a set of consistent sentencing guidelines were formidable ones. Many people throughout the federal criminal justice system were involved at various points. By early 1987 the first draft of guidelines was distributed for review among judges, prosecutors, and probation officers. At first, these guidelines evoked fear and dismay from many quarters. Mock cases and unusual scenarios were presented in most federal districts to explain how the guidelines were designed to function and be applied.

From the outset it was apparent to many probation officers that compared with pre-guidelines conditions, very few offenders would be eligible for straight probation sentences without some other accompanying sanction. Another fear prevalent among probation officers throughout the nation was that their integrity would be placed on the line and that they would be held to a much higher standard of PSI report preparation and refinement compared with past times. Some probation officers expressed the feeling that defense attorneys, prosecutors, and judges would "tear them apart" in court over minor mistakes made in PSI report preparations or other challenges of their authenticity and accuracy. One very capable defense attorney confronted me one afternoon in mid-1987 on an elevator in the federal courthouse. "How do you like the new guidelines?" he asked. I replied that I wasn't "thrilled" by them and expressed the concern that the U. S. Probation Officer role would become considerably more visible than at present. He remarked, "Don't worry about that, because over the years, defense lawyers, judges, and prosecutors have been unable to determine what justice is. And so now it's your turn. You can't do any worse than we have done."

Regardless of my feelings and those of other probation officers, we reasoned that the guidelines were here to stay and we would be required to become familiar with them. At the time, it was believed that President Reagan or Congress would postpone the implementation of these guidelines pending some more extensive investigation of their appropriateness and implications for federal offenders and correctional institutions. This was not the case and the guidelines were implemented on November 1, 1987.

Probation officer training relative to the guidelines was problematic throughout most federal districts, since the guidelines seemed to be undergoing continuous revision. The U. S. Probation Office in Philadelphia was better off than most. We had an experienced officer, Sharon Henegan, who grasped the content and intent of the guidelines and helped us learn them. She made our learning efforts as painless as possible.

GUIDELINES, PROBATION, AND DIVERSION

Since the guidelines have been implemented, how have probation and diversion been affected? In order to understand the implications of these guidelines for such adjudicatory alternatives, we must examine briefly the guidelines themselves. As we have seen in previous chapters, the guidelines are weighted according to several criteria. The primary criteria are (1) offense seriousness and (2) offender criminal history. Each federal offense is rated on a point system, where more points are assigned for more serious crimes. The range of points on offense seriousness is from 1 (least serious) to 43 (most serious). Some of the offense levels for specific crimes include a base number of 4 for possession of stolen mail and a base number of 26 for distribution of cocaine. There are "adjustments" in these points upward or downward, determined from any existing aggravating or mitigating circumstances.

The offender's criminal history ranges from I (the lowest) to VI (the highest). Offenders are placed in one of these categories based upon their prior convictions, status at the time of their present conviction offense (e.g., on parole from prison for other offenses), and other factors. However, prior convictions have a time window of 15 years. Any conviction older than 15 years must be reported but receives no numerical value. As with offense levels, adjustments in one's criminal history score are made according to various criteria in order to arrive at the final category for sentencing.

When these two categories, offense level and criminal history, are crosstabulated, a 258-cell table is derived. Each cell contains "numbers of months" of possible incarceration with the exception of life sentences without parole eligibility for the most serious crimes.

Appendix B illustrates this table. Thus, the extreme incarceration ranges in the table are between (1) an offense level score of 1 and a criminal history score of I, yielding a "0–1" or "no months to one month" incarceration term judges could impose, to (2) an offense level score of 43 and a criminal history score of VI, yielding life imprisonment. These point values are calculated by probation officers in their preparation of PSI reports. Thus, it is imperative that every important detail about offenses and offenders be included when these reports are prepared. Otherwise, minor point fluctuations on either offense level or criminal history can make a significant difference of several years in time to be served by convicted offenders.

These guidelines have had a major impact on the diversion and probation options available to federal judges. If we remove the option of statutory probation, the possibility of probation is dependent almost entirely on the resulting offender score received from the sentencing table. The Comprehensive Crime Control Act of 1984 made probation a sentence in and of itself (18 U.S.C. Sec. 3581, 1989). Probation may also be used as an alternative to incarceration, provided that the terms and conditions of probation can be fashioned so as to meet fully the statutory purposes of sentencing, including promoting respect for the law, providing just punishment for the offense, achieving general deterrence, and protecting the public from further crimes committed by the defendant (U. S. Sentencing Guidelines, 1987b, Part B).

Subject to statutory restrictions, a sentence of probation is authorized:

1. if the minimum term of imprisonment in the range specified by the Sentencing Table is zero months;
2. if the minimum term of imprisonment specified by the Sentencing Table is at least one but no more than six months, provided that the court impose a condition or combination of conditions requiring intermittent confinement or community confinement as provided in Section 5C2.1(c)(2) of the guidelines ("Imposition of a Term of Imprisonment").

A sentence of probation may not be imposed in the event:

1. the offense of conviction is a Class A or B felony, (18 U.S.C. Sec. 3561(a)(1));
2. the offense of conviction expressly precludes probation as a sentence (18 U.S.C. Sec. 3561(a)(2));

3. the defendant is sentenced at the same time to a sentence of imprisonment for the same or a different offense (18 U.S.C. Sec. 3561(a)(3)).

When the minimum term of imprisonment specified in the guideline range from the Sentencing Table is more than six months, the guidelines do not authorize a sentence of probation. Under the guidelines, a term of probation shall be at least one year but no more than five years if the offense level is 8 or greater, and no more than three years in any other case.

The guidelines require the same types of conditions of probation that have become traditional throughout the criminal justice system over the years. This is an area where each district court will continue to add conditions to probation, if granted, which are unique to that district court.

What constitutes "community confinement" under these new guidelines? It may include confinement in a jail or prison, or it may indicate detention in a community treatment center, halfway house, or similar residential facility. It does *not* include house arrest or home confinement. Since the federal system currently lacks adequate space to accommodate growing offender populations resulting from guidelines implementation, it is reasonable to expect that one of the next guideline revisions will include the consideration of house arrest as a viable judicial sentencing option and condition qualifying for "intermittent confinement."

If judges adhere to the guidelines stringently at the time of sentencing, the actual number of offenders who will qualify for probation under the conditions described above will be extremely limited. Defendants with offense levels of 6 or less will be the only exceptions. Furthermore, probation will be adversely affected by prevailing statutes that now require mandatory minimum prison terms. These minimums are also devoid of parole. Therefore, between the guidelines and mandatory prison statutes, probation as a sentence is even more limited.

THE EMERGING ROLES OF PROBATION AND PROBATION OFFICERS

At least for the immediate future, probation is considered a luxury sentence for some types of crimes. Some good examples are fraud and business-related crimes. These typically involve very low-risk criminals or "gravy" cases. Gravy cases are those involving little or no probation service provisions. Thus, in the Eastern District of Pennsylvania, gravy cases would be placed in our Administrative Caseload Program, which does not currently require any ongoing personalized contact with probationers on any regular basis.

While the distinction is purely cosmetic, parole and special parole, the most common types of supervision categories for offenders sentenced under pre-guidelines sanctions, will be replaced by "supervised release." The major implication of the new guidelines for changing the supervised release functions for probation officers when parole is completely abolished will be that tasks formerly performed by the U. S. Parole Commission will now be performed by probation officers exclusively. An important change will be how probation officers handle program violations by offender-clients.

Under the pre-guidelines system, judges placed certain offenders on probation under the supervision of probation officers. Parole and special parole cases were handled by the U. S. Parole Commission. Currently, there is only probation, and those supervised by probation officers (including parole and special parole cases) will be accountable only to the original sentencing court. Probation officers have been given the responsibility for acknowledging and reporting *all* violations to original sentencing judges. Basically, this means that an already overburdened judiciary will be increasingly overburdened by assuming sanctioning responsibility for both probationers and parole/special parole cases. There will be hundreds, perhaps thousands, of extra judicial proceedings conducted annually to hear allegations of program violations. The extra courtroom work anticipated will be overwhelming. Program infractions (e.g., drug or alcohol abuse, curfew violations, nonpayment of fines or victim restitution) will merit full hearings involving all court players including the judge, Assistant U. S. Attorney, probation officers, defense attorneys, and all other supporting court personnel. The additional cost to taxpayers is staggering. The time consumed by such formal court proceedings will also be overwhelming. Considering the length of time it currently takes to schedule these types of proceedings, it is likely that our federal court system will gradually grind to a halt in a few short years, unless alternatives are initiated as resolutions to these problems.

It is unlikely that justice for offenders will be served any better under the new lethargic system envisioned by these guidelines changes. Presently for those still operating under the pre-guidelines sanctions (parolees and probationers alike), a parole or special parole violation involves few court personnel. A few field agents from the U. S. Parole Commission, the probation officer who supervised the case originally and prepared the PSI report, and possibly another officer who serves as the initial hearing officer for the Commission will convene to determine whether probable cause exists for the al-

162 *Part IV* Corrections

leged infraction. A second hearing is held to determine the possible punishment. Since prison overcrowding is critical, reconfinement is an unpopular option.

DIVERSION

The new guidelines and laws have eliminated diversion as a judicial sanctioning option. The only diversion remaining will be whether to bring a case forth for prosecution. This decision is purely discretionary and rests with the U. S. Attorney. Diversion procedures under the pre-guidelines period will be unlikely to undergo dramatic transformation in the post-guidelines period. In fact, it is likely that diversion may be returned to service as probation officer caseloads escalate and existing resources continue to diminish.

THE FUTURE

Now that I have painted a bleak picture of the future of probation and diversion under the new federal sentencing guidelines, is there any viable solution to the problems that are anticipated? From my own experience with the guidelines thus far, I believe that we will see many modifications and changes over the next two or three years that will restore greater judicial discretion to federal courts. It is merely a matter of time before the increased confinement costs and overcrowding accompanying these new guidelines will generate sufficient public interest in federal correctional change.

On the one hand, longer jail and prison sentences have political appeal. The "get tough on crime" movement has rallied around public officials who have endorsed larger fines and longer sentences for drug dealers and other criminals. However, it is questionable that these enhanced punishments will have a perceptible effect on the current rate of drug use in the United States or a serious reduction in international drug trafficking. Occasional "busts" dramatize that something is being done to fight crime and defeat it. However, these busts are miniscule compared with the current level of world drug activity. Arrests, convictions, and confinement for life of drug kingpins will only prompt their lieutenants to rise to new kingpin positions.

On the other hand, longer jail and prison sentences have profound adverse consequences for corrections. The financial resources and personpower simply do not exist presently to accommodate the deluge of convicted offenders emanating from federal district courts into federal prisons and correctional facilities. Furthermore, judicial discretion in sentencing may not be completely bad. It is probably true that no two criminal cases are identical, and that even where codefendants in the same criminal action appear before the same judge to be sentenced, each deserves proportionately different penalties for their different roles in the crime committed.

From the viewpoint of a probation officer, I offer the following as some of the changes I believe will occur in the near future to increase probation as an option under the new sentencing guidelines:

1. The minimum guidelines qualifications for probation eligibility will be decreased, thus making it possible to sentence convicted offenders to this nonincarcerative option.
2. The guidelines will allow for increased straight probation without accompanying intermittent confinement conditions.
3. House arrest or home confinement will be added as a sentencing option to fulfill present intermittent confinement conditions.
4. There will be a dramatic increase in the use of electronic monitoring services to enforce house arrest/home confinement. One problem will be who will have to pay for the increased costs associated with these services.
5. There will be a general reduction in the guidelines range of prison sentences, including reductions in minimum and maximum "months of incarceration" provisions.
6. A liberalization of the criteria enabling judges to depart from these guidelines will occur. This will permit judges to exercise greater discretion in the sentences they impose and to consider important facts and offender needs for their deterrent effect.
7. A liberalization will occur of the reasons for *downward departures* from the guidelines, including mitigating factors other than assistance and cooperation with police and others.

These are only a few of the many changes I expect to occur in federal sentencing practices. I believe the sentencing guidelines will undergo drastic revision and overhaul. The task will be arduous, and the Commissioners will have considerable responsibility for making required changes.

SUMMARY

In this chapter I have attempted to delineate some of the problems inherent in the new federal sentencing guidelines and how they will likely affect both offenders and probation officers. While there is nothing wrong with attempting to create a better sentencing system than we presently use, and while there is nothing particularly wrong with devising harsher punishments for certain types of offenders, there are several problems that these changes have created for various actors in corrections. It may be that the "baby has been thrown out with the bath water," as some of the good elements of the old sentencing system have been discarded with many of the bad ones.

I do not regard judicial discretion as particularly problematic. While it is apparent that some federal judges have abused their discretionary powers, most judges have made significant attempts to attain consistency in the imposition of punishments in their courtrooms. Have we disenfranchised all judges because of the imprudent actions of a few? In making the old system work better, it is significant that we remember to leave the ability to "do the right thing" in the hands of judges. Federal judges are not infallible, but they do deserve the benefit of the doubt and an element of trust.

As a federal probation officer I will continue to solicit judicial cooperation and encourage them to depart from the new sentencing guidelines whenever the situation merits departures. I say this knowing full well that my recommendations will mean that these judges will be required to provide in writing the justification for their guidelines departures. The judicial process is not out of control or unbridled. It never has been out of control. However, the new guidelines have seemingly "overregulated" the federal courtroom. In the end, more problems will have been generated than solved, and it will be up to future Commissioners to remedy the defects that have already been detected in this new sentencing system. Such remedying will be costly.

9

The Impact of Federal Sentencing Guidelines on Community Corrections and Privatization

Deborah G. Wilson

INTRODUCTION

"The sentencing decision is complex, difficult, and of fundamental importance; yet we lack a common law of sentencing. The purposes to be achieved by sentencing are not agreed upon, nor are our procedures" (Morris, 1977). Consequently, sentencing practices in our criminal justice system have taken the form of a number of short-lived trends that are the product of reforms. These reforms occur as frustration develops over the efficacy of current sentencing schemes. The reforms become standard practice and then themselves generate additional reforms as they fail to meet the often excessive expectations set for sentencing.

The recent trend in sentencing which has received much attention is the transition from indeterminate to determinate sentencing. Numerous states have adopted some form of determinate sentencing. Determinate sentencing is based on two premises: (1) that treatment and rehabilitation should be replaced by deterrence and incapacitation, and (2) that the traditional inherent judicial discretion in determining the type and length of sentence should be reduced and/or regulated (Hepburn and Goodstein, 1986). The establishment of the U. S. Sentencing Commission in 1984 and the resulting Sentencing Guidelines are a part of this national trend.

The guidelines were developed primarily to achieve fair sentencing through honesty. Honesty in sentencing was to be achieved through the use of guidelines that would reduce judicial discretion by setting criteria to determine type of sentence, length of sentence, and duration of time to be served. This would result in uniform sentencing that would be proportional to the severity of the crime and would eliminate disparities within and across jurisdictions.

The Commission established guidelines containing sentencing ranges for all federal crimes according to their seriousness as well as according to offender background characteristics. These two categories created a grid, with the vertical axis consisting of 43 levels of offense seriousness and the horizontal axis consisting of six offender categorizations arranged according to progressively more extensive criminal histories. A sentencing range (measured by months) is determined by cross-tabulating offense seriousness with one's criminal history index on the 43 X 6 grid. Sentences may be enhanced or reduced by considering Special Offense Characteristics. These are aggravating or mitigating circumstances or factors which include generic adjustments such as the offender's role in the offense, perjury, vulnerability of the victim, and multiple-count indictment adjustments which take into account the nature of the multiple counts filed.

Consistent with their ideological emphasis on punishment and deterrence, prison time is required for virtually all convicted offenders unless the minimum term is one to six months. In this event, the court may impose conditions of probation requiring intermittent confinement or community-based supervision. Probation for Class A and Class B felonies is not an option, and probation for white-collar offenders is discouraged. Criminal history has a significant impact on sentencing. Repeat offenders are generally considered inappropriate candidates and unacceptable risks for probation and, in some instances, they may receive incarcerative sentences on the average three times as long as those given to first offenders (Lowe, 1987).

As with any change in the criminal justice system, there is a great deal of interest in the impact of these guidelines on sentencing practices among the federal judiciary as well as upon other components of the criminal justice system. The highly interdependent nature of the components of the criminal justice system necessarily results in a "ripple effect." That is, a change in one part of the system (e.g., sentencing) will necessarily change the nature and operation of other parts of the system (e.g., corrections). While these changes in sentencing will produce alterations throughout the criminal justice system, the specific concern of this assessment is the potential impact of these guidelines on community corrections and the privatization movement within corrections.

SENTENCING GUIDELINES AND THE ABOLITION OF PAROLE

The most obvious change in community corrections associated with the guidelines actually predates the formulation of them. This was the scheduled abolition of the U. S. Parole Commission and, consequently, the termination of all parole in the federal prison system. In anticipation of the guidelines work of the Commission, Congress acted to eliminate several potential obstacles (Lowe, 1987). Parole was considered one of these "obstacles." Parole, or the discretionary early release of incarcerated offenders prior to serving their incarcerative sentences in their entirety, is the product of the rehabilitation and treatment ideology and a cornerstone of indeterminate sentencing. Within a system utilizing indeterminate sentencing, parole provides the vehicle whereby adjustments to inmates' sentences may be made in relation to their progress and good behavior while incarcerated.

The link between behavioral change, adjustment, and early release theoretically creates the motivation to become rehabilitated. The sentence imposed by the court is translated into a maximum and minimum range of actual hard time to be served. The maximum equals the actual time designated by the court in the sentence and translates into punishment for offenders who cannot or will not make the expected and appropriate adjustments. The minimum becomes the reward, the early release, that may be earned by the offender in exchange for evidence of rehabilitation and responsiveness to treatment.

Therefore, parole serves the following major functions: (1) early release via parole provides rewards and motivation for individual change and adjustment; (2) the emphasis placed on institutional adjustment and individual change by the parole process supports prison discipline and addresses a number of the problems of prison administration (Allen, Eskridge, Latessa, and Vito, 1985); (3) the post-release supervision provided by parole promotes positive adjustment to the community and provides a means of monitoring releases for indications of pending failure to adjust; and (4) parole provides a calculated population safety-valve which can be utilized to alleviate prison overcrowding through the process of careful review of inmates for a reduction in their time to be served (Breed, 1984).

Proponents of parole argue that the abolition of it will result in an inability of correctional authorities to motivate and control their inmates both inside correctional institutions and under conditions of supervised release in the community. However, the literature investigating inmate reactions to determinate sentencing and the existence of mechanisms which will exist under the new guidelines to compensate for the absence of parole suggests that the adverse effects upon offenders will be minimal.

The determinate sentence may introduce greater predictability in an otherwise unpredictable institutional environment. Goodstein (1980) found that the indeterminate sentence produced higher levels of anxiety and less tolerance for frustration among inmates, especially as inmates approached their parole review dates. Similarly, inmates who were given determinate sentences in South Carolina evidenced less stress compared with their counterparts in several other states where indeterminate sentences were imposed, regardless of sentence lengths. Both inmates receiving indeterminate and determinate sentences did not differ significantly in their attitudes or behaviors while in prison (Goodstein, 1982). Additional data from California and Oregon (Forst and Brady, 1983) compared prison rule violation rates before and after determinate sentencing. They found no direct relation between prison misconduct and the implementation of determinate sentencing. Instead, the researchers suggested that overcrowding, racial tensions, declining median age of inmates, gang membership, and variations in the form of prison administration should be assesssed as more directly contributory to prison misconduct.

These studies suggest that while the parole process may offer the option of serving only a portion of the original sentence, parole also introduces uncertainty, frustration, anxiety, and feelings of powerlessness. These factors may be more facilitative of misconduct than lengthy determinate sentences. The treatment process, seemingly promoted by parole via the participation-parole linkage, may instead be undermined as insincere, unmotivated inmates enter various prison programs for their cosmetic value and to enhance their chances for parole. Under determinate sentencing, however, prison program participation by inmates may encourage participation by interested, motivated, and more amenable inmates (Goodstein, 1980).

The fact that determinate sentences have not been associated directly with significant problems in correctional institutions may be related to the existence of "good time" provisions which are retained when sentencing guidelines (one form of determinate sentencing) are implemented. The guidelines purport to ensure "honesty in sentencing" by requiring offenders to serve the actual type and duration of sentence prescribed by the guidelines. The abolition of parole theoretically institutes integrity into sentencing by requiring offenders to serve the full duration of their sentences. However, the realities of prison administration and control introduce indeterminacy into a seemingly determinate sentencing system. Even a system based on "just deserts" must motivate offenders to abide by prison regulations. Adherence to these regulations must be rewarded. The greatest reward and motivation is a reduction in time served. The Commission has provided this mechanism through "credit toward service of a sentence for satisfactory behavior" (U. S. Sentencing Commission, 1987d; Ch. 229, Sec. 3624(b)). This provision allows offenders serving sentences of more than a year, but not life sentences, to accrue 54 days of credit toward their sentences annually. This is essentially good time credit that is awarded for compliance with institutional rules and regulations. If maximum time is accrued, it will reduce the actual time served on sentences by about 15 percent. While this reduction may not be comparable to reductions of sentences through a parole system, it is nevertheless a means for reducing actual time served. But because it is discretionary, however, it brings a degree of indeterminacy into the sentencing process. Prison officials may interpret minor infractions of rules in ways that reduce inmate credits earned as a form of sanction or penalty.

The concept of "good time", though not new, takes on a new meaning in the absence of parole. It becomes the only means for reducing the amount of time served in the institution. Like parole, it shifts the responsibility for length of time served to inmates and should enhance their motivation to adjust and change. While good-time credits to be earned cannot guarantee compliance with prison rules precisely the same way that parole functions (e.g., parole boards seldom require service of 85 percent or more of inmate sentences), it becomes the exclusive means for reducing time served and, if utilized properly, may generate a higher degree of compliance.

Like parole, credits toward service of sentence have the potential to be discretionary, since correctional officers make decisions to report or not report noncompliance. To provide motivation, this credit must be awarded fairly, judiciously, and consistently. Inmates must know prison regulations and the sanctions (i.e., the non-accrual of credit) that accompany specific violations of rules. Regulations governing the accumulation of this credit must be specific, uniform, and carefully administered. Credit should be accrued annually following a detailed assessment of the level of each inmate's adjustment. It should not be awarded at the beginning of the time period and then taken away for noncompliance as is the case with automatic good time in many jurisdictions. It must be perceived as a fair reward if it is to motivate inmates without increasing their anxiety and frustration, as may accompany parole systems.

Other early release and post-release functions of parole can be met, in part, by the "supervised release" sentencing option set forth in the federal guidelines. Under these guidelines, judges may order terms of supervised release following incarceration when sentences are more than one year, when required by statute, or to follow imprisonment in any other case. The length of supervision varies from one to five years, depending on the offense. While under supervised release, offenders are monitored by probation officers and are subject to conditions that may be imposeed if they are reasonably related to (1) the nature and circumstances of the offense and (2) the history and characteristics of the offender.

While supervised release has the potential for providing the post-release supervision of parole, the mandatory imposition for some crimes and the imposition of this post-release status at the time of sentencing imply an emphasis upon surveillance following release, rather than facilitating one's community reintegration. The nature of supervised release is not to reward evidence of adjustment but rather, to take precautions for public safety at the time of release.

While inherently different from parole by implication, supervised release is a reasonable provision if the guidelines fulfill their intended objectives. If the guidelines increase sentences which can only be reduced at best by 15 percent, offenders at the time of their release may be "increased risks" simply because of their longer sentence lengths. Offenders will be more institutionalized, more socially distant, and more isolated from community-based support systems because of their lengthy incarcerative periods. Ties with the institutional community will be strong and community reintegration more difficult. These offenders will have a much greater need for pre- and post-release services to facilitate their successful completion of supervised release. The system will be producing more long-term offenders with enhanced reintegration needs.

These enhanced reintegration needs will place increased demands on probation officers who currently supervise caseloads in excess of a size that would facilitate service provision and adequate surveillance. If their caseloads are not reduced, then the lack of surveillance and service provision may result in increased failure rates and recidivism. Further pressure on probation officer caseloads will occur during the transition phase as parole is completed by inmates sentenced under pre-guidelines sentencing. The guidelines will create transitional stress, as inmates under the old federal system are phased out while new offenders enter incarceration under post-guidelines conditions. Benjamin Baer, Chairman of the U. S. Parole Commission in 1988, estimated that by 1992, there will be 8,000 inmates requiring parole hearings and other procedures to which they were entitled in the pre-guidelines period. At the same time, there will be from 12,000 to 15,000 parolees and mandatory releasees under some form of correctional supervision (Clark, 1988). These offenders will be transferred to the jurisdiction of courts which are already overcrowded and cannot afford to take on additional supervisory responsibilities.

The last consequence of the abolition of parole will be an increase in the institutional population and an elimination of a prominent safety-valve to offset prison overcrowding. Regardless of whether this early release, safety-valve function is regarded as legitimate (Morris, 1977), offenders will serve a minimum of 85 percent of their original sentences. This will represent a substantial increase in time served, since federal prisoners in the past have served an average of 33 percent of their original sentences (Lowe, 1987). Additionally, many of the offenders traditionally probated will now be serving partial, if not full, sentences under incarceration. Without parole, inmates will serve 156 percent longer sentences at the minimum. This will have a substantial impact upon the size of the prison population.

PROBATION UNDER THE FEDERAL SENTENCING GUIDELINES

Probation is " . . . a conditional sentence that avoids incarceration of the offender" (Allen, Eskridge, Latessa, and Vito, 1985). It is considered one of several sentencing alternatives available to the court following one's conviction. Practically, probation means that convicted offenders are released into their communities, under various conditions, and under the supervision of probation officers. Probation is a central component of the rehabilitation philosophy within corrections and is based on the assumption that incarceration is unnecessary or even harmful for some offenders who do not pose serious threats to public safety. While in their communities, offenders are able to avoid some of the costs of incarceration and take full advantage of a wide range of formal and informal services and support systems not readily available to them while incarcerated.

Probation is the most frequently utilized form of sentencing. In some instances, over 70 percent of all convicted felony offenders are placed on probation (Petersilia, 1985; Allen, Eskridge, Latessa, and Vito, 1985). In the federal system, about 50 percent of all sentences have specified probation (Lowe, 1987). In some jurisdictions such as Ohio, probation has been combined with incarceration to create the sentencing alternative of split-sentencing or "shock probation." Under this alternative, an offender is sentenced to incarceration but "shock probated" (released under supervision) after a given period of time (usually 30, 60, 90, or 120 days) (Vito, 1978, 1984). The assumption is that by providing offenders with a "taste of the bars" (Parisi, 1981), offenders experience the deprivations of incarceration without permanent harm and are presumably deterred from future criminal activity. The "shock" of prison becomes the motivation for success on probation and for non-criminal behavior.

Specifically, those qualified for probation are ordinarily specified by statute. First-offenders and/or offenders who commit less serious crimes are considered the most appropriate candidates for probation. Although they are few in number, even some offenders convicted of second-degree murder, robbery, or aggravated assault have been placed on probation rather than incarcerated. However, studies of the criminal histories of prospective probationers generally reveal that first-offenders who commit minor crimes are those most likely to be granted probation in most jurisdictions (Parisi, 1981:111–112).

The critical element for determining who will be probated under the new federal sentencing guidelines is set by the sentencing requirements of these guidelines. Lowe (1987) has provided a detailed discussion of the "in/out" line created in the sentencing table and the implications of this line for prospective probationers. The "in/out" line is a "threshold boundary" (Lowe, 1987:36) which determines who will be incarcerated and who will be probated. Cases falling well below or well above this line in the sentencing table pose few problems for judges when applying sentencing options and achieving uniformity and fairness originally functioning as the rationale for guideline development. The cases well under the line will be probated. Those well above the line will result in incarceration.

The cases that pose the greatest sentencing problems within the guidelines are **intermediate crimes** (Lowe, 1987:36). These are crimes that are clustered close to the in/out lines rather than in the extremes of the sentencing grid. Under the guidelines, for example, these intermediate crimes include "economic crimes, frauds and deceptions, assaults, burglary, and public welfare offenses" (Lowe, 1987:36). The placement of white-collar offenses in this range was a policy decision made by the Commission. The decision was based on the belief that " . . . [the] courts sentence to probation an inappropriately high percentage of offenders guilty of certain crimes such as theft, tax evasion, antitrust offenses, insider trading, fraud, and embezzlement . . . " (U. S. Sentencing Commission, 1987d:1.8).

Because these intermediate crimes are situated at the threshold between incarceration and probation, this area becomes the section of the sentencing grid that has the potential to generate discretionary decisions and sentence variability in the absence of policy to govern sentencing decisions. According to Lowe (1987), the guidelines could be govered by three sets of options in these cases. The first option would be to treat all intermediate crimes as cases deserving of probation. Departures would be specified for first-offenders who commit crimes under especially serious circumstances. This policy would result in less complex judicial decision-making, reduced variability in sentencing, and would additionally provide a means of reducing the impact of these guidelines on the size of the prison population (Lowe, 1987).

The second option would be to treat all "intermediate crimes" as necessarily requiring incarceration. Those cases deserving of leniency would receive probation. This option would increase the rate of incarceration and increase the impact of the guidelines on the prison population. It would serve retributive goals and incapacitate offenders, but it would not result in the level of crime control sought through incapacitation, because of the large numbers of first-offenders who would receive incarceration (Lowe, 1987). The final option would be to develop a policy of judicial discretion or to simply develop no policy to guide their decision-making involving these crimes. Judges would then make a determination on each individual case. This option would result in extreme variability and unfairness in sentencing.

According to Lowe (1987), the guidelines and related policy statements do not coincide completely with any of the three options concerning the in/out line. Instead, various policy statements appear to divide the sentencing table into three areas: probation, incarceration, and intermediate crimes. The probation cases are those which fall under level 7 in crime seriousness and level I in one's criminal history. The line moves down to progressively less serious crimes as the rating for criminal history increases. Cases requiring incarceration include those crimes above level 12 for first-offenders and decrease in severity level as criminal history increases. Crimes above level 5 receive incarceration when criminal history is within the maximum category.

The area between the two lines is the intermediate area. This ranges in severity from levels 7 to 12 for first-offenders, and levels I to VI at the extreme of one's criminal history. Within this category, some cases may be probated following the completion of the minimum sentence in prison, while other, more serious crimes may not be probated. Rather, these crimes may include sentencing penalties split between incarceration and probation based on the minimum sentence (Lowe, 1987). The specific offenses that fall into this range include several economic, fraud/deception, and/or white-collar offenses. A number of aggravating factors (e.g., number of victims, vulnerability of victim, and amount of financial loss) exist as enhancements to increase offense severity. However, many of the potentially mitigating factors related to these crimes are unspecified. Consequently, many first-offenders who commit white-collar and economic offenses may face minimum prison terms, provided that judges adhere to the guidelines (Lowe, 1987). While a large number of federal district judges refused to comply with these guidelines during 1988 (citing several constitutional challenges of them before the U. S. Supreme Court), the Court upheld the constitutionality of the guidelines in early 1989 in *Mistretta v. United States*. Thus, considerable ambiguity about the legitimacy of these guidelines was resolved and federal judiciary compliance with them was mandated.

What impact these guidelines will have on probation is unclear. Economic-based crimes comprise the greatest proportion of federal offenses (U. S. Sentencing Commission, 1987d:1.6). The usual practice of federal judges has been to imprison only approximately half of these offenders, including many first-offenders. The remainder have been probated or sentenced to split sentences (Lowe, 1987). While the guidelines would appear to limit the mitigating factors that could reduce sentences and to specify that white-collar offenders should be treated more harshly (U. S. Sentencing Guidelines, 1987d), the nature of these guidelines and stipulated means of departure would appear to easily allow judges to continue in their pre-guidelines sentencing patterns. It is also apparent that a critical part of an offender's ability to receive probation in cases of intermediate crimes will be the plea agreement. Negotiations surrounding the proceedings for intermediate crimes will have as the primary objective the sentence of probation.

Unless judicial departures are extreme, a major change in the probation clientele will occur. The number of probationers who have served portions of their sentences in prison will increase, given the numbers of offenders who will fall into the category of those who may be probated following a minimum prison sentence. The probation officer's job will then include some of the additional reintegrative functions that have been traditionally associated with parole.

Another major change in the probation officer's function will occur as the result of the increased importance of presentence investigation (PSI) reports under the federal guidelines. All offenders are required to have a PSI report prepared. Defendants may not waive the preparation of this report. The information contained in this report will be critical to the offender's sentence under the guidelines, since the report will provide facts related to mitigating or aggravating circumstances that will influence the sentencing outcome. While it is possible for judges to find that there have been ample facts presented at trial to make sentencing decisions and PSIs may not be essential, most judges will continue to have these PSIs prepared as supportive evidence for the sentences they impose. This will mean that probation officers will spend more time in PSI preparation and less time supervising offenders. Prior to the application of the new guidelines, average federal caseloads for probation officers were 55 offender-clients including PSI preparations. The increased PSI preparation—more PSI reports with more time spent preparing each report—will predictably strain probation officer workloads (Clark, 1988).

While the number of offenders serving exclusively probationary sentences (i.e., probation with no form of confinement) will decrease, the caseloads of probation officers will continue to escalate. As discussed earlier, the increased emphasis on PSIs, the general increases in the federal inmate population, and the resulting offenders released under split-sentencing probation and other forms of supervised release will continue to expand the range of responsibilities and numbers of clients supervised. Without a simultaneous increase in sheer numbers of probation officers to accommodate this anticipated increased caseload, the quality of probationary services will decline.

FEDERAL SENTENCING GUIDELINES: IMPETUS FOR PRIVATIZATION

Privatization is the provision of public services by nongovernmental for-profit and not-for-profit entities. It is not and has not been unique to corrections. In fact, government services through contractual agreements with the private sector was a major means of providing many govermental services in early American history. "Transportation, fire protection, police, and even armies were often provided on contract" (Allen and Simonson, 1989:604). Gradually, as government became more efficient and specialized, these services were transferred to the public realm. Recently, as the costs of these services have increased, there is a movement toward the transference of these functions back to the private sector via contractual agreements.

Currently, the most publicized area of privatization involves the delivery of correctional services by private organizations and agencies. Like privatization in government generally, private sector involvement in corrections is not new. During the early to mid-19th century, privatization was frequently utilized in prison industries (Saxton, 1988). Similarly, many services in corrections such as medical, food, and maintenance services have been contracted for in the past. In community corrections, work-release centers and halfway houses have been operated via contractual or fee-for-services agreements for many years.

These services and arrangements are still part of the the privatization movement in corrections. However, what is generating the current controversy over privatization is the transfer of complete correctional operations to private, for-profit companies. This means transferring the operation of a local, state, or federal correctional facility from the government to a private enterprise (Robbins, 1988). The proponents of privatization argue that government has inadequately performed these correctional services. The costs of these services are high and continue to climb annually, while recidivism rates also remain high. Confinement conditions, even with increased appropriations, are often inhumane and continue to precipitate federal involvement (Robbins, 1988).

The private sector can construct facilities quickly at lower costs. The limited bureaucracy minimizes impediments to creative ideas and the implementation of programs or the procurement of equipment to meet correctional needs. For example, at the Bay County Jail in Florida, employees were often isolated and had communication problems. Corrections Corporation of America was managing this facility and immediately issued employees two-way portable radios (Hutto, 1988). There was no need to request additional appropriations and wait for legislative or bureaucratic approval.

The critics of privatization cite the impropriety of incarceration based on the profit motive where there is no incentive to reduce the institutional population. Instead, greater motivation will exist to construct more prison and jail space. There is concern that this motive will promote cost-cutting measures that will affect adversely present prison and jail conditions. Additionally, a number of legal and quasi-legal issues have not been resolved and raise concern among critics. These include:

1. The constitutionality of passing public safety duties and state responsibilities for incarceration to private companies.
2. Whether liability will be the responsibility of the private company or the government.
3. Which entity is responsible for monitoring standards and making classification and transfer decisions?
4. Can private companies refuse inmates (i.e., those with AIDS)?
5. What options are present if a private company goes bankrupt or raises fees beyond the means of the government agency (Robbins, 1988)?

While many organizations such as the American Bar Association recommend caution (ABA Resolution, February 1988), privatization of the operation of correctional facilities has become a reality in a number of jurisdictions in the United States. Currently, at least 1,600 adults are housed in private correctional facilities. These include both felons and misdemeanants in secure state and local facilities in Kentucky, Florida, Tennessee, Minnesota, and New Mexico (National Institute of Justice, 1987b). Additional facilities are under construction in Texas. Many states also contract for nonsecure detention space (i.e., work release, prerelease, and restitution centers), and twelve states operate private juvenile facilities (National Institute of Justice, 1987b).

Most of the impetus for privatization comes from prison overcrowding. As the numbers of offenders sentenced to incarceration continues to grow and places increased demands on limited prison, jail, or other incarcerative space in correctional facilities and programs, governments at all levels have been forced to consider several alternative means for addressing the overcrowding problem. One option seriously explored is privatization.

Traditionally, one objective of the Federal Bureau of Prisons was to serve as a model for state and local corrections. Federal courts have emphasized diversion and community-based treatment. Federal offenders have been primarily property offenders and were frequently probated. Those who were institutionalized were usually multiple offenders with lengthy histories of serious and/or violent crimes. While these offenders were incarcerated, the Federal Bureau of Prisons sought to implement a "balanced approach" that recognized individual rather than "all-purpose" treatment as most effective (Allen and Simonson, 1989).

Recently, however, the Federal Bureau of Prisons has developed many of the problems that traditionally typified state facilities. The detention of refugee groups in federal facilities and the increase in the number of serious, violent offenders have strained correctional resources. To these strained resources will come further stress as the new federal guidelines take effect. The guidelines will increase the federal prison population as

—probation with confinement increases;
—average time for violent crimes increases;
—confinement for serious drug offenders increases; and
—confinement for burglary increases.

However, the sentencing guidelines will not have an effect comparable to that of the Anti-Drug Abuse Acts of 1986 and 1988 and the career offender provision of the Comprehensive Crime Control Act of 1984 (National Institute of Justice, 1987a). The latter acts will significantly increase the prison population. The guidelines will simply aggravate this growth.

The National Institute of Justice has projected low and high inmate population growth scenarios. The low growth scenario projects that the population will grow almost threefold by the year 2002 to 105,000. The high growth scenario predicts almost a fourfold increase to 156,000 by the year 2002 (National Institute of Justice, 1987a). Without major government expenditures, this growth cannot be accommodated by existing facilities. The high cost of prison construction, length of time required to design, approve, and construct government-owned facilities, and long-term obligations to operate government facilities will act to facilitate the consideration and eventual use of private facilities by the federal government.

Private facilities may be brought on-line rapidly and without major capital construction costs. Contracting with private corporations may be used to accommodate currently growing populations but does not require permanent expansions. The flexibility of private contractors permits specialization in facilities which could relieve pressures on general purpose institutions as offenders with special needs are confined in these specialized facilities.

All of these benefits will need to be utilized to meet the growing prison population. Without a massive outlay in public funds, the private sector may be the only option given the current sentencing practices and ideologies. Given the current strain on federal monies and the necessity to respond quickly, privatization remains one of the most viable options and will most certainly be utilized in the future for both secure and nonsecure correctional facilities.

Another area of private sector involvement that will be precipitated by these guidelines is the increased use of an independently produced PSI report. As mentioned earlier, the PSI report will take on greater importance under the new guidelines. This report has traditionally provided information needed by the court to set sentences, and it has also been used by appellate courts for reviewing appeals of sentences. Since the guidelines set highly specific sentencing requirements involving mitigating and aggravating factors, and require judges to justify departures via circumstances not adequately covered by the guidelines, the importance of the detail of PSIs will grow substantially.

Ideally, PSI reports contain summary information that is both objective and subjective in nature. This information, if comprehensive, should include information such as: present offense (including the offender's attitude and role in the commission of the offense), criminal record (if any), family relationships, education (including academic and behavioral history), employment skills, emotional stability, and efficiency, associates and companions, type and quality of participation with peers and associates, habits (e.g., substance abuse, gambling, sexual problems), and physical and mental health (Reckless, 1967).

Much of the objective data (e.g., age, marital status, number of children, nature of offense) are readily available. However, the subjective data that may be difficult and time-consuming to collect are most crucial. These subjective data summarize offender attitudes, approach to life, and factors that have significantly influenced their development and behaviors—factors that often provide the most insight into the offender's past and present (Reckless, 1967). With caseloads averaging 55 (sometimes 80 to 100 or more) clients, probation officers simply do not have the time to prepare adequate PSIs that provide these important details.

Since the PSI report will be paramount in determining an offender's sentence, it will become a major tool for the defense in attempts to obtain less stringent sentences. Because of the highly specific nature of the guidelines, it will also become a central means whereby sentences may be appealed. Particularly defense counsels will want detailed and accurate PSIs and may even obtain privately prepared ones to supplement those provided by probation officers. If probation officers are unable to provide the detail required by defense counsels because of the increased demands on their time, the use of PSIs prepared by independent sources may become more frequent.

In California, private corporations currently provide PSI reports and other relevant documents for a fee. The personnel who prepare these reports are often former probation officers and investigators who specialize in collecting and preparing valuable details required by defense counsels. These private PSI reports may be accepted by the court in lieu of reports prepared by probation officers, as supplemental reports, or they may be used by the defense in challenging the content of various points made in PSI reports prepared by public agencies. This "service for a fee" arrangement could guarantee that much time and energy would be allocated to providing much detail about offenders to be sentenced. It could also avoid certain biases that may be evident in reports prepared by agents of the state, although it could equally introduce defense counsel biases favorable to the offender. Nevertheless, privately prepared PSI reports is an option involving privatization and will undoubtedly assume greater significance under the new federal sentencing guidelines.

CONCLUSION

The federal sentencing guidelines will most certainly have an effect on all components of the federal criminal justice system. And since the federal system is generally viewed as a model for many states to emulate, it is expected that some state systems will be influenced accordingly to follow federal procedures to some degree. While the impact of these guidelines may be projected with some degree of confidence, the critical factor in the nature and extent of this impact will be judicial sentencing behavior. The greater the judicial departures from these guidelines, the more unpredictable will be the long-range impact. If the judiciary depart in the direction of greater leniency toward offenders, the less extreme will be the impact on probation. If judicial departures are toward greater sentencing severity, the greater the impact of the abolition of parole, the greater the impact on probation, and the greater the impetus for privatization in corrections. Harsher sentencing practices would increase the existing federal prison population as well as the use of PSI reports by the private sector through larger numbers of defense counsel requests.

Precisely what the impact of these guidelines will be on community corrections is presently unknown. However, it is apparent that there will be definite changes in present pre- and post-incarcerative practices and significant consequences for offender-clients. If the Commission functions as it was originally intended to function, the implications of these guidelines for community corrections will be closely monitored and revised accordingly through experience. Congress has enabled the Commission to make adjustments to accommodate ideological and administrative shifts and to address pragmatic needs and new issues that arise as the guidelines are applied.

10

The Impact of Federal Sentencing Guidelines on Jail and Prison Overcrowding and Early Release

G. Larry Mays

INTRODUCTION

As part of a general dissatisfaction with the processes of indeterminate sentencing, Congress passed the Comprehensive Crime Control Act of 1984 which established the United States Sentencing Commission. The prevailing discontent with sentencing and correctional policy may be stated as three closely related propositions:

1. The use of indeterminate sentences allows judges a tremendous amount of virtually unchecked discretion leading to a lack of uniformity among defendants convicted of similar offenses;
2. As a result of the first proposition (and actual release dates being determined by paroling authorities), there is a lack of proportionality, and, thus some would argue, "injustice" in sentencing;
3. Because of the second proposition, the actual sentencing authority of judges is abdicated to paroling authorities who may or may not weigh public safety and related issues in determining release dates for prison inmates.

This chapter will consider the effects of federal sentencing guidelines on jail and prison overcrowding and the processes of early release. However, because these guidelines have been operational only for a short time, and their existence has been a source of great controversy among the federal judiciary, no data presently exist to assess their short- or long-range impact. Therefore, in order to predict what some of the anticipated effects might be, several states will be examined where determinate and/or presumptive sentencing guideline patterns have been adopted.

As states have increasingly grown disaffected with traditional or indeterminate methods of sentencing, the trend has been toward implementing determinate sentences, often coupled with elimination or severe restriction, of parole (Blumstein, 1984b; Knapp, 1982, 1984, 1986). Indeterminate sentences provide ranges established by the legislature (e.g., one to five years), they are imposed by judges, but the actual release dates are determined by parole boards. Determinate sentences involve precise terms of incarceration decided at the time of disposition, and normally reducible only through the accumulation of "good time" credits (Blumstein, 1984b; Lipson and Peterson, 1980; McCoy, 1984).

A variation of determinate sentencing involves the use of guidelines to provide the basic parameters within which judges should sentence convicted offenders (Block and Rhodes, 1987; Hewitt and Little, 1981; Knapp, 1982; von Hirsch, 1982). However, it is also important to note that guidelines can be employed under indeterminate sentencing schemes, as is the case in Pennsylvania.

In 1984 Congress passed the Comprehensive Crime Control Act that, among other things, created the United States Sentencing Commission. This Commission, functioning within the judicial branch of government, was designed to establish federal sentencing policies and practices. It was charged especially with producing "guidelines that would avoid unwarranted sentencing disparities while retaining enough flexibility to permit individualized sentencing when called for by mitigating or aggravating factors" (Block and Rhodes, 1987:2).

Determinate (and/or presumptive) sentencing imposes a fundamental alteration in the sentencing behavior of judges, and such policy initiatives have clear implications throughout the network of criminal justice agencies. A manual prepared by the Federal Bureau of Prisons (1984) says that sentencing guidelines can impact at different points in the processing of cases including at the point of sentencing, with "front-end" policy considerations like uniformity or equity of sentencing; at the point of incarceration, concerning issues such as lengths of prison sentences and the size of prison populations; and at the point of release from incarceration, especially on questions of prison crowding and the availability of early release mechanisms.

The first of these issues will not be addressed here, in order to retain a focus on institutional crowding and early release. The sections that follow will address some of the explicit provisions of the U. S. Sentencing Guidelines that will likely impact on prison populations, the examples of selected states that have developed and implemented determinate/presumptive sentencing (some using sentencing guidelines), the mechanisms for controlling the flow of inmates in and out, and finally, some of the policy options facing the federal government.

THE INFLUENCE OF SENTENCING GUIDELINES ON CORRECTIONS

Many provisions contained in the enabling legislation creating the U. S. Sentencing Commission (28 U.S.C., Sec. 991, 1988) and the guidelines developed by the Commission (18 U.S.C., Sec. 3551) will likely affect the population of federal prisoners. However, certain of these policy changes will more directly influence federal correctional populations.

Sentencing Philosophies

Congress mandated that the Commission is to "provide **certainty** and **fairness** in meeting the purposes of sentencing, **avoiding unwarranted sentencing disparities** among defendants with similar records who have been found guilty of similar criminal conduct while **maintaining sufficient flexibility to permit individualized sentences** when warranted by mitigating or aggravating factors not taken into account in the establishment of general sentencing practices. . ." (28 U.S.C., Sec. 991(b)(1)(8), 1988) [emphasis added]. While these purposes certainly are lofty sounding, the Commission complicated the picture when it stipulated that the sentence imposed **shall** consider the need "(A) to reflect the seriousness of the offense, to promote respect for the law, and to provide just punishment for the offense; (B) to afford adequate deterrence to criminal conduct; (C) to protect the public from further crimes of the defendant; and (D) to provide the defendant with needed educational or vocational training, medical care, or other correctional treatment in the most effective manner. . ." (18 U.S.C., Sec. 3553(a)(2), 1988). In other words, the guidelines are to "establish a uniform, determinate federal sentencing system that will accomplish the purposes of just punishment, deterrence, incapacitation, and rehabilitation" (U. S. Department of Justice, 1984). Such far reaching, and perhaps conflicting, sentencing philosophies mean that the federal sentencing guidelines purport to be all things to all people.

Abolition of Parole and Early Release Alternatives

In order to achieve honesty in sentencing, Congress dictated that the process of parole, overseen by the U. S. Parole Commission, would be abolished. Congress held the view that with indeterminate sentencing, the sentence **imposed** was not the sentence **served**. Under the authority of the U. S. Parole Commission to grant early releases, most inmates served about one-third of their original sentences (U. S. Sentencing Commission, 1987:2). Thus, while the ostensible sentences imposed under indeterminate sentencing might appear quite lengthy, the time served was actually much less. For example, a convicted offender might be sentenced to a prison term of 2–10 years, but under indeterminate sentencing, the first parole eligibility date is set at some fraction of the minimum sentence. This means that a sentence of 2–10 years actually could translate into an 8–9-month active prison sentence.

In place of parole, most states that have adopted determinate sentencing employ a system of "good time" credits that function to reduce sentences from one-third to one-half (Lipson and Peterson, 1980). Under the new federal sentencing guidelines, the maximum **good conduct time** (GCT) allowable for sentence reductions is 54 days per year or .148 days per day served, and not applicable to sentences of less than one year (U. S. Department of Justice, 1984). The clear implication of the elimination of parole and the institution of GCT credit is that sentencing guidelines should have an effect on the length of prison sentences, the size of prison populations, and the flexibility of early release mechanisms.

Probation Restrictions

Block and Rhodes (1987:2) note that before the implementation of the federal sentencing guidelines, 41.4 percent of the convicted defendants received "straight probation" (i.e., traditional community supervision not preceded by a period of incarceration). After November 1, 1987 (the effective date of implementation of the guidelines), straight probation sentences are expected to fall to 18.5 percent of all of those sentenced (Block and Rhodes, 1987). Along with a reduction of straight probation sentences, the Commission permitted courts to impose split sentences, short periods of incarceration followed by traditional community supervision (U. S. Sentencing Commission, 1987:8–9).

Other Sentencing Provisions

The major effects on federal prison populations likely will come more from the Anti-Drug Abuse Act of 1986 and the career offender component of the Comprehensive Crime Control Act of 1984 than from the sentencing guidelines themselves (Block and Rhodes, 1987:2; U. S. Sentencing Commission, 1987:11). The 1986 Anti-Drug Abuse Act provides for substantial increases in the minimum and maximum prison sentences for most federal drug offenses. Career offender sections of the Comprehensive Crime Control Act of 1984 provided that "certain repeat offenders—those 18 or older who were convicted of a violent crime or drug offense and who had been convicted of two or more such crimes previously—receive sentences at or near the maximum term authorized" (Block and Rhodes, 1987:3). As Figure 10.1 shows, the combined impacts of all three changes potentially could be quite dramatic.

Addressing Prison Capacities

When developing sentencing guidelines, some states, such as Minnesota, have used **current** prison capacity as a policy constraint when determining the categories of who will go to prison and for how long (Blumstein, et al., 1983; Knapp, 1982, 1984, 1986). The federal sentencing guidelines recognize the limitations of prison capacities, but only to a certain extent. The enabling legislation provides that the Commission "shall take into account the nature and capacity of the penal, correctional, and other facilities and services available, and shall make recommendations concerning any change or expansion in the nature or capacity of such facilities and services that might become necessary as a result of the guidelines. . ." and the "sentencing guidelines prescribed under this chapter shall be formulated to minimize the likelihood that the Federal prison population will exceed the capacity of the Federal prisons, as determined by the Commission" (28 U.S.C., Sec. 994(g), 1988).

Although the Commission was admonished to "take into account" prison capacities, unlike Minnesota, its work was not constrained by present capacity limits. The danger, then, is that the sentencing changes will drive populations higher, a critical element since federal prisons already are operating at 58 percent over rated capacity [see Endnote 1]. This means that should populations increase beyond institutional capacities, the Commission could recommend a variety of options to absorb or deflect the overflow. An array of these options will be discussed in the final section of this chapter.

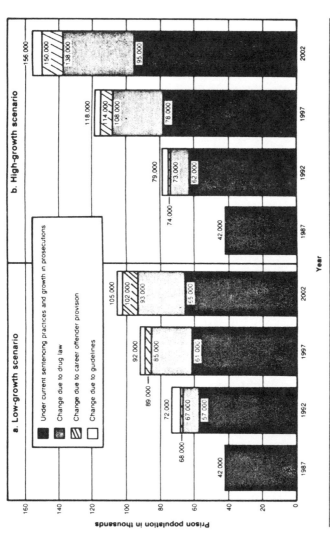

Figure 10.1 Prison Population Projections (Source: Michael K. Block and William M. Rhodes, "The Impact of the Federal Sentencing Guidelines." *NIJ Reports*, September/October 1987, p. 6).

POPULATION CONTROL MECHANISMS

When relating sentencing policy changes, like the implementation of sentencing guidelines, to prison populations, Gottfredson (1987:144–148) says there are four approaches to controlling prison crowding: front-door guidelines, trap-door guidelines, side-door guidelines, and back-door guidelines. Each of these will be discussed in this section, and the following section will deal with selected state experiences concerning determinate sentencing, sentencing guidelines, and prison crowding.

Front-Door Guidelines

Blumstein et al. (1983:225) note that prison populations are affected by the number of people sent to prison, the length of sentences, and the amount of time each inmate actually serves. This means that to control prison populations, on the front-end of the process (at the point of sentencing, or even earlier, at the point of establishing penalties) the choices may be to sentence fewer offenders to prison or to reduce sentence lengths (Knapp, 1986:47).

The first front-end policies include preprosecution or pretrial diversion programs (Blumstein, 1983:461; Clear and Cole, 1986:282). Such programs may exist regardless of prison populations and capacities, but they can remove from the adjudicatory process minor offenders, first offenders, and those charged with nonviolent, property offenses. Also, community corrections programs involving halfway houses and community-based residential or nonresidential treatment programs typify front-end mechanisms intended to minimize prison crowding.

Front-end policies, controlling the inflow of prison inmates, have had the greatest impact in those states that have chosen to follow one of two courses of action: to use current prison capacity as the absolute limit for future sentencing decisions, or actually to reduce the population from current figures to some defined percentage of institutional capacity (e.g., 90–95 percent). When prison bedspace constraints are ignored, or when operating capacity is treated as a limitless resource, front-end sentencing considerations will not be major policy determinates.

Trap-Door Guidelines

By mid-1988, at least seven states (Michigan and Illinois among them) maintained statutory-based emergency release mechanisms

(Gottfredson and McConville, 1987:146). For these states, certain population target numbers trigger a shutdown in new admissions and/or release of inmates 60 to 90 days earlier than anticipated (Blumstein, et al., 1983:254; Gottfredson and McConville, 1987:146, 168).

Emergency release mechanisms can provide an effective short-term solution to the problems of prison crowding, but they suffer from two deficiencies. These releases cannot solve the long-term crowding problems caused by front-end "loading" exacerbated by sentencing policies, and early release provisions tend to be publicly and politically unpopular. When prison administrators speak of releasing "several hundred" inmates at the same time, even when most are within a few months of release anyway, the general public has the perception of deranged ex-convicts running loose over the countryside. This becomes upsetting to the citizenry and complaints begin to state legislators who often move to limit such emergency release provisions.

Side-Door Guidelines

Side-door sentencing policies allow offenders to be sentenced to relatively short periods of confinement followed by some period of mandatory community supervision. These "split sentences" are provided for under the new federal sentencing laws in 28 U.S.C., Sec. 994, 1988 (Block and Rhodes, 1987). Such provisions often permit trial court judges to review cases and to resentence offenders to intensive community supervision programs (Gottfredson and McConville, 1987:147). Side-door policies are directed more at the length of time served than they are at the numbers and types of offenders sentenced to prison.

Back-Door Guidelines

Parole has been characterized as the most important "safety valve" mechanism available to prison officials facing increasingly crowded prisons (Blumstein et al., 1983:253; Lipson and Peterson, 1980:37–38). However, as states have moved toward determinate sentencing systems, the processes of parole decision-making have been eliminated or severely limited (Blumstein, 1984b:131; Blumstein et al., 1983:254; Knapp, 1986:38).

Parole boards have been effective in controlling prison populations by selectively increasing discharge rates (Lipson and Peterson, 1980:37). However, the discretion exercised by parole boards in making release decisions often has been criticized as being arbitrary. As a result, the federal government, followed by a number of states, has experimented with the use of parole guidelines as an intermediate step toward sentencing guidelines (Alschuler, 1980; Fischer, 1987; Gottfredson, 1979; Hoffman et al., 1986; Hussey, 1978; Krauth, 1987; Sullivan, 1987).

Parole guidelines are intended to provide more objective ways for making early release decisions (Fischer, 1987; Gottfredson, 1979; Sullivan, 1987; Taylor, 1979). This structuring of discretion is meant to accomplish two objectives. From the inmate's point of view, parole guidelines are intended to make the review and release process less arbitrary and clearly more explicit. At the same time, parole guidelines should contribute to community well-being by not releasing those inmates who have a high probability of recidivating or who pose a continuing threat to public safety (Fischer, 1987).

STATES' EXPERIENCES WITH DETERMINATE SENTENCING

The previous section has discussed the control points and flow mechanisms that tie determinate sentencing (especially coupled with sentencing guidelines) and prison populations together. It should be noted here, though, that the federal government has limited experience with sentencing guidelines (specifically, since November 1, 1987). Thus, to assess the potential impact of sentencing guidelines on federal correctional populations, it seems most reasonable to examine guideline provisions and the experiences of different states (some having prison populations as great as the federal government, and some substantially smaller) that have adopted various determinate sentencing systems.

Changing Sentencing Patterns

Several states adopted determinate sentencing schemes prior to the movement by Congress to mandate determinate sentencing for the federal courts. This means that with greater frequency, jurisdictions are imposing sentences of definite terms, rather than those with statutory minimums and maximums. The experience of nine states with determinate sentences should be instructive for the federal government.

Table 10.1 shows the general trends in prison populations in nine of the states with the longest experience with determinate sentencing. As can be seen, five of these states (California, Illinois, Maine, New Mexico, and Washington) have had percentage increases during the 1980s that exceed the average increase for all states. Three of these

Table 10.1 Nine States With Determinate Sentencing and Prison Population Trends

States	Prison Population 1987	Percentage Change 1986-1987	Percentage Change 1980-87	Incarceration Rate/100,000 1987
California	66,975	12.6	178.6	231
Florida	32,445	.6	60.1	265
Illinois	19,850	2.0	85.1	171
Indiana	10,827	6.4	69.3	192
Maine	1,328	.9	88.8	106
Minnesota	2,546	3.4	27.8	60
New Mexico	2,648	9.6	113.6	169
North Carolina	17,249	- 2.5	11.7	250
Washington	6,131	- 7.1	139.4	134
U.S. Total	581,609	6.7	76.5	228
Federal	48,300	8.8	91.8	16
State	533,309	6.5	75.4	212

Source: Bureau of Justice Statistics. <u>Prisoners in 1987</u>. Washington, D.C.: U.S. Department of Justice, 1988, pp. 2-3.

states present useful case studies when pondering the possible effects of the new federal sentencing guidelines.

In 1976, Maine became the first state in recent history to abolish indeterminate sentencing and parole release (Lagoy, Hussey, and Kramer, 1978; Tilton, 1987; von Hirsch and Hanrahan, 1981). However, while Maine employs what is termed a determinate sentencing system, von Hirsch and Hanrahan (1981:295) reject this classification because "it lacks the essential element of determinacy: explicit standards governing the quanta of penalty."

Maine's sentencing system, which has been characterized as a "judicial model" (Lagoy et al., 1978), has some distinctive features. One is that while judges impose sentences of a definite period, they have a wide range of penalties from which to choose (e.g., 0–5 years or 0–20 years). Thus, state statutes contrain judicial discretion only at the upper limits of the penalties (Lagoy et al., 1978:387–388). The result is the potential for even more disparate sentences rather than the uniformity normally associated with determinate sentences.

On July 1, 1977, determinate sentencing took effect in California [see Endnote 2]. Lagoy et al. (1978:388) describe the California sentencing system as a "legislative model." That is, the state legislature has set a very narrow range of options within which convicted defendants may be sentenced. Statutes prescribe a middle range, or "presumptive sentence," to which the average offender should be sentenced, and this range is fairly narrow, thus differentiating California's approach from Maine's. Additionally, judges may depart from the presumptive sentence, for aggravating or mitigating circumstances, but they must state the reason(s) in writing and impose a higher or lower term as prescribed by the legislature (Brewer et al., 1981:204; von Hirsch and Hanrahan, 1981:295).

California prison populations must be viewed in two time frames: general trends prior to the passage of the determinate sentencing law (DSL), and changes in populations subsequent to the DSL. One of the chief assumptions under the DSL was that prison populations would not be affected (Nagin, 1979:72). Average sentence length was to remain essentially the same, and much of the disparity evident under indeterminate sentencing would be removed (Brewer et al., 1981:227). However, the reality was that between December 1977, and December 1978, the state was faced with a "sharp increase in the commitment rate to prison" that was somewhat offset by surplus bedspaces and early releases (Lipson and Peterson, 1980:36–37).

The initial increases in population have been explained as continuations of upward trends existing before adoption of the DSL. Ideally, however, good time credits taken into account, determinate sentences should be shorter than indeterminate sentences (Lipson and Peterson, 1980:20, 31). The differences can be explained by increasing rates of incarceration for certain categories of offenders (Brewer et al., 1981; McCoy, 1984).

Current figures show California's prison population has continued to grow. During 1987 the state's inmate population grew by 7,500, accounting for 21 percent of the nation's total prison population increase (Bureau of Justice Statistics, 1988:1). Since 1980, California prison populations have increased by 179 percent (Bureau of Justice Statistics, 1988:2); however, determinate sentencing alone is not responsible for these dramatic increases [see Endnote 3]. For one thing, the California legislature has continued to adopt increasingly punitive sentences, despite increasing capital, operational, and programmatic costs (Brewer et al., 1981; Lipson and Peterson, 1980; McCoy, 1984; Nagin, 1979). For another thing, California has experienced state population growth and changing demographic characteristics that increase the number of individuals in the most crime-prone and incarceration-likely years (Blumstein, 1984a; Cohen and Tonry, 1983).

The State of Washington represents one of the most recent attempts at developing and implementing guidelines to structure the discretion inherent in the sentencing process (State of Washington, 1983). The Washington Sentencing Guidelines Commission chose to be bound by the 1984 prison capacity in designing its sentencing plan (State of Washington, 1983:20). In fact, the Commission plan was to reduce the population of the state's overcrowded prisons to capacity by 1986. As can be seen from Table 10.1, while Washington experienced dramatic prison population increases from 1980 to 1987 overall, during 1986–1987 there was an impressive decrease.

In designing its sentencing guidelines, the State of Washington also gave explicit consideration to the linkages between jail and prison populations. There was a desire on the part of the state to reduce prison populations without backing up convicted felons in local jails.

The implications of determinate sentencing for the federal government seem clear. Without careful consideration, changes in sentencing policies can drive prison populations substantially higher. There are some exceptions, however, and these are worth discussion.

The most notable exception to the general upward spiral of prison populations is the State of Minnesota. Minnesota's move toward determinate sentencing introduced a new element: an independent, nonlegislative sentencing commission to determine and review criminal penalties and the impacts those penalties might have on correctional populations.

For most states, criminal offense penalties are determined by the legislature. Legislatures suffer from two deficiencies, however (von Hirsch, 1982:167). These are that most legislative bodies do not have the time to compare each new or revised penalty with all other criminal offenses to assure consistency and proportionality; and legislative bodies tend to be acted upon by political forces that can skew sentencing provisions, especially in more punitive ways (Knapp, 1984). In order to avoid these problems, Minnesota created a sentencing guidelines commission charged with the tasks of increasing the uniformity and proportionality of sentences, and coordinating sentencing policies and practices with correctional resources, especially prison bedspace (Blumstein, 1984b:138; Knapp, 1986:38).

Minnesota authorities view correctional resources as finite, very expensive commodities. The state has had a long history of low prison commitment rates, and the likelihood of massive capital spending to support sentencing changes seemed remote to the sentencing guidelines commission (von Hirsch, 1982:177; Bureau of Justice Statistics,

1988). Therefore, beyond merely considering the prison capacity available, the sentencing guidelines commission viewed state prison capacity (in 1980) as the maximum limit within which they could work. Thus an artificial, but very meaningful, limit was placed on the commission, the legislature, and the state corrections department.

One of the primary assumptions of the guidelines commission was that when prisons became crowded, criminal justice system actors (especially prosecutors, judges, and prison administrators) would engage in adaptive behaviors that largely would nullify the objectives of the guidelines (Knapp, 1982:254–256; von Hirsch, 1982:177). To forestall this possibility, Minnesota's sentencing guidelines provide not only durational standards for imprisonment, but also indicate to the judge whether the presumptive sentence would indicate imprisonment (von Hirsch and Hanrahan, 1981:297). Minnesota's experience with sentencing guidelines can be summarized in two important areas: prison populations, and jail and workhouse populations. First, in regard to prison populations, the State of Minnesota had 2,072 prison bedspaces in 1981 when the sentencing guidelines took effect (Knapp, 1984:188) [see Endnote 4].

From the end of 1981 to the end of 1982, prison populations increased from 1,936 to 2,015 (Knapp, 1986:46). In recent Bureau of Justice Statistics figures (1988:2), Minnesota's 1987 prison population was 2,546. This represents a 3.4 percent increase over 1986, but less than the average state increase of 6.7 percent and the Midwest regional average of 7.9 percent. The main point is that even with explicit consideration of prison capacities, as has been done with the Minnesota sentencing guidelines, prison populations have continued to rise, albeit at a relatively slow rate. This means that if prison capacities are not considered definite constraints, a state (or the federal government) could find itself in worsening shape in terms of prison crowding.

One final point concerning Minnesota's experience with determinate sentencing is that the relatively small, but perceptible, growth in the state's prisons must be viewed in conjunction with the population growth of local jails and workhouses (Blackmore, 1978). Since the sentencing guidelines originally did not address sentences of less than one year (von Hirsch, 1982:192; Carney, 1982; Taft, 1979), jails serve as overflow facilities for state prisons (Mays and Bernat, 1988; Mays and Thompson, 1988a).

North Carolina is another state that seems not to have followed the pattern of tremendous increases in prison populations. The state's Fair Sentencing Act took effect July 1, 1981 and, like California, set presumptive terms for felony convictions. Unlike Minnesota, North Carolina did not use sentencing guidelines nor presumptive thresholds for the decision to incarcerate.

Soon after adoption, the FSA had a number of discernable effects. First, the rate of convicted felony offenders receiving an active prison sentence increased from 55 percent in 1979 to 63 percent by 1982 (Clarke, 1984:148). This seemed to portend increasing prison populations, but the second impact was a decrease in sentence lengths.

Clarke's (1984:151) assessment of the FSA, after one year, was that "it will probably not increase the felon population and may even reduce it somewhat." Table 10.1 indicates that Clarke's prediction was accurate. During the 1970s, North Carolina had one of the nation's highest rates of incarceration; however, from 1980 to 1987, the state's prison population only grew by 11.7 percent, compared with the national average for states of 75.4 percent.

Washington's experience with sentencing changes already has been discussed, but one note needs to be added. Figures supplied by the Bureau of Justice Statistics [see Table 10.1] indicate something of the impact of sentencing changes on Washington's prison populations. From 1980 to 1987, the state's inmate population grew by 139.4 percent, ranking it as the state with the eighth largest percentage increase during the 1980s. However, for the 1986–1987 period, Washington had a 7.1 percent decrease in prison populations and a rate of incarceration much less than the national average for all states or for states in the Western region [see Endnote 5]. Thus, it seems likely that Washington's sentencing changes, including the guidelines that took effect in 1984, are having an impact on the state's prison population.

Parole Elimination and Substitution of Good-time Credits

Another feature the new federal sentencing guidelines share with the nine states included in Table 10.1 is the elimination of discretionary parole decision-making authority. This section will explore the experiences of three states—Maine, California, and North Carolina—that have eliminated parole, and the State of Oregon, that has taken a different approach to parole decision-making.

Prior to 1976, and the adoption of determinate sentencing, almost 77 percent of Maine's prison inmates were paroled on the first date of eligibility (Tilton, 1987:59). The director of Maine's Division of Probation and Parole says prison crowding in the wake of sentencing changes, has forced the state "to open four new institutions, handle overflow populations from county jails, order a major lockdown in 1981 of the Maine State Prison [a maximum security facility], reduce programmatic availability to all inmates and deal with what is, to a large extent, the most serious problem of all within the prison system, the idleness resulting from a lack of work for inmates" (Tilton, 1987:60) [see Endnote 6].

Like Maine, California's determinate sentencing law also eliminated parole board discretion to determine early release dates for inmates (Lagoy et al., 1978:390; Nagin, 1979:70–71). In place of parole, there was a provision for reduction of sentences by one-third for good-time credits accumulated (Lipson and Peterson, 1980:6) [see Endnote 7].

In order to address the institutional crowding problems created by presumptive sentences, elimination of parole, and a general trend toward punitiveness, California has been faced with a series of policy options. The choice least favored by determinate sentencing opponents is expanding prison capacity (Nagin, 1979:97), but in 1984 California voters approved a prison construction bond levy of $300 million (McCoy, 1984:274, fn. 113). While California has chosen to expand maximum good time credits from one-third to one-half of the sentence, this approach is slow to respond to problems of prison crowding. For example, if the average felony sentence is three years, it takes at least eighteen months before the effects of such changes would be realized.

Finally, discretion employed by judges and prosecutors to mitigate the effects of sentencing changes seems to have little apparent effect on prison populations (Nagin, 1979:97; McCoy, 1984). Lipson and Peterson (1980:37) best summarize California's experience by saying that determinate sentencing's "greatest impact on corrections has been to aggravate the problem of prison crowding."

Like a number of other determinate sentencing states, North Carolina eliminated discretionary parole and provided in its place good time and "gain time" reductions (Clarke, 1984:142) [see Endnote 8]. Unlike some states (notably Minnesota), and now the federal government, North Carolina did not provide for sentencing guidelines nor for presumptive thresholds on the decision whether to incarcerate.

Clarke (1984:152) suggests that three conclusions are warranted from North Carolina's experience. First, while prosecutorial and judicial discretion provided opportunties to "evade the policies of the legislation . . . little evasion seems to have taken place." Second, the likelihood of imprisonment increased for convicted felons. Third, the length of most prison terms was decreased; thus, prison populations largely have been stabilized.

Similar to California, Oregon has adopted "durational standards" (von Hirsch and Hanrahan, 1981:295); however, Oregon has retained parole and the parole board is responsible for establishing durational guidelines. Thus, "in Oregon the parole board is required to notify prisoners of their expected release dates shortly after they enter prison" (von Hirsch and Hanrahan, 1981:295). Instead of presumptive sentences, as in California, Oregon has presumptive paroles.

Several features distinguish Oregon's move toward determinacy from the efforts of other states. First, although not done so initially, the parole guidelines have been tied to prison capacities (McCoy, 1984:260). Second, the state has worked to prevent an escalation in average sentences served. For example, Oregon sentences few inmates to terms five years or longer, even for crimes against persons (von Hirsch and Hanrahan, 1981:298).

The result of Oregon's sentencing policies is relatively slow growth of prison populations. While Oregon ranked fifth of all states in 1986–1987 percentage growth (14.9 percent), the state's correctional population grew only 72.8 percent from 1980 to 1987, ranking it 29th of the fifty states (Bureau of Justice Statistics, 1988:3). In order to keep prison populations in check, Oregon's policy makers have chosen to increase penalties for some serious crimes, while decreasing penalties for many lesser offenses (von Hirsch and Hanrahan, 1981:298).

FEDERAL GUIDELINES AND PRISON POPULATIONS

Since the federal government is just beginning its experience with sentencing guidelines, the previous section illustrates the experiences of some states that have adopted determinate sentencing schemes (whether presumptive or not, and with or without sentencing guidelines). It seems that the collective experiences of these states are worth analyzing in anticipating some of the effects of sentencing guidelines on federal prison populations.

The Pitfalls of Determinate Sentencing

Currently, several observations about determinate sentencing seem warranted, and each of these should be considered a caveat for federal legislative, judicial, and correctional officials. First, in most states, and now the federal government, determinate sentencing has spelled the doom of parole. In reality, this statement needs two points of clarification. For some states determinate sentencing legislation has ended parole altogether. For most states, however, determinate sentencing merely has ended discretionary parole release decision-making, while the functions of parole planning, supervision, and revocation have remained (Nagin, 1979; von Hirsch and Hanrahan, 1981).

The second observation is that such a dispositional approach **generally increases** prison populations. The experience of some states such as Minnesota is that initially prison populations stabilize or decline, then they start to increase again. These changes in population occur through the interaction of several factors: durations of sentences and early release mechanisms (how long), types of offenders incarcerated (who), and the number of individuals incarcerated (how many). It should be emphasized, however, that states without determinate sentencing have experienced some of the same dramatic increases in prison populations as determinate sentencing states (Bureau of Justice Statistics, 1988).

Third, it seems to make a difference who has authority to design and modify sentencing standards. Von Hirsch and Hanrahan (1981:298) note that there are three common mechanisms for developing sentencing standards. The first, legislative development, is the most traditional. This method suffers from a lack of coherence over a period of time and from the whims of short-term political pressures. The second, a sentencing commission, may be more systematic but must establish political legitimacy. The third, parole guidelines, has a particular advantage—these standards are carried out by their adopters—and a special disadvantage—they only deal with length of incarceration, and not who will be incarcerated. The clear implication is that the type of body drafting sentencing standards results in qualitative and quantitative differences in the standards (von Hirsch and Hanrahan, 1981:298). Fourth, the tendency over time is for sentencing to become more punitive, even with dispositional guidelines. This can be seen especially in states like California and Pennsylvania, where state legislatures have responded to public pressure (or perceived public pressure) to make sentences longer, good time credits fewer, and mandatory minimums more broadly applicable.

Fifth, good-time credits normally range from one-third to one-half of the original sentence imposed in most states. Under the new federal sentencing guidelines, however, good-time credits are limited to 54 days per year, or no more than 15 percent of the original sentence. This may mean, with the elimination of parole and a restrictive good-time policy, that federal prison populations will increase quickly and dramatically. Even with a more generous good time policy, it is important to recognize that this back-end release mechanism is not as responsive as front-end, flow-control policies.

The sixth consideration, therefore, is that sentencing standards, like the federal sentencing guidelines, must be constructed with an eye toward prison populations/capacities. Otherwise, inmate populations will grow substantially beyond capacity. When this happens, prosecutors, judges, and/or correctional administrators likely will take adaptive steps that may nullify the impact of the guidelines (von

Hirsch, 1982:177). Such actions send a signal to legislators that guidelines are unimportant, unrealistic, or unworkable.

Seventh, we must conclude that prison and jail populations are intimately linked (Allinson, 1982; Carney, 1982; Taft, 1979). This causes a tremendous criminal justice dilemma, for no matter how bad prison conditions may be, jails often are so much worse (Mays and Bernat, 1988; Mays and Thompson, 1988b; Thompson, 1986). In over 30 state prison systems that were under court order in 1988 to reduce overcrowding and other health and safety deficiencies, convicted felons "back up" in local jails (Taft, 1979; Mays and Thompson, 1988b). Jail crowding will present an especially acute problem for federal authorities, since the federal government does not operate its own jails and must rely on local facilities to house short-term detainees [see Endnote 9].

Finally, determinate sentencing must not be viewed as a cause of sentencing and correctional change, but more as an effect (Lipson and Peterson, 1980). In most states determinate sentencing has been a solution proposed by liberals and conservatives alike to make sentences more fair and sure, to limit broad judicial and parole decision-making discretion, and to make many actors in the criminal justice system more accountable for their actions. Thus, determinate sentencing is one manifestation of the disaffection with "traditional" (i.e., indeterminate/rehabilitative) methods for dealing with offenders.

Federal Policy Alternatives

Given the preceding implications, it should be obvious that Congress and the Federal Bureau of Prisons are faced with certain policy choices. Lipson and Peterson (1980:15) say that when prison crowding results from sentencing changes, decision-makers are faced with at least three politically unattractive choices. The first choice is to build more prisons (McCoy, 1984:274; Nagin, 1979:97). This is an expensive option, given capital construction and operating costs, but one that seems acceptable to some authorities. In fact, the federal government has engaged in a regular program of repair, replacement, and expansion of its prison facilities. Additionally, for some functions (e.g., detention of illegal aliens), the federal government has started contracting with private corporations to provide some incarcerative services (National Institute of Justice, 1984). This may mean that federal authorities are resigned to expanding prison capacities, at least temporarily, either publicly or privately.

The second option is to selectively reduce prison terms—for example, for property crimes—or to reduce all terms by some specified amount. The danger of such "tinkering" over a period of time is the resulting inconsistency that has traditionally characterized criminal penalty structures (Lipson and Peterson, 1980:15; Nagin, 1979:97). The approach chosen by Minnesota is to constantly monitor prison populations and make policy adjustments that will prevent prison crowding, rather than simply responding to it.

A third choice is to develop additional community release programs as supplements to, or in place of, incarceration (Blackmore, 1978; Lipson and Peterson, 1980). These programs can serve as non-incarcerative alternatives for nonviolent offenders, in lieu of prison terms or as part of "shock probation" programs (Block and Rhodes, 1987). This is not to suggest that community corrections programs are not without their own problems, chief among them being "net widening" (Austin and Krisberg, 1981; Decker, 1985). Research has shown, for example, that many of the offenders placed in community corrections programs are "good risks," and by definition, they would not be incarcerated under normal circumstances.

In the final analysis, the federal government may choose the course of action chosen by most states; namely, to do nothing until a crisis in crowding or litigation occurs. This means the existence of two default policy choices. One approach that can be taken by legislative bodies is to do nothing and leave criminal justice decision-makers to exercise discretion and adapt the best way possible (Nagin, 1979:97). Alternatively, legislatures can put in place emergency release mechanisms, like Michigan's, that allow inmate discharges sufficient to bring prison populations down to the level of capacity.

However, both of these approaches seem to avoid the issue of the relationship between sentencing policy and prison populations. The basic question now confronting the federal government is whether to try and influence sentencing policy by adjusting prison policy, or to control prison policies/resources by changing sentencing policies. The two are so closely linked that we cannot ignore the interrelatedness and consequent changes in one resulting from alterations in the other.

ENDNOTES

1. The August 22, 1988 issue of *Monday Morning Highlights*, the weekly newsletter of the Federal Prison System, reported rated capacity of all Bureau of Prison facilities as 27,555 and the current population as 43,500.
2. For an extended discussion of California's Determinate Sentencing Law (DSL) including its legislative history and impacts, see Lipson and Peterson (1980).

3. At the end of 1987, California correctional facilities housed 66,975 inmates compared with 21,525 in 1977 (Bureau of Justice Statistics, 1988:3; McCoy, 1984:272).
4. A maximum security facility with a capacity of 400 was finished subsequent to the adoption of the sentencing guidelines (Knapp, 1984:188).
5. Washington's rate for 1987 was 134 per 100,000 residents, compared with the average for all states of 212 and for Western states of 214 (Bureau of Justice Statistics, 1988:2).
6. For a discussion of the problems that have plagued Maine's jails, see Miller and Clark (1987).
7. In 1984, the California legislature passed a bill increasing the maximum good-time credits allowable from one-third to one-half of the sentence (McCoy, 1984:274, fn. 13).
8. North Carolina is fairly generous with its good-time provisions, allowing for reductions up to one-half of the original sentence, plus the possibility of "gain time" for work or meritorious conduct (Clarke, 1984:142, fn. 3). These sentence-reducing mechanisms may greatly contribute to stable or declining prison populations in North Carolina.
9. The federal government does operate several Metropolitan Correctional Centers (MCCs) in Miami, Chicago, New York, San Diego and Tucson, and while these facilities do provide some short-term detention, they are not jails in the traditional sense of the word.

11

Inmate Litigation Trends and Constitutional Issues

John W. Palmer

INTRODUCTION

Mistretta v. U.S. (1989) has upheld the constitutionality of the U. S. Sentencing Guidelines. One result of this decision is that the guidelines will be fully implemented and convicted offenders will receive longer prison sentences. By 1997, it is anticipated that the federal prison population alone will escalate from 42,000 to 92,000. As the inmate population rises, history teaches that there will be a corresponding increase in law suits involving appeals and civil actions challenging the conditions of confinement.

The *Mistretta* case indicates that for nearly a century, the federal government used indeterminate sentencing for sanctioning convicted offenders. Federal statutes stipulated penalties for crimes, but almost always, judges exercised wide discretion in the application of these penalties. The length of confinement, place of confinement, fine, or some lesser sanction such as probation were within judicial purview. Indeterminate sentencing was subsequently supplemented by a parole system operated by the U. S. Parole Commission, whereby offenders were granted early release from confinement and returned to society under the "guidance and control" of parole officers.

Both indeterminate sentencing and parole were based on concepts of the offender's possible, indeed probable, rehabilitation. The rehabilitation perspective viewed offender reform as real, and legitimate attempts to rehabilitate inmates would thereby minimize the risk that offenders would re-offend when returned to society. It was the responsibility of both judges and parole officers to make their respective sentencing and early release decisions based upon their own assessments of any offender's amenability to rehabilitation. As a result, the court and parole officers were in positions to exercise broad discretion, and they did so.

Decisions about whether to parole inmates were believed to be "predictive and discretionary." Consequently, correctional officials possessed almost absolute discretion over the parole decision. Essential to the parole decision was the inmate's institutional conduct. Minor rule infractions could have unintended yet serious consequences for inmates if this information were brought to the attention of paroling authorities. Thus, trivial violations of institutional rules often resulted in parole denials. Minor misconduct could and did usually result in longer prison terms.

Although the system of parole is scheduled for abolition in 1992, institutional conduct will continue to influence how long prisoners remain confined. Even under the new federal sentencing guidelines, the time prisoners serve is reduced by credits earned through good behavior while in custody [see Endnote 1]. Consequently, institutional conditions of confinement may be expected to play an even greater role in promoting litigation than in past years. The history of inmate litigation is clear: the longer prisoners spend in prison, the more likely they are to engage in civil rights litigation against prison officials and others.

BACKGROUND

The experience of inmate litigation in Ohio that has been reduced by administrative reform serves to highlight what can be done by enlightened leadership. During the spring of 1971, a seminar in criminal justice administration was offered to law students at Capital University in Columbus. The various institutions making up the criminal justice process were studied during the semester. Local representatives of various criminal justice agencies were invited to participate. The Assistant Commissioner of Corrections spoke about the Ohio prison system. As a prelude to class discussion, he gave a brief overview of case law concerning the constitutional rights of prisoners [see Endnote 2]. The most recent U. S. Supreme Court decision dealt with an inmate's right to counsel and authorized jailhouse lawyers to advise other inmates of their rights (*Avery v. Johnson*, 1969). Furthermore, the administration of the Lucas County Jail in Toledo had recently been taken over by a federal judge, and the jail was being run by judicial fiat (*Jones v. Wittenberg*, 1971). This incident was making headlines in most Ohio newspapers.

Following the seminar, the professor was asked to address the next monthly meeting of the superintendents of the Ohio prison system. Following the meeting, Commissioner Bennett J. Cooper asked the professor if he would be interested in helping his Department during the following summer with its emerging legal problems. These were the days of almost unlimited Safe Street Funds, and an ample budget was provided to retain ten law students for the summer project, as well as two professors.

The summer project was divided into three parts. First, all federal and state cases involving conditions of confinement and parole were read and digested. The important issues were highlighted and emerging issues identified. Second, a comprehensive series of questions were prepared dealing with each area of constitutional concern. The questions were intended to obtain a thorough understanding of the daily operations of the Ohio prison system. Next, the team visited each of Ohio's prisons. The researchers interviewed the superintendent, deputies, senior officers, junior officers, correctional workers, and two inmates selected at random. Each of those interviewed was asked identical questions. Answers were then collated so that prevailing practices could be determined for each of the institutions and for the state as a whole. Third, a comprehensive report was prepared and recommendations were made for the implementation of change.

The results of the study were staggering. Several of the conclusions are summarized as follows:

1. In many instances, the senior officers in each institution were completely unaware of what was happening among prisoners and staff within their own institutions.
2. There were no uniform correctional policies within any institution or within the state system as a whole.
3. Recognized constitutional rights of inmates were being systematically violated, not intentionally, but because officials had little or no idea about their legal responsibilities in caring for the inmates or of the potentially large civil liability they incurred in the event they were sued.
4. Each superintendent and staff had virtually unlimited discretion about regulating and disciplining inmates. The system individually and as a whole could best be described as irrational and capricious.
5. The majority of superintendents and staff wanted to perform their tasks humanely, legally, and honestly, although they were not provided with administrative, financial, and legal support from the State of Ohio to provide such minimal assistance.

Several examples highlight the problems and conditions that were found:

Example 1: The inmates at the Ohio State Penitentiary, the maximum-security prison, were permitted to subscribe to and possess "men's magazines" by the warden. However, when inmates were transferred to a medium- or minimum-security facility, they were immediately given a "ticket" and placed in a disciplinary cell for "possession of obscene material." Obscenity standards were determined on an individual basis by prison officials in each institution according to their personal views. Many of these officials lacked a high school education.

Example 2: It was a disciplinary infraction for inmates to have "menacing eyeballs" or to display "silent insolence" toward guards.

Example 3: Those inmates involved in fights were given identical punishments by correctional officials with no attempt made to assign fault for the fight. The doctrine of self-defense was nonexistent.

Example 4: There was no system for dealing with unauthorized use of force by correctional officers toward inmates.

Example 5: Inmates who violated vaguely defined disciplinary rules were placed in correctional cells for ten days or more and then "shipped to the wall," or transferred to the maximum-security prison. Correctional officials interviewed reported that their rationale was that "we always have done it this way."

Example 6: Health services were nonexistent.

Example 7: Jailhouse lawyers were permitted to operate in some institutions, but they were ruthlessly punished in others.

One experience is worth mentioning. During one of the prison visits with the team, the professor received a telephone call from the Governor's office. The Commissioner of Corrections was on the telephone and stated that the Governor had requested him to do something significant involving prison reform. He asked for our ideas. Our studies revealed that if inmates wanted materials sent out of the prison, they could do so easily. However, correctional officers censored mail at their discretion. The only practical result of mail censorship was bribery and corruption of the correctional officers. It was irrational to monitor letters through censorship when those to whom letters were addressed could easily visit prisoners and obtain the same information orally. Conversations during visiting hours were unmonitored.

As a result of this conversation, the following morning a directive was issued from the office of the Commissioner abolishing mail censorship in the prisons. The directive consisted of three parts. First, mail censorship was immediately abolished. Second, each superintendent had the authority to monitor specific mail for good cause shown, based upon "reasonable suspicion." Third, the authorization for the monitoring had to be in writing, with justifications, and forwarded to the office of the Commissioner. In effect, we had instituted into the Ohio prison system the doctrine of an administrative search warrant. To our knowledge, this was the first time this had occurred in any American prison.

Later that evening, Ohio was featured on CBS News for abolishing its mail censorship. During the first week following the issuance of the directive, over 100,000 pieces of mail were sent out of the Ohio prisons by inmates. Less than ten complaints were received, these being from parents of teenage girls who did not want inmate-boyfriends continuing their relationships with daughters through the mail.

Prisons are like pressure-cookers, and they will explode if no outlets for "steam" are provided. That fall, Attica (New York) exploded and prisons throughout the United States were in turmoil (*Inmates of Attica Correctional Facility v. Rockefeller*, 1971). Ohio experienced no major problems and had few incidents. It was reported that at the subsequent hearings investigating the causes of the Attica rebellion, a senior prison official stated that it was not possible to run a prison without mail censorship. The Ohio experience proved this statement false. Needless to say, tape recordings and interview statements were ultimately trashed to avoid having them used by inmates or others in any subsequent civil litigation.

During the following years, and as a result of the findings disclosed by the Capital University team, detailed administrative regulations were adopted by the newly formed Ohio Department of Rehabilitation and Correction, comprehensively covering all areas of constitutional concern. Administrative regulations were promulgated to anticipate problems before they arose, and administrative control over the institutions was retained. Control over the various institutions was centralized through the Office of the Director through the rule-making process. Most Ohio institutions subsequently exceeded the minimal constitutional standards. One result of these internal controls and enlightened management was that Ohio avoided the debilitating effect of inmate litigation for many years. In short, competent management channeled problems of constitutional concern through a rational, controlled administrative process.

There were unfortunate side effects resulting from the mass of administrative regulations that were subsequently issued from the central office. Several superintendents took early retirement, as they felt they no longer could cope with new administrative policies. Second, budgetary constraints made it impossible to educate and train correctional staffs properly in the application of the new policies. Consequently, there was a period of low morale and resulting administrative chaos as regulations were misunderstood, misapplied, and/or disregarded. Fortunately, a newly established grievance procedure, an **ombudsman program,** and an avenue for administrative review reduced most of the problems.

It is self-evident that inmate litigation cannot be avoided despite the application of the best of administrative remedies for inmate complaints. It is unfortunate that in the American social scene, those arguably aggrieved often turn to the courts for resolutions of their disputes. Litigation solves many problems, but litigation also has adverse and counterproductive implications for effective prison administration. Some problems with inmate litigation include:

1. Many suits are frivolous and lack merit. Nevertheless, they must be investigated and defended. Valuable administrative time must be spent answering interrogatories, participating in depositions, and obtaining documentation for the discovery process. It has been estimated that between 30 percent and 50 percent of senior administrative time is allocated to matters of inmate litigation. Administrators eventually develop a bunker mentality and take no action for fear of being sued. Occasionally, there is a complete abdication of administrative responsibility.
2. There is no effective sanction against inmates who file frivolous or false lawsuits. Prisoners are mostly indigent and file their legal actions *in forma pauperis*. It is unheard of that formal legal sanctions are applied against inmates for filing false statements or committing perjury.
3. Inmates frequently sue many prison personnel as defendants in the same lawsuit. This places the attorney assigned by the State in a potential conflict-of-interest situation. The interests of the key administrators or government officials often conflict with those of the front-line institutional workers and correctional officers. The alternative of providing each defendant with separate counsel is impractical and economically unsound.
4. The personal credit of a defendant is damaged when named as a defendant in an inmate's "shotgun" naming of all available defendants. Banks view unfavorably the prospect of making loans to those with potential civil tort liabilities climbing into six figures. In short, inmate litigation must be regarded as an occupational hazard.

INMATE LITIGATION

Inmates become involved in litigation for essentially two reasons. First, they are interested in appealing their original sentences. Second, they wish to challenge the conditions of their confinement. As a general rule, inmates are interested in essentially one thing: release from confinement and return to the outside world. Their foremost concern is to have their original sentences reversed or vacated.

Litigation to overturn or to vacate their convictions assumes two forms. The first form is a direct apppeal of their conviction and sentence. The direct appeal must be made within a short time after the judgment entry of conviction has been filed. Timing is critical. It is important to make a timely filing of a notice of appeal in order to obtain a transcript of the trial as a matter of right. This takes time to acquire. Only too often, appellate review has been precluded by the absence of a trial transcript clearly showing that errors were made by trial judges during the trial. The second form is a delayed appeal through the use of **post-conviction remedies**. There may be statutory remedies under color of state law or in the form of a *habeas corpus* petition. Both of these remedies, direct or collateral appeals, involve only the propriety of the original conviction and sentence. Neither of these remedies involves challenges of the conditions of confinement.

Inmates who challenge the conditions of their confinement may do so either through federal or state litigation. They often have a choice of forum, although increasingly, federal judges are remanding certain types of inmate litigation back to state courts under 42 U.S.C. Sec. 1997 (U. S. Code, 1989). However, practice has shown that state remedies are not as adequate as federal remedies. As a result, most inmate litigation occurs in federal district courts. In many instances, federal court cases involving conditions of prison confinement arise under 42 U.S.C. Sec. 1983 (U. S. Code, 1989), commonly known as the Civil Rights Act. This federal statute provides that:

> Every person who, under color of any statute, ordinance, regulation, custom, or usage, of any State or Territory, subjects, or causes to be subjected, any citizen of the United States or other person within the jurisdiction thereof to the deprivation of any rights, privileges, or immunities secured by the Constitution and laws, shall be liable to the party injured in an action at law, suit in equity, or other proper proceeding for redress.

Inmates may sue for monetary damages, although they most often sue for injunctive relief. Suits for damages access defendants to a trial by jury if they desire, whereas suits "in equity" are decided by federal judges without juries. There is no constitutional right to trial by jury in equity cases. Inmates with unsavory histories may decide to forego monetary remedies that must be decided by an unsympathetic jury, and they may opt for judges who will decide the merits of the issues between the suing inmates and the prison officials.

Furthermore, for the past several years, successful inmate plaintiffs have been entitled to have their attorney fees paid by the defendant under 42 U.S.C. Sec. 1988 (U. S. Code, 1989). This places a great incentive on private litigation to remedy constitutional wrongs. In fact, the attorneys become "private attorneys general" to protect the constitutional rights of their clients. Litigation is encouraged as a matter of public policy.

Until recent years courts have deemed it necessary to refrain from hearing inmate suits filed against their keepers. This practice was known as the "hands-off doctrine." There were three major reasons which justified this doctrine. First, the administration of prisons was regarded as an executive function, and the courts were prevented from intervening because of separation of powers. Second, courts believed they lacked judicial expertise in penology to effectively review decisions of prison officials. Third, it was believed that judicial interference would subvert prison authority and discipline.

The "hands-off" doctrine met its demise in 1964 when the U. S. Supreme Court held in *Cooper v. Pate* that state inmates may bring suits against administrators and other correctional officials and staff under 42 U.S.C. Sec. 1983. From this point on, the federal courts were open to inmate litigation and were encouraged to hear their complaints. Currently, it is generally recognized that inmates are not slaves of the state, and that they retain all constitutional rights they possessed as free citizens excepting those which of necessity must be withdrawn from them as a condition of their confinement.

Although *Cooper v. Pate* (1964) opened the doors of federal courtrooms for inmates, the anticipated flood of litigation did not begin until *Avery v. Johnson* (1969). *Avery* established the principle that inmates have the Sixth Amendment right of access to the courts, and of necessity, they must be provided some form of legal assistance in securing this right. Should the state not provide counsel or other equivalent legal services, inmates could use the services of jailhouse lawyers. In other words, states were precluded from restricting the activities of jailhouse lawyers unless adequate alternatives were provided by their penal institutions. Further, states could not constitutionally restrict prisoners from petitioning the federal courts to challenge the conditions of their confinement.

In short order, all aspects of the prison regime came under attack, with the federal courts being inundated with inmate lawsuits. Over the next twenty years, the U. S. Supreme Court clarified the application of the Constitution to prisons through several important landmark decisions [see Endnote 3]. *Gilmore v. Lynch* (1971) and *Bounds v. Smith* (1977) followed up on *Avery v. Johnson* (1969) and established the duty of the state to make legal materials such as lawbooks available to inmates. *Cruz v. Beto* (1972) provided inmates protection from religious discrimination. However, in *O'Lone v. Estate of Shabazz* (1987), religious practices were restricted.

Morrissey v. Brewer (1972) and *Gagnon v. Scarpelli* (1973) established due process and right to counsel requirements for parole and probation revocation proceedings, although the right to an immediate hearing was restricted under *Moody v. Daggett* (1976). *Procunier v. Martinez* (1974) established standards of review over censorship of inmate correspondence by prison officials, and *Wolff v. McDonnell* (1974) made it clear that censorship of legal mail interfered with an inmate's access to the courts. *Turner v. Safley* (1987) indicates that there are limits to mail censorship.

Pell v. Procunier (1974), *Houchins v. KQED* (1978), and *Saxbe v. Washington Post Company* (1974), while recognizing the First Amendment rights of prisoners to communicate with the media, refused to grant newspersons superior rights over other citizens, and restricted unlimited media access to the prisons and personal interviews with inmates. Similarly, *Jones v. North Carolina Prisoner's Labor Union, Inc.* (1977) held that the First Amendment did not give prisoners the unfettered right to form prisoner labor unions and to bargain collectively with prison authorities.

Hutto v. Finney (1978) and *Rhodes v. Chapman* (1981) set the standards for determining when prison overcrowding was "cruel and unusual" punishment and a constitutional violation. Procedural due process requirements in prison disciplinary proceedings were set by *Wolff v. McDonnell* (1974), *Hewitt v. Helms* (1983), *Baxter v. Palmigiano* (1976), and *Enomoto v. Clutchette* (1976). Deliberate indifference by prison officials to the medical needs of prisoners also violates the Constitution according to *Estelle v. Gamble* (1976).

However, inmates do not always win their suits. *Bell v. Wolfish* (1979) approved special institutional regulations regarding the receipt of books and packages. The U. S. Supreme Court recognized that prisons have a legitimate governmental purpose to provide security and order. The reality that parole was not an absolute right was made clear in *Greenholtz v. Inmates of the Nebraska Penal and Correctional System* (1979) and *Connecticut Board of Pardons v. Dumschat* (1981). Furthermore, a state's placing civil disabilities on inmates was severely restricted in *Turner v. Safley* (1987), although states may lawfully disenfranchise convicted felons under *Richardson v. Ramirez* (1974). Transfers from one prison to another do not involve any constitutional issues under *Meachum v. Fano* (1976), *Montanye v. Haymes* (1976), *Cuyler v. Adams* (1981), *Vitek v. Jones* (1980), *Howe v. Smith* (1981), and *Olim v. Wakinekona* (1983).

SCOPE OF LITIGATION

A review of prisoner petitions filed June 30, 1978 and December 1987 is instructive. These figures indicate a steady rise of civil rights cases of approximately 10 percent each year through 1985, but a substantial decrease for the years 1986 and 1987 among federal prisoners. Petitions filed by state prisoners have steadily increased each year, from 9,730 in 1978 to 22,972 in 1987. Total filings of all kinds, including motions to vacate sentence, *habeas corpus*, mandamus and injunctions, and civil rights, have shown a consistent increase of about 10 percent annually. As the projected prison population increases over the next several years due to the full implementation of the federal sentencing guidelines and the adoption of similar guidelines by various states, the implications for the federal judiciary are enormous.

Based on the statistics shown in Table11.1 [see Endnote 4], it would appear that federal inmates file more petitions concerning their convictions, sentencing, and parole than about their conditions of confinement. For example, in 1987, of the 4,519 legal actions filed by federal prisoners with diverse records, only 725 (16 percent) involved condition of confinement cases or civil rights actions. The statistics indicate a substantial difference between the litigation activity of federal and state prisoners in this regard. However, legal actions of all kinds are filed more often by federal prisons contrasted with state inmates.

By comparison, of 32,797 cases filed by state prisoners, 22,972 (70 percent) involved civil rights cases. The relative number of civil rights suits filed by state prisoners has increased from less than one suit filed per 100 inmates in 1962 to 1.65 per 100 inmates in 1971, 2.95 per 100 in 1976, 4.59 per 100 in 1981, 4.14 per 100 in 1986, and 4.39 per 100 inmates in 1987.

Several explanations account for the substantially greater number of state prisoners who seek relief from their conditions of confinement. Unlike their federal counterparts, state prisoners who seek release on *habeas corpus* must first exhaust their state post-conviction remedies. Because of the time consumed by these cases, state prisoners are often released before their court cases have been decided. In 42 U.S.C. Sec. 1983 litigation, except for alleged damage to property (*Parratt v. Taylor*, 1981), there is no exhaustion-of-remedies requirement, and suit may immediately be filed in federal court, even if an adequate state remedy exists. Further, if inmates are represented by counsel, the counsel is entitled to attorney's fees. Federal inmates do not have the jurisdictional right to bring actions under 42 U.S.C. Sec. 1983, since this remedy is only available to state inmates. Federal inmates must sue under the Federal Tort Claims Act (28 U.S.C. Sec. 2674, 1989), or under

Table 11.1 U.S. District Courts Prisoner Petitions Filed During the 12-Month Periods Ended June 30, 1978 through 1987.*

TYPE OF PETITION	YEAR (NUMBERS OF PETITIONS)			PERCENT CHANGE

Petitions Filed
by Federal
Prisoners:

	1978	1979	1980
Motions to			
Vacate Sentence 1,924	1,907	1,322	
Habeas Corpus........1,851	1,664	1,465	
Mandamus, etc......... 544	340	325	
Civil Rights.......... 636	588	603	

Petitions Filed
by State
Prisoners

	1978	1979	1980
Habeas Corpus........7,033	7,123	7,031	
Mandamus, etc......... 206	184	146	
Civil Rights.........9,730	11,195	12,397	

	1981	1982	1983

Federal continued:

Motions to Vacate			
Sentence.............1,248	1,186	1,311	
Habeas Corpus........1,680	1,927	1,914	
Mandamus, etc......... 342	381	339	
Civil Rights.......... 834	834	790	

State Prisoners:

Habeas Corpus........7,790	8,059	8,532	
Mandamus, etc......... 178	175	202	
Civil Rights........15,639	16,741	17,687	

	1984	1985	1986	1987

Federal continued:

Motions to Vacate				
Sentence............ 1,427	1,527	1,556	1,659	
Habeas Corpus....... 1,905	3,405	1,679	1,812	
Mandamus, etc........ 372	373	427	313	

Table 11.1 U.S. District Courts Prisoner Petitions Filed During the 12-Month Periods Ended June 30, 1978 through 1987 *(continued)*.

```
Civil Rights.........  822        957       770       725

State Prisoners:

Habeas Corpus........8,349      8,534     9,045     9,542
Mandamus, etc........  198        181       216       283
Civil Rights........18,034     18,491    20,072    22,972
```

TOTALS BY YEAR	1978	1979	1980	1981	1982
Federal	4,955	4,499	3,713	4,104	4,328
State	16,969	18,502	19,574	23,607	24,975

	1983	1984	1985	1986	1987
Federal	4,354	4,526	6,262	4,432	4,519
State	26,421	25,581	27,206	29,333	32,797

TOTALS ALL INMATES	1978	1979	1980	1981	1982
	21,924	23,001	23,287	27,711	29,303

TOTALS ALL INMATES CONT'D	1983	1984	1985	1986	1987
	30,775	31,107	33,468	33,765	37,315

```
                        PERCENT CHANGE
                          1986/1987

TOTAL........................    10.5

Federal Prisoners..............   2.0
   Motions to Vacate Sentence...  7.3
   Habeas Corpus................  7.9
   Mandamus, etc................ -26.7
   Civil Rights................  -5.8

State Prisoners................  11.8
   Habeas Corpus................  5.5
   Mandamus, etc................ 31.0
   Civil Rights................  14.4
```

*Source: Administrative office of the U.S. Courts (Table 3C.)

the so-called Federal Constitutional Tort Theory (*Bivens v. Six Unknown FBI Agents*, 1971).

Returning to the Ohio cases, the numbers of civil rights suits filed against the State prison system have decreased proportionately in relation to the inmate population between 1983–1988. During this period, the prison population increased from approximately 18,000 to 23,000 inmates. However, the number of suits filed in federal court under 42 U.S.C. Sec. 1983 (1989) during the same period decreased from 1,107 to 334 [see Endnote 5]. Of these filings, most are filed *pro se* by the inmates without the assistance of legal counsel. Many of these cases are summarily dismissed. However, it has been suggested that these *pro se* cases may be used by federal judges to manipulate their dockets. A large number of *pro se* cases that are accepted on their merits make the court caseload appear excessive. Thus, larger court staffs are justified. In short, since the discretion rests with federal judges to accept or reject *pro se* petitions by inmates, they are able to slant the caseload statistics accordingly to show precisely what they wish to show. It may be argued that federal judges have created an "industry" in *pro se* prisoner complaints.

CONCLUSION

There have been several suggestions made to reduce inmate litigation (Thomas, 1988:124–127). These include the following:

1. Increase the use of alternative dispute settlement techniques in the prisons. Litigation often occurs due to a breakdown in communication between the prisoners and their keepers. Grievance procedures, the use of ombudsmen, and other traditional methods of alternative dispute settlement can help to eliminate the causes of real or imagined inmate discontentment and abuses. In Ohio, a system was developed to provide channels of appeal to the Director from both grievance procedures and prison administrative bodies. In this way, the Director was apprised of problems concerning inmates and dissimilar, discriminatory inmate treatment within the prison system as a whole. Conflict resolution needs to be stressed.
2. Consolidation of suits through class actions can reduce the total number of suits and adjudicate common problems in a single suit. Continuing problems that occur regularly in state prisons and jails should not be litigated individually or separately.
3. Since most civil rights cases are filed *pro se*, it is only too common that prisoners do not understand the legal process or do not have

appropriate legal assistance when they prepare their civil complaints. Prison administrators should realize that a comprehensive legal program within the prison can alleviate many problems that otherwise would end up in federal courts. Practical experience has shown that federal judges have a tendency to work with prison legal programs and give them more consideration than those filed by *pro se* prisoners without the "blessing" of the prison legal advisor. A legal advisor program can also serve to spot troublesome areas and resolve conflicts before judicial intervention is sought.

4. As a part of a prison litigation clinic or prisoner assistance program, the "jailhouse lawyer" can be controlled if not entirely eliminated. "Compensation" of whatever kind charged an inmate for legal advice should be strenuously suppressed. It is a practice that should and can be prevented through viable alternatives.

The U. S. Supreme Court has made it abundantly clear that federal judges should not be too quick to intervene in the administration of correctional systems. As was stated in *Bell v. Wolfish* (1979),

. . . There was a time not too long ago when the federal judiciary took a completely "hands-off" approach to the problem of prison administration. In recent years, however, these courts largely have discarded this "hands-off" attitude and have waded into this complex arena. The deplorable conditions and draconian restrictions of some of our Nation's prisons are too well known to require recounting here, and the federal courts rightly have condemned these sordid aspects of our prison system. But many of these same courts have, in the name of the Constitution, become increasingly enmeshed in the minutiae of prison operations. Judges, after all, are human. They, no less than others in our society, have a natural tendency to believe that their individual solutions to often intractable problems are better and more workable than those of the persons who are actually charged with and trained in the running of the particular institution under examination. But under the Constitution, the first question to be answered is not whose plan is best, but to what branch of the Government is lodged the authority to initially devise the plan. This does not mean that constitutional rights are not to be scrupulously observed. It does mean, however, that the inquiry of federal courts into prison management must be limited to the issue of whether a particular system violates any prohibition of the Constitution, or in the case of a federal prison, a statute. The wide range of "judgment calls" that meet constitutionally and statutory requirement are confined to officials outside of the Judicial Branch of Government.

Further, in *Rhodes v. Chapman* (1981), the U. S. Supreme Court admonished the lower federal courts that they cannot assume that state legislatures and prison officials are insensitive to the requirements of the Constitution, or to the sociological problems of how best to achieve the goals of the prison function in the criminal justice system. Most of the "law" that controls prison life, both federal and state, is not found in statutes or case law. Most, if not all, correctional departments have promulgated extensive rules and regulations during the past ten years that cover all aspects of prison life. Courts will defer to carefully drafted administrative rules and regulations. Issues before the courts most often result in factual disputes between inmates and prison officials rather than constitutional issues. Despite the increased litigation that will naturally flow from the application of the federal sentencing guidelines, patience, education, and intelligent decision-making can find the balance between legitimate state interests in administering an economically sound prison system and protecting the constitutional rights of prisoners.

ENDNOTES

1. 18 U.S.C. Secs. 3624(a) and (b).
2. The author of this chapter, John W. Palmer, was subsequently retained by the Ohio Department of Rehabilitation and Corrections. Over a period of five years, he assisted the Department in all legal matters and was the principal draftsman for detailed rules and requirements that covered all aspects of prison life.
3. For a more complete discussion of these and other cases, see John W. Palmer, *Constitutional Rights of Prisoners* (3rd Ed.). Cincinnati, OH: Anderson.
4. These figures are contained in the Annual Report of the Director of the Administrative Office of the U. S. Courts, Table 3c.
5. These statistics were provided by the Litigation Section of the Office of the Ohio Attorney General.

12

Federal Sentencing Reform in Light of Incapacitation and Recidivism

William G. Doerner   Benjamin S. Wright

INTRODUCTION

The legislative mandate for the recently established U. S. Sentencing Guidelines can be traced to the Comprehensive Crime Control Act of 1984. This reform package proposed an abrupt change in prevailing sentencing practices. The variation in punishments imposed by different judges for the same violations traversed such a broad spectrum that sentencing practices defied reasonable explanation. Congressional leaders, shocked to discover substantial inconsistencies in criminal sentencing at the federal level, wished to revamp existing sentencing practices. Disenchantment with the failure of the rehabilitative promise, coupled with a losing effort in the war against crime and voter demand for greater accountability, prompted Congress to initiate a strategy geared towards greater structuring of federal judicial discretion.

The basic thrust of this reform effort has been a movement away from offender-based sentencing toward offense-based sentencing. Past sentencing practices depended largely upon the personal philosophy of presiding judges. For some judges, social variables figured more prominently than legal factors in the sentencing equation. Often judges relied more heavily upon a "just deserts" philosophy and applied a more stringent calculation. The net result, according to one prosecutor, was a whimsical system in which defendants had "the deprivation of liberty dependent solely on the luck of the draw in judicial assignment" (Eakin, 1987:6). At the same time, however, critics counter that offense-based guidelines do not provide the necessary balance. They contend that resorting to categorical sentencing is not a panacea and represents an unwarranted intrusion into judicial sentencing authority (Weinstein, 1987).

As can be seen, the debate continues. Instead of turning in yet another direction, this chapter relies heavily on the preceding materials. Several authors in this book have provided ample discussion of the philosophical underpinnings of the question of why society punishes its transgressors. As noted earlier, these perspectives include retribution or atonement, rehabilitation or treatment, social defense or the protection of societal members from any menace, and deterrence or the threat of punishment. Rather than explore each of these views separately, this chapter will be confined to a consideration of how the new U. S. Sentencing Guidelines affect the criminal population. The incapacitation argument will be explored as well as the influence of these new guidelines on offender recidivism. However, before examining these topics, an examination will be undertaken of what the federal system did prior to these sentencing reforms. Then, the discussion will move to a consideration of our present understanding of the guidelines, in order to set the stage for subsequent comments.

SOME GENERAL CHARACTERISTICS OF THE FEDERAL SYSTEM

One way for us to better appreciate just what the new sentencing guidelines are designed to accomplish is to describe the nature of the federal sentencing system prior to the enactment of these reforms. Table 12.1 shows the number of federal defendants and convictions for various offenses during the 1984–1985 period. These crime categories were devised so as to coincide with the *Uniform Crime Reports* format. An inspection of Table 12.1 shows that fewer than 5 percent of the federal defendants were charged with violent offenses, while property offenses accounted for another 10 percent. Almost three-fourths of all federal charges were included within Part II Offenses, with the remainder included in other federal crime categories. These figures demonstrate a close correspondence with the national distribution of persons arrested.

Two other points deserve consideration here. First, Table 12.1 shows that 81 percent of the defendants charged with criminal violations by federal authorities eventually were convicted. As we might expect, there is some degree of interoffense variation that has occurred. For example, the government is able to successfully prosecute 90 percent of all robbery cases, but it only is successful in prosecuting 77 percent of all homicide cases. Second, the federal system processed 47,360 criminal defendants during the 1984–1985 period. The 1985 *Uniform Crime Reports* show that law enforcement agencies effected over 13

Table 12.1   Criminal Defendants Convicted in U.S. District Courts by Offense, 1984–1985

OFFENSE CATEGORY	NUMBER OF DEFENDANTS	NUMBER CONVICTED	PERCENT CONVICTED
Violent Index:			
Robbery	1,387	1,247	90%
Assault	555	427	77%
Homicide	171	131	77%
Nonviolent Index:			
Larceny and Theft	4,141	3,399	82%
Auto Theft	461	388	84%
Burglary	165	126	76%
Part II Offenses:			
Fraud	7,109	5,832	82%
Narcotics	11,208	9,231	82%
Forgery and Counterfeiting	2,343	2,041	87%
Embezzlement	1,951	1,733	89%
Weapons and Firearms	1,746	1,448	83%
Sex Offenses	200	163	82%
Other	9,914	7,245	73%
Immigration Laws	2,631	2,394	91%
Federal Statutes	3,357	2,707	81%
Internal Revenue Liquor	21	18	86%
TOTALS	47,360	38,530	81%

Adapted from Administrative Office of the U. S. Courts (1986: Table D-4).

million arrests that same year (Federal Bureau of Investigation, 1986). Even though the number of defendants standing trial and the number of arrests involve slightly different domains within the criminal justice system, these figures are still instructive. The federal system handles far fewer cases compared with local courts. In fact, the federal system handles only a small fraction of all criminal cases nationally.

We know that criminal convictions do not always result in sentences of incarceration. Sparks (1983) recognized this dual feature and called for a separate analysis of these two system junctures. As a result, Table 12.2 provides information that describes federal sentencing pratices by offense for the 1985–1986 period.

The imprisonment rate in Table 12.2 exhibits substantial variation by offense within each crime category. For example, 94 percent of the robbery convictions resulted in incarceration compared with 29 percent of the embezzlement cases. However, it should be noted that the imprisonment column includes only those defendants sentenced to straight prison terms. It does not include split sentences, indeterminate sentences, nor individuals remanded under the Youth Corrections Act or the Youthful Offender Act. In general, however, only half of the convicted offenders received a sentence of incarceration.

Table 12.2 also contains average sentence lengths for various offense categories. An inspection of the table shows that homicide and rob-

Table 12.2 Defendants Sentenced in U. S. District Courts, by Offense and by Length of Sentence, 1985–1986.

OFFENSE CATEGORY	NUMBER SENTENCED	NUMBER IMPRISONED	PERCENT	NUMBER OF MONTHS OF SENTENCE
Violent Index:				
Robbery.........	1,141	1,068	94%	161
Assault.............	411	228	55%	58
Homicide...........	123	91	74%	194
Nonviolent Index:				
Larceny and Theft...	3,395	1,366	40%	34
Auto Theft.........	374	274	73%	45
Burglary...........	101	71	70%	35
Part II Offenses:				
Fraud..............	6,646	2,801	42%	42
Narcotics..........	10,764	8,152	76%	39
Forgery and Counterfeiting...	2,286	1,059	46%	37
Embezzlement.......	1,766	511	29%	40
Weapons and Firearms	1,648	1,063	65%	42
Sex Offenses.......	226	135	60%	42
Other.............	6,837	1,600	23%	17
Immigration Laws.....	2,443	1,431	59%	41
Federal Statutes.....	2,564	767	30%	30
Internal Revenue				
Liquor.............	15	4	27%	40
TOTALS..............	40,740	20,621	51%	65

Adapted from Bureau of Justice Statistics (1987:2).

bery carry the harshest penalties (194 and 164 months respectively). Most of the other penalties related to the remaining offense categories range from 2 to 3 years. However, the assigned sentence is different from the actual amount of time served. An analysis of entries into the federal prison system during the 1979–1980 period reveals that the average convicted offender served slightly more than half the sentence imposed by judges after deducting time off for good behavior and early release through parole (Bureau of Justice Statistics, 1987:4).

Several caveats must be delineated before we draw conclusions, however. First, these crude figures fail to include other relevant variables. For example, Tables 12.1 and 12.2 do not include information about the prior records of offenders. Second, each offense category lumps a variety of offenses into single entries. For instance, homicide includes first- and second-degree murder as well as manslaughter. Fraud includes income tax violations, banking irregularities, postal violations, stock exchange manipulations, passport restrictions, and other assorted violations. As a result, there is greater heterogeneity than what appears to be an otherwise homogeneous grouping. Third, imposed sentences may partially be an artifact of the criminal justice system. In short, judges may impose harsher sentences with the knowledge that if they do not do so, parole boards will release offenders earlier than whatever judges consider appropriate incarcerative periods (Sparks, 1983:209–211).

THE U. S. SENTENCING GUIDELINES

As other chapters in this book have explained, the manifest goal of the new federal sentencing guidelines is to reduce sentencing disparities. The avenue chosen for achieving this goal is to limit judicial discretion when determining an appropriate length of imprisonment. While the Commission constructed a grid of permissible ranges for various offenses, it is still possible to express sentencing patterns in a very elementary fashion. Following the example furnished by Fisher and Kadane (1983), the current federal sentencing plan may be presented as follows:

Length = a + Social + Legal + Crime + Judge + e;   Where:
Length = sentence length;
a   = some constant;
Social = offender social characteristics;
Legal   = offender legal characteristics;
Crime = punishment specified for the offense in the sentencing
             guidelines;

Judge = judge's discretion when considering aggravating and
mitigating circumstances; and

e = an error term.

According to this formulation, sentence length is a function of the offender's social characteristics, the offender's legal characteristics, crime characteristics, and the judge's predisposition. As we will demonstrate momentarily, the Commission made several deliberate and significant decisions which ignored a substantial amount of criminological literature. As a result, the guidelines fail to represent the zenith of accumulated scientific knowledge about offenders and how they ought to be punished.

Social variables represent the first input into the equation. Empirical studies of criminal justice decision-making commonly separate what are referred to as social or nonlegal variables from legal characteristics of offenders. Nonlegal variables include race, age, gender, employment status, and education. The legal variables refer to prior record, offense seriousness, type of plea, and other case characteristics. Researchers ordinarily include both social and legal variables within the same equation in order to determine whether differential processing exists. In those instances where nonlegal variables take precedence over legal variables, researchers interpret these results as an indication of the presence of discriminatory sentencing practices (Terry, 1967; Hepburn, 1978; Visher, 1983). Unfortunately, many researchers do not hesitate to attribute theoretical primacy to discrimination even though they typically fail to include any direct measure of this construct.

The new sentencing guidelines reject any consideration of an offender's social characteristics and set the effective value equal to zero. This position probably results from a heavy reliance upon the Minnesota sentencing reform effort which specifically prohibits any reference to offender social characteristics (Silets and Brenner, 1986:1075–1076). As will be seen later in this chapter, this decision has important policy implications for the nature of incapacitation effects we might expect to derive from this type of sentencing reform.

The second input into the equation consists of offender legal characteristics. The sentencing guidelines explicitly mandate a consideration of an offender's criminal history. Thus, having one or more prior convictions becomes a definite liability because it increases sentence lengths.

The third input is the crime itself. The Commission considered a lengthy list of federal offenses and then assigned a corresponding sentence based upon presumed offense severity. Unfortunately, the actual punishments associated with the crimes are far from systematic. As Robinson (1986) explains, the deliberations surrounding this ranking scheme failed to entertain the enormous body of literature which was generated after the survey conducted by Rossi et al. (1974) of public perceptions of offense seriousness. Thus, punishment length does not correspond evenly to commonly held public views of punishment.

The final factor in the model permits judges to either enhance or reduce sentence lengths according to a weighing of aggravating and mitigating circumstances. This procedure closely resembles the strategy taken by various states when they revised their capital punishment in the wake of the *Furman v. Georgia* (1972) decision (Ehrhardt et al., 1973). Circumstances that render the crime more heinous allow judges to increase sentences by 25 percent. Mitigating circumstances likewise permit 25 percent reductions in sentencing severity. This part of the equation is hailed by supporters because it regulates actions permissible under the rubric of judicial discretion.

As can be seen, this formulation allows a heuristic portrayal of the federal sentencing reform effort. Defendant social characteristics fall outside of the boundaries of judicial consideration, the offender's prior record becomes more important, and judicial discretion in sentencing is more tightly regulated. In the following section, several reservations are noted about whether this reform effort is achieving its goals and targeting the offender population in an appropriate and reasonable manner.

INCAPACITATION

The new federal sentencing guidelines were designed as a crime reduction strategy. One of the more salient gains comes from the incapacitation effect. **Incapacitation means that offenders are unable to commit additional crimes while confined.** Thus, society benefits temporarily through the incarceration of these offenders.

Criminologists generally recognize two types of incapacitation. **Collective incapacitation is restricted to the imposition of offense-based sentencing.** Violators receive a prison term commensurate with the seriousness of the crime. Minimum mandatory sentences are included here as well. For example, some states require a fixed period of incarceration for any offender who uses a firearm during the commission of a crime. On the other hand, **selective incapacitation concentrates on individual-based sentencing.** Punishment is tailored to the offender, and incarceration decisions are based on the offender's predicted propensity for future criminal involvement. Under this approach, the same offense could result in two quite different sentences for two offenders.

Both forms of incapacitation rely heavily upon the idea of a **criminal career**. An offender's life can be blocked into two conceptual segments. One segment marks the time during which the offender is active in criminal pursuits. The other portion reflects the time prior to entry and the time subsequent to retirement from criminal pursuits. It is this intervening portion of an individual's life that researchers refer to as the criminal career.

If the criminal justice system were 100 percent effective, then every criminal event would be detected and every offender would be apprehended and subjected to punishment. The incapacitation as well as the deterrent effect would be sufficient. However, the present system does not operate in this ideal fashion. Approximately half of the serious crimes go unreported, overall police clearance rates are in the teens, and not all discovered offenders are punished. Despite these facts, the system is capable of exerting some incapacitative effects. If offenders commit X number of crimes annually, then an imprisonment of S years represents a savings of (X)(S) crimes during that period (Cohen, 1983).

The incapacitation model is predicated upon three assumptions (Cohen, 1983; Visher, 1987). First, all offenders share an equal risk of being inducted into the criminal justice system. No single group is immune from detection, apprehension, conviction, and punishment. Second, the removal of offenders from the free world does not create a vacuum which is filled automatically by criminal replacements. Obviously, this assumption is flawed by organized criminal activity including narcotics distribution, the pornography industry, automobile chop shops, and other syndicate-operated enterprises. It would seem that this assumption would be violated more frequently in those instances where greater economic profits may be realized. Finally, it is assumed that the incarceration period does not alter the offender's criminal career. It merely represents a temporary interruption. In other words, the offender will not necessarily embark on a new crime spree or engage in new criminal activity immediately upon release from incarceration. By the same token, it is also assumed that offenders will not necessarily desist from criminal activities and terminate their criminal careers after being released back into society. In short, these three assumptions are advantageous because they permit researchers to make mathematical projections concerning the impact of various incapacitation strategies on crime.

Both Cohen (1983) and Visher (1987) have reviewed the empirical incapacitation literature and independently arrived at similar conclusions. As far as collective incapacitation is concerned, both researchers caution that future returns from this approach will be minimal. Although collective incapacitation made substantial inroads in crime between 1970 and 1988, the net result was a burgeoning inmate population whose effects are now being observed. Given the current crisis in prison and jail overcrowding, advocates intent on pursuing a collective incapacitation policy need to increase prison space first. However, filling these newly constructed prison bedspaces is expected to have an imperceptible effect on crime, at least in the short-term. The gains associated with expanding prison facilities will not furnish a similar incremental foothold into the crime problem.

The pessimism associated with the collective incapacitation approach does not extend nearly as much to all selective incapacitation strategies. The criminal career literature generally shows that a very small proportion of offenders account for the majority of the crime volume. Wolfgang and his colleagues (1972) refer to this group of perpetrators as "chronic offenders." This discovery prompted others to engage in cohort analyses of offenders and their crimes (Lab, 1988). This research avenue has made substantial contributions to criminological thought through such concepts as desistance, age of onset, and the escalation hypothesis.

Proponents of selective incapacitation would point to this literature and argue that accurate identification and proper processing of these chronic offenders would do much to produce a sizeable reduction in crime. However, critics of selective incapacitation would counter with myriad problems and arguments. For one thing, criminologists have yet to devise an accurate technology for identifying chronic offenders. A second concern is that if the technology for the early identification of chronic offenders or career criminals does become available in the near future, then a fundamental dilemma results. Is it appropriate for the criminal justice system to punish offenders for what they **might** do in the future rather than for what they have done in the past? Although selective incapacitation does have a certain appeal, some important and basic issues will continue to prevail.

Using the issues associated with collective and selective incapacitation as a backdrop, let us return to the equation presented earlier which presented a schematic portrayal of the new sentencing guidelines. The guidelines specifically set the input value of the offender's social characteristics equal to zero. What this means, then, is that selective incapacitation is being rejected in favor of a collective incapacitation strategy. Sentence length becomes a function of legal characteristics (i.e., prior record and current offense seriousness), the value listed in the sentencing matrix, and the judge's balancing of any aggravating or mitigating circumstances. If we adhere to the three assumptions characterizing incapacitation research, then the anticipated returns from this sentencing reform are disappointing. However, rather than simply embrace these assumptions blindly, let us critically examine the last condition, which stipulates the absence of either a rehabilitative or a criminogenic effect.

RECIDIVISM

As we stated earlier, the Comprehensive Crime Control Act of 1984 charged the Commission with the task of drafting suitable guidelines that would allow more equitable sentencing of federal offenders. This directive also stipulated that these reforms simultaneously consider the needs of offenders as well as the public. Since one of the purposes of the new sentencing guidelines is to reduce sentencing disparity and, ultimately, crime itself, an outcome measure is needed to assess the success or failure of offenders sentenced under these new criteria. One concept that observers commonly use is recidivism.

While recidivism might be targeted as an outcome measure, the literature suggests no consensus as to what might be the most accurate definition of the concept. Numerous operationalizations of this concept exist. Some researchers define recidivism as reinvolvement in criminal activity within a specific period of time that results in a new arrest (Griswold, 1978; Menard and Covey, 1983), a new conviction (Nacci, 1978; Maltz, 1984; Shover and Einstadter, 1988), a new prison sentence (Brookhart et al., 1976; Gottfredson et al., 1977; Kitchener et al., 1977; Pritchard, 1979; Gatz and Vito, 1982; Hoffman and Beck, 1984; Wormith and Goldstone, 1984; Zatz, 1984), or a violation of felony probation (Vito, 1986). Even though one may regard these measures as standard operating definitions, they reflect basically different underlying concepts and system processes. As a result of this diversity, researchers often experience difficulty whenever comparing the results of recidivism studies.

It is not unexpected that problems arise from using different measures of recidivism. The first difficulty is constructing an unambiguous measure of success. Webb et al. (1976) maintain that if parolees are returned to confinement for technical violations instead of committing new crimes, this should be regarded as a partial success of particular parole programs. The irony of this position is clear. If the commission of a new crime is our measure of recidivism, then a technical violation emerges in the success column even though the parolee is reincarcerated.

Another shortcoming is that some definitions of recidivism do not consider the length of time between an offender's release from prison and subsequent reincarceration. In this instance, ex-convicts who stay clean for long periods are scored the same way as ex-convicts who recidivate immediately after release. Indifference about this point obscures the distinction between short-term and long-term objectives.

A third obstacle is that some recidivism rates are inherently misleading. This point rests upon two key variables: criterion measure and follow-up period. Hoffman and Stone-Meierhoefer (1980) discovered that the selection of either new arrest, new conviction, or new incarceration as the criterion could affect their conclusions substantially. When rearrests were counted over a one-year period, the failure rate was 29 percent. When reincarcerations were tallied during this same time interval, the failure rate was only 9 percent. Extending the time frame from one to six years produced a 60 percent rearrest rate, while the reimprisonment rate remained steady. These results indicate that future researchers must be wary of fluctuating indicators due to particular operationalizations of recidivism.

A fourth concern stems from the procedure researchers frequently use when sampling from the recidivist population. According to Blumstein and Larson (1971), the most common error associated with recidivism sampling methods is random incidence. This means that the enumeration of recidivists is biased toward selecting those offenders with known instances of failure. Individuals who acquire formal recognition through arrests, convictions, or incarcerations are counted. Those fortunate enough to escape official detection and apprehension go uncounted. As a result, recidivism measures based solely upon official records do not necessarily reflect the real amount of recidivism.

As can be seen, the Commission cannot afford to overlook the problems associated with recidivism as an outcome measure. Prior experience illustrates that system officials do rely heavily upon recidivism rates to measure the effectiveness of sentencing and various programs. In a pragmatic sense, the Commission also will utilize recidivism rates to determine whether the sentencing reforms are successful. However, unless the Commission proceeds with at least a modicum of caution, it will continue to perpetuate the same shortcomings highlighted here.

The Commission can alleviate some of these definitional problems by seeking greater impact specification through the use of multiple outcome measures. For example, the Minnesota Sentencing Guidelines Commission has encouraged assessments as to whether the legally mandated guidelines have provided more predictable sentences and less judicial discretion (Miethe and Moore, 1985). Another avenue would be to devise more effective definitions of recidivism. For example, most recidivism research makes inferences about individual behavior from group statistics (Maltz, 1984). However, there is some indication that ex-offender characteristics, such as the degree of familial support, educational attainment, and age at first arrest, collectively influence the adjustment process. Finally, the use of system junctures to mark recidivism may invite some distortion. While arrest-based measures carry some liabilities of their own, they avoid some of the muddling that taints prosecution and conviction data. System researchers are well aware that the funnelling effect owes a great deal to the technical distinction between the terms "not guilty" and "innocent." Even so, mere reliance upon arrest-based definitions will not automatically cure every ailment. There is still a need for greater precision in conceptual and operational formulations.

CONCLUSIONS

The purpose of this chapter was to address various issues related to incapacitation and recidivism in light of the new U. S. Sentencing Guidelines. One depiction of these new guidelines stresses that sentence length is a function of the offender's social characteristics, legal characteristics, offense characteristics, and the judge's predisposition. A close inspection of the equation reveals that the Commission seeks a crime reduction strategy by relying upon collective incapacitation. The effectiveness of that particular crime reduction approach may be judged in terms of its immediate impact as well as its long-term influence on recidivism rates. However, an exact and precise evaluation of the sentencing reforms awaits the resolution of several definitional and measurement problems associated with the use of recidivism as an outcome measure. Barring the unexpected, it is recommended that multiple indicators should be used to reflect the broad and diverse legislative mandate that Congress has placed upon the U. S. Sentencing Commission.

Part V

The Guidelines in Retrospect

13

The U. S. Sentencing Guidelines:
A Summary of Selected Problems and Prospects

Dean J. Champion

INTRODUCTION

This chapter has been written after I received and carefully read all contributed materials from each of the chapter authors. Several observations are in order about the guidelines established by the U. S. Sentencing Commission. First, despite the "lead time" given the Commission in formulating its current sentencing guidelines and the many discussions, evaluations, and deliberations it conducted, it is apparent that these guidelines have many critics. The fact that nearly 150 federal district judges refused to abide by them when sentencing convicted offenders during the entirety of 1988 tips the scales of the controversy that surrounded the birth of the guidelines, the hearings that preceded their implementation, and the legal dialogues, commentary, and appeals that led eventually to the precedent-setting case of *Mistretta v. United States* (1989).

The constitutionality of these sentencing guidelines has been resolved rather resoundingly in an 8-1 decision by the U. S. Supreme Court in *Mistretta*. However, much work remains to be done by the Commission and other interested factions in devising adjustments to calm the unsettled waters of corrections created by the Commission's splash.

This project, in all frankness, survived by a wing and a prayer. Two contributing authors, both attorneys and legal scholars in their own right, recommended to me and advised at the eleventh hour during December 1988 that perhaps the publication of this book ought to be postponed until the U. S. Supreme Court had ruled one way or the other in a pending case (*Mistretta*) challenging the constitutionality of the November 1987 guidelines implementation. My "gut-level" reaction at the time was that the U. S. Supreme Court, in all of its wisdom, would hardly reject outright a four-year endeavor involving the work of thousands of experts, statisticians, correctional authorities, federal district judges, Congressional leaders, and a host of other actors too numerous to mention. Yet, the advice of these experienced attorneys and legal scholars was personally unsettling. Despite these admonitions to the contrary, I pushed for completion deadlines for chapters that would provide intellectual fodder and the basis for heated dialogue among criminologists and criminal justice scholars, regardless of future Supreme Court holdings about these guidelines.

I believe that I express the sentiments of the entire contributing author aggregate when I say that none of us had much good to say about the guidelines and their implementation. In fact, the collective tone of this entire work may be conservatively portrayed as **skeptical** and **apprehensive**. However, a seasoned Commission consisting of respected scholars, jurists, and politicians conceived an alternative scheme whereby current federal sentencing injustices could be remedied. I do not believe that the Commission's efforts were regarded by their membership or others as the final word on the subject of federal sentencing. Rather, a lengthy list of provisos has been incorporated into these guidelines as well as recommendations to render them flexible and amenable to change should the occasion warrant it. In defense of the Commission, significant attempts were made to incorporate conservativism into the resulting guidelines. Indeed, these attempts are clearly a part of the formal documentation issued by the U. S. Sentencing Commission in late 1987, shortly before the guidelines went into effect.

We must remember that prior to the implementation of these guidelines, considerable research existed to show evidence of unfairness, discrimination, and general sentencing disparities attributable to racial, ethnic, gender, and socioeconomic factors under the previous federal indeterminate sentencing scheme. The federal system was not alone in this regard. Many states with indeterminate sentencing schemes have been intellectually and methodologically indicted for disparate sentencing practices due to the aforementioned factors and others. Thus, sentencing reform was a logical step toward the improvement of an imperfect sentencing system. I might add that the Commission charged with the overwhelming task of revising the previous federal sentencing scheme seemed very much aware of its own imperfections while formulating these new guidelines.

Lest federal district judges be labeled as the exclusive distributors of disparate sentencing, we should also recognize that the U. S. Parole Commission has been equally culpable in the view of critics, by engaging in disparate dispensations of parole according to nonrational criteria. Therefore, parole abolitionists have been able to persuade influential and significant others that perhaps parole ought to be abandoned as an unobjective and unfair enterprise together with indeterminate sentencing. However, the guidelines devised by the Commission did not fully remedy in any absolute sense the discretionary unfairness of actors at any particular adjudicatory or correctional stage. If anything, the major power shift regarding the life chances of criminal defendants gave prosecutors even broader powers despite their previously broad discretionary latitude, and judges were disenfranchised of only a small degree of sentencing discretion.

As Deborah Wilson, Albert Alschuler, Larry Mays, and others have noted in the present volume, a hydraulic effect has been incurred by the federal criminal justice system through the implementation of a guidelines sentencing scheme. It is unlikely that the rate of plea bargaining will escalate beyond its already high 90 percent level. However, since sentencing guidelines are "guidelines" and mandate, more or less, *some* amount of incarceration for the majority of convicted criminals [see Endnote l], there will be greater pressure exerted on corrections in the near future to cope with rising incarcerated and supervised release offender populations. Prison and jail space in most jurisdictions is at a premium, and many states are under court order to reduce their inmate populations. Furthermore, nonincarcerative supervisory personnel, including probation and parole officers, will have to assume greater caseloads as larger offender aggregates are pushed into their sector through the guidelines sentencing scheme. In other words, the feds currently have little elbow room within which to distribute their future, convicted, prison-bound offenders short of massive construction of new incarcerative facilities or substantial redesign and modification of existing, unused federal buildings for incarcerative purposes.

Anticipating this possible state of affairs, Congress has specified that "[F]our years after the sentencing guidelines [have gone into effect] the General Accounting Office shall undertake a study of the guidelines in order to determine their impact and compare the guidelines system with the operation of the previous sentencing and parole release system, and, within six months of the undertaking of such study, report to the Congress the results of its study" (U. S. Sentencing Commission, 1987b:B.23). Thus, this Congressional "checks and balances" system is a safeguard measure to ensure that these guidelines have been effective, are still effective, and probably will continue to be effective if extended to future years. Have these guidelines accomplished their explicit objectives as set forth by the Comprehensive Crime Control Act of 1984? The Commission is charged with providing the General Accounting Office with its own study of the impact of the guidelines in addressing each of the goals they sought to achieve throughout the criminal justice system. Collectively, the authors of this volume are doubtful that these goals, either cumulatively or separately have been achieved thus far. Also collectively, we are apprehensive that these ambitious goals will have been achieved by the time the mandated four-year investigation by the General Accounting Office is conducted. Of course, no one can predict with certainty the state of affairs of our correctional system during the next four- or five-year period.

For instance, we will not know for some time whether these guidelines have functioned effectively as "deterrents" to further criminal activity. Such answers are not easily obtainable in the short-range. Longitudinal studies must be conducted carefully to assess whether the desired effect has occurred. However, since federal felons and misdemeanants account for only a fraction of all felons and misdemenants, it is probably the case that federal sentencing practices will not affect recidivism rates to a significant degree. Carefully conducted follow-ups of those offenders convicted under the new guidelines will be required. Thus, the best we can do for now is to speculate about the possibility of the deterrent influence of these guidelines on future federal criminal activity. Of course, those states which have implemented guidelines similar to those devised by the Commission (e.g., Minnesota, Washington, California) have issued favorable reports thus far.

If we examine each of the purposes of punishment expressed by the Comprehensive Crime Control Act of 1984, the guiding doctrine within which these federal sentencing guidelines were supposedly couched, perhaps a tentative appraisal about the probable effectiveness of these guidelines may be made. These purposes include:

1. deterring crime
2. incapacitating the offender
3. providing just punishment
4. rehabilitating the offender.

DETERRING CRIME

Will the U. S. Sentencing Guidelines deter crime? Certainty of punishment in relation to the commission of crimes has been debated for centuries. We appear to be no closer to answering this question now compared with the philosophical debates on the subject during the time of Cesare Beccaria. Some convicted murderers have claimed that knowing "for certain" that they would probably be executed for committing murder had no apparent impact on their behavior "at the time." After they had occasion to contemplate the penalty, they seemed regretful. However, as many of them have indicated in interviews with the press, they aren't thinking of getting caught during their acts of violence.

Is there any reason to expect that guidelines are more effective as crime deterrents compared with the discretionary power of judges under indeterminate sentencing? Would the absence of parole and greater flat time be taken into account more by would-be federal criminals contrasted with their impressions of the certainty and duration of incarceration under the pre-guideline sentencing scheme? Again, research of the before-after variety is sorely needed in order to provide reasonably accurate answers to these questions. The propensities of offenders to engage in criminal activity must be weighed against their expectation or likelihood of apprehension and conviction. Thus, the motivation to violate federal laws is pitted against the calculable risks associated with these violations.

It is unlikely that many federal offenders, apprehended or unapprehended, are going to order a copy of the U. S. Sentencing Guidelines and study them intently, or even know of their existence. Even under a "best-case" scenario, it is doubtful that knowledge of the certainty of incarceration will prevent those intent on committing crimes to refrain from committing them. Like many of my colleagues, I tend to agree with the pessimistic view originally expressed by the late Robert Martinson that nothing seems to work. Although he modified his views in later years, he aptly portrayed many of the strategies of lawmakers and others to establish effective crime deterrents. Even Delaware lawmakers were considering in 1989 bringing back the "Red Hannah" whipping post as a corporal punishment measure for drug dealers. Several Delaware legislators said that since nothing else seems to be effective, why not resort to lashing convicted offenders with a cat o' nine tails? While I am not advocating a return to Plymouth, stocks and pillories, and whipping posts, I am indicating that drastic measures to deal with escalating crime are being pursued by some frustrated politicians and interest groups.

INCAPACITATING THE OFFENDER

Will the federal sentencing guidelines incapacitate offenders? Definitely. This is one of the purposes of criminal punishment stated by the 1984 act that will become a reality. More convicted offenders will be incarcerated. This certainly scares correctional officials, and it **should** scare them. Not only are many of the nation's jails and prisons old and unfit for human habitation, but they are also in various conditions of overcrowding, bulging at the seams with record numbers of new inmates. Where are we going to house the sudden gush of convicted offenders who will be placed at the correctional doorsteps for custody? Some professionals have recommended the concept of *selective incapacitation* as the solution. But even this concept is not operative under the present guidelines system. Selective incapacitation of offenders means discretion, and the guidelines effectively eliminate discretion, unless in writing. Even then, departures are subject to appellate review for correctness.

PROVIDING JUST PUNISHMENT

Another troubling dimension of the new guidelines is whether they comply fully with "providing 'just' punishment" for convicted offenders. What does it mean to "provide just punishment"? We think we know what it means, that each punishment should be tailor-made for the criminal committing the crime. Yet, a cursory examination of the guidelines suggests that numerous flaws exist that detract from "just" punishment. One flaw unaddressed by any of the works here is that the punishments for certain crimes are based on dollar-amount "increments" in terms of the amount embezzled or the value of the theft or robbery. Some blatant examples of "just" punishment abuses are as follows.

Let us take "money laundering and monetary transaction reporting," theft, embezzlement, receipt of stolen property or property destruction," and "fraud and deceit" as three examples of the extent to which "just" punishment has been abused, intentionally or unintentionally. Money laundering punishes offenders according to an ordinal scale rather than an interval one. Offense level scores are adjusted upward from 1 to 13 points for money-laundering transactions ranging from $100,000–$200,000 to more than $100,000,000. The categories are not ordered according to interval properties. Adding 2 points to one's offense level occurs if the value of funds ranged between $200,000 and $350,000, yet we must add 3 points if the value of funds ranges from $350,001 to $600,000. There is neither rhyme nor reason to these disproportionate and unequal increments. If we increase one's offense level by 2 points for a range of dollars of $150,000 (i.e., between $200,000 and $350,000), this would mean logically that each point increment would be worth about $150,000/2 or $75,000. Yet, this logic breaks down when we find that a "third" point has been added if the value of the funds ranged between $350,001 to $600,000, a difference of about $250,000. Thus, 1 point is worth $250,000. Or is it? There is a $25 million gap in the range for "L" level offenses, requiring an 11-point addition to one's original offense level score (23), and a $40 million gap in the range in level "M" offenses, requiring a 12-point addition to one's original offense level score.

Fraud and deceit and "theft, embezzlement, etc." are similar. Standard gradations between offense level scores are not found. For instance, in the theft, embezzlement category, there is a $1 million gap (between $1 million and $2 million) for a raise in offense level of 11 points, but there is a $3 million dollar gap (between approximately $2 million and $5 million) to raise the offense level by 12 points. Thus, a point raise of "1" is worth anywhere from $100 to "over $3 million," depending upon the amount taken. Over $5 million, no points are added beyond 13 points. This doesn't make sense. The rationale for these unusual allocations of points to offense level scores has not been explained at all. We are left with "Ouija Board" mathematics as determinants for these various increments. ALL crimes involving monetary loss which have been tabulated in the guidelines manual are plagued by this nonrational or irrational problem. Thus, I just as well might steal or attempt to steal $20 million as $5 million, because my penalty will be the same, regardless.

The injustice of such incremental schemes undermines our confidence in those who devised these unequal incremental scales. This confidence, once undermined, is generalized such that our confidence in other aspects of these guidelines and point adjustment instructions is undermined accordingly. It is little wonder that Frank Marshall said that probation officers had their work cut out for them in attempting to learn to apply these guidelines to individual criminal cases. No, the guidelines do not provide "just" punishment. Theft is an example. The value of a theft is not merely a rational "enhancement," but rather, it is neatly spelled out in unequal dollar increments. This is at least one punishment problem associated with the guidelines that is in need of a remedy.

REHABILITATING THE OFFENDER

Do the guidelines seek to rehabilitate offenders? No. In fact, rehabilitation is the only goal absolutely overlooked and omitted by the Commission. I feel quite comfortable stating that nowhere in the new guidelines are provisions for offender rehabilitation. Under the "Supervised Release" and "Recommended Conditions of Probation and

Supervised Release" provisions, the ONLY provisions for "rehabilitation" are the "optional" provisions for participation in a "substance abuse program" or "mental health program." Other than these, the rest of the "special conditions" are regulatory in nature, indicating that offenders refrain from this or that or conduct themselves this way or that.

The following "special conditions of probation" (and remember that probation is only an "option" within a very limited spectrum of low offense level and criminal history scores) enhance offender control rather than address any rehabilitative need: (1) do not possess weapons (rehabilitation?), (2) make restitution (rehabilitation?), (3) pay fines (rehabilitation?), (4) pay debt obligations (rehabilitation?), (5) give probation officers access to financial information (rehabilitation?), (6) undergo community confinement (living in a halfway house as rehabilitation?), (7) undergo home detention (rehabilitation?), (8) community service (rehabilitation?), and (9) submit to occupational restrictions (rehabilitation?). The recommended conditions governing "probation" whenever it is imposed are considered standard, non-rehabilitative conditions: Don't leave the judicial district, report to the probation officer regularly, answer the probation officers' questions truthfully whenever they ask questions, support dependents and family, work regularly, notify probation officers about changes in employment or residency, refrain from "excessive" alcohol use, don't frequent places known to be frequented by other criminals and do not associate with such persons, permit probation officers to visit your work or residence whenever they feel like it, notify your probation officer about a police investigation in which you are involved or if you are arrested as a criminal suspect, do not enter into informer agreements with various law enforcement agencies, and notify others of your past criminal conduct in certain types of employment.

Where's the beef? If there is rehabilitation there, perhaps a Commission member would prepare a rejoinder to the above paragraph and point out the therapeutic or rehabilitative value of these "special conditions" or "standard conditions" apart from obligatory participation in alcohol, substance abuse, or mental health programs. Perhaps I am being overly critical and am overlooking "judicial discretion" in certifying that particular offenders should be rehabilitated through the sentences imposed. More logically, the Commission has shifted the rehabilitative burden to formal and less formal correctional institutions and agencies for providing rehabilitative programs. Since most jails are intentionally custodial in nature, involving short-term incarcerations, it is logical that they should not be expected to provide lengthy therapeutic and rehabilitative programs. However, prisons are long-term incarcerative facilities and do provide some inmate access to rehabilitative programs. But most critics would concede outright that regardless of the sophistication of the prison and where it is located (e.g., downtown New York City or in the Smoky Mountains of Tennessee), prisons generally don't "rehabilitate" their inmate populations.

For federal criminal offenders, at least, these guidelines insure their secure detention for specified periods, less allowances of 54 days per year for compliance with institutional rules and regulations. This is "good-time" credit, even though it is not acknowledged as such. Thus, the dominant objective fulfilled by these guidelines is incapacitation of more federal criminals for more or less definite incarcerative periods. This objective is ideally achieved in tandem with three other, equally important, objectives: deterrence, "just" punishments, and rehabilitation. Operationally, however, these other aims have not been addressed either adequately or at all by the existing guidelines.

The fundamental logistical problem of jail and prison overcrowding will cause the preparation of an unfavorable GAO report, regardless of the picture painted by the Commission in its own mandated report to the GAO after four years' worth of sentencing guidelines. As some of our authors have suggested, this will likely reactivate the U. S. Parole Commission, but with a different title. After all, citizens don't like the word "parole." But citizens also don't like the excessive taxation required to find adequate space to house enormous numbers of offenders. This book has not resolved the various and sundry problems associated with the U. S. Sentencing Guidelines. Rather, it has attempted to highlight certain of these problems as priorities for future Commissions to remedy. One hopes this aim has been achieved.

ENDNOTE

1. For instance, a majority of first-offenders and nonviolent convicted felons under previous sentencing schemes have been prime candidates for probation in lieu of incarceration. Under the guidelines, probation for any first-offender, violent or nonviolent, is not authorized for *any* offense carrying an offense level score larger than 10, absent any mitigating circumstances that would lessen the offense seriousness and the offense level to a lower value where probation eligibility would obtain. Burglary of a residence (ordinarily defined as a property or nonviolent crime) carries a base offense level of 17, whereas robbery (ordinarily defined as a violent crime or crime against the person) has a base offense level of 18. Thus, by definition, all residential burglars, regardless of their first-offender or nonviolent status as good public risks for probation, will serve a minimum of two years of incarceration, absent any mitigating circumstances.

Statutory Mission of the
U. S. Sentencing Commission

The Comprehensive Crime Control Act of 1984 foresees guidelines that will further the basic purposes of criminal punishment, i.e., deterring crime, incapacitating the offender, providing just punishment, and rehabilitating the offender. It delegates to the Commission broad authority to review and rationalize the federal sentencing process.

The statute contains many detailed instructions as to how this determination should be made, but the most important of them instructs the Commission to create categories of offense behavior and offender characteristics. An offense behavior category might consist, for example, of "bank robbery committed with a gun/$2500 taken." An offender characteristic category might be "offender with one prior conviction who was not sentenced to imprisonment." The Commission is required to prescribe guideline ranges that specify an appropriate sentence for each class of convicted persons, to be determined by coordinating the offense behavior categories with the offender characteristic categories. The statute contemplates the guidelines will establish a range of sentences for every coordination of categories. Where the guidelines call for imprisonment, the range must be narrow: the maximum imprisonment cannot exceed the minimum by more than the greater of 25 percent or six months (28 U.S.C. Sec. 994(b)(2)).

The sentencing judge must select a sentence from within the guideline range. If, however, a particular case presents atypical features, the Act allows the judge to depart from the guidelines and sentence outside the range. In that case, the judge must specify reasons for departure (18 U.S.C. Sec. 3553(b)). If the court sentences within the guideline range, an appellate court may review the sentence to see if the guideline was correctly applied. If the judge departs from the guideline range, an appellate review may review the reasonableness of the departure (18 U.S.C. Sec. 3742). The Act requires the offender to serve virtually all of any prison sentence imposed, for it abolishes parole and substantially restructures good behavior adjustments.

The law requires the Commission to send its initial guidelines to Congress by April 13, 1987, and they took effect on November 1, 1987 (Pub. L. No. 98–473, Sec. 235, *reprinted at* 18 U.S.C. Sec. 3551). The Commission may submit guideline amendments each year to Congress between the beginning of a regular session and May 1. The amendments will take effect automatically 180 days after submission unless a law is enacted to the contrary. 28 U.S.C. Sec. 994(p).

The Commission emphasizes, however, that it views the guideline-writing process as evolutionary. It expects, and the governing statute anticipates, that continuing research, experience, and analysis will result in modifications and revisions to the guidelines by submission of amendments to Congress. To this end, the Commission is established as a permanent agency to monitor sentencing practices in the federal courts throughout the nation.

. . .

The Commission emphasizes that its approach in this initial set of guidelines is one of caution. It has examined the many hundreds of criminal statutes in the United States Code. It has begun with those that are the basis for a significant number of prosecutions. It has sought to place them in a rational order. It has developed additional distinctions relevant to the application of these provisions, and it has applied sentencing ranges to each resulting category. In doing so, it has relied upon estimates of existing sentencing practices as revealed by its own statistical analyses, based on summary reports of some 40,000 convictions, a sample of 10,000 augmented presentence reports, the parole guidelines, and policy judgments.

The Commission recognizes that some will criticize this approach as overly cautious, as representing too little a departure from existing practice. Yet it will cure wide disparity. The Commission is a permanent body that can amend the guidelines each year. Although the data available to it, like all data, are imperfect, experience with these guidelines will lead to additional information and provide a firm empirical basis for revision (U. S. Sentencing Commission, 1987:1.1–1.2, 1.12).

The Sentencing Table

The Sentencing Table below contains sentence lengths expressed in months. Thus, "12–18" means 12 to 18 months of possible incarceration. Offender sentences are based upon one's criminal history score and level of offense seriousness. The mandatory element of these guidelines is that sentences which carry a minimum incarceration of more than 10 months must be satisfied by a term of imprisonment, less good behavior adjustments. Otherwise, judges may sentence offenders to probationary terms for sentences up to 6 months. For those sentences carrying incarcerative penalties of from 6 to 10 months, judges may impose nonincarcerative penalties as long as one half (½) of the sentence is imprisonment.

Departures from these guidelines are permitted, provided that judges specify the reasons for their departures in writing. These departures are subject to appellate review for a determination of their reasonableness. Additional departures from these guidelines may be determined by judges on the basis of numerous factors beyond the scope of this book. However, an example of one of these departures is in order. "If defendants clearly demonstrate a recognition and affirmative acceptance of personal responsibility for the offense of conviction," the offense level may be reduced by 2 levels (U. S. Sentencing Commission, 1987:3.21). Although "acceptance of personal responsibility" is not explicitly defined, a partial list of applications is provided. Several of these applications parallel closely certain mitigating factors, including voluntary termination or withdrawal from criminal conduct, voluntary payment of restitution prior to adjudication of guilt, voluntary admission to authorities of involvement in the offense, and voluntary assistance to authorities in recovering fruits and instrumentalities of the offense. Guilty pleas are not the equivalent of "acceptance of personal responsibility." However, the Commission has noted that "a guilty plea may show some evidence of acceptance of responsibility" (U. S. Sentencing Commission, 1987:3.22).

CRIMINAL HISTORY

Determining a defendant's criminal history score is outlined below. The total points from items (a) through (e) determine the criminal history category in the Sentencing Table.

> (a) Add 3 points for each prior sentence of imprisonment exceeding one year and one month.
> (b) Add 2 points for each prior sentence of imprisonment of at least sixty days not counted in (a).
> (c) Add 1 point for each prior sentence not included in (a) or (b), up to a total of 4 points for this item.
> (d) Add 2 points if the defendant committed the instant offense while under any criminal justice sentence, including probation, parole, supervised release, imprisonment, work release, or escape status.
> (e) Add 2 points if the defendant committed the instant offense less than two years after release from imprisonment on a sentence counted under (a) or (b). If 2 points are added for item (d), add only 1 point for this item.

OFFENSE LEVEL

According to Commission dicta, "For technical and practical reasons it [the Sentencing Table] has 43 levels. Each row in the table contains levels that overlap with the levels in the preceding and succeeding rows. By overlapping the levels, the table should discourage unnecessary litigation" (U. S. Sentencing Commission, 1987:1.11). It has been further noted by the Commission that "In determining the appropriate sentencing ranges for each offense, the Commission began by estimating the average sentences now being served within each category. It also examined the sentence specified in congressional statutes, in the parole guidelines, and in other relevant, analogous sources" (U. S. Sentencing Commission, 1987:1.10–1.11).

For most federal crimes, the Commission has provided specific "Base Offense Level" scores for judges to follow. These are accompanied by point additions or subtractions from the Base Offense Level score, depending upon a variety of circumstances that are closely related to mitigating and/or aggravating factors. For offenses such as tax evasion or price-fixing, the monetary damages incurred by victims are calculated and result in changes in Base Offense Level scores of varying numbers of points. For example, price-fixing carries a Base Offense Level score of 9. If the volume of commerce is less than $1 million, 1 point may be subtracted from the Base Offense Level score of 9. However, if the volume of commerce is over \$50 million, 3 points may be added to the Base Offense Level score of 9. Monetary figures are published for various offenses where applicable.

Table B.1 Sentencing Guidelines

Offense level	Criminal history category					
	I 0 or 1	II 2 or 3	III 4, 5, 6	IV 7, 8, 9	V 10, 11, 12	VI 13 or more
1	0–1	0–2	0–3	0–4	0–5	0–6
2	0–2	0–3	0–4	0–5	0–6	1–7
3	0–3	0–4	0–5	0–6	2–8	3–9
4	0–4	0–5	0–6	2–8	4–10	6–12
5	0–5	0–6	1–7	4–10	6–12	9–15
6	0–6	1–7	2–8	6–12	9–15	12–18
7	1–7	2–8	4–10	8–14	12–18	15–21
8	2–8	4–10	6–12	10–16	15–21	18–24
9	4–10	6–12	8–14	12–18	18–24	21–27
10	6–12	8–14	10–16	15–21	21–27	24–30
11	8–14	10–16	12–18	18–24	24–30	27–33
12	10–16	12–18	15–21	21–27	27–33	30–37
13	12–18	15–21	18–24	24–30	30–37	33–41
14	15–21	18–24	21–27	27–33	33–41	37–46
15	18–24	21–27	24–30	30–37	37–46	41–51
16	21–27	24–30	27–33	33–41	41–51	46–57
17	24–30	27–33	30–37	37–46	46–57	51–63
18	27–33	30–37	33–41	41–51	51–63	57–71
19	30–37	33–41	37–46	46–57	57–71	63–78
20	33–41	37–46	41–51	51–63	63–78	70–87
21	37–46	41–51	46–57	57–71	70–87	77–96
22	41–51	46–57	51–63	63–78	77–96	84–105
23	46–57	51–63	57–71	70–87	84–105	92–115
24	51–63	57–71	63–78	77–96	92–115	100–125
25	57–71	63–78	70–87	84–105	100–125	110–137
26	63–78	70–87	78–97	92–115	110–137	120–150
27	70–87	78–97	87–108	100–125	120–150	130–162
28	78–97	87–108	97–121	110–137	130–162	140–175
29	87–108	97–121	108–135	121–151	140–175	151–188
30	97–121	108–135	121–151	135–168	151–188	168–210
31	108–135	121–151	135–168	151–188	168–210	188–235
32	121–151	135–168	151–188	168–210	188–235	210–262
33	135–168	151–188	168–210	188–235	210–262	235–293
34	151–188	168–210	188–235	210–262	235–293	262–327
35	168–210	188–235	210–262	235–293	262–327	292–365
36	188–235	210–262	235–293	262–327	292–365	324–405
37	210–262	235–293	262–327	292–365	324–405	360–life
38	235–293	262–327	292–365	324–405	360–life	360–life
39	262–327	292–365	324–405	360–life	360–life	360–life
40	292–365	324–405	360–life	360–life	360–life	360–life
41	324–405	360–life	360–life	360–life	360–life	360–life
42	360–life	360–life	360–life	360–life	360–life	360–life
43	Life	Life	Life	Life	Life	Life

Source: U.S. Sentencing Commission (1987: 5.2).

U.S. Sentencing Commission Establishment and Purposes

Under Chapter 58, 18 U.S.C. Sec. 991,

(a) there is established as an independent commission in the judicial branch of the United States a United States Sentencing Commission which shall consist of seven voting members and one nonvoting member. The President, after consultation with representatives of judges, prosecuting attorneys, defense attorneys, law enforcement officials, senior citizens, victims of crime, and others interested in the criminal justice process, shall appoint the voting members of the Commission, by and with the advice and consent of the Senate, one of whom shall be appointed, by and with the advice and consent of the Senate, as the Chairman. At least three of the members shall be Federal judges selected after considering a list of six judges recommended to the President by the Judicial Conference of the United States. Not more than four of the members of the Commission shall be members of the same political party. The Attorney General, or his designee, shall be an ex officio, nonvoting member of the Commission. The Chairman and members of the Commission shall be subject to removal from the Commission by the President only for neglect of duty or malfeasance in office or for some other good cause shown. (b) The purposes of the United States Sentencing Commission are to:

(1) establish sentencing policies and practices for the Federal criminal justice system that—

(A) assure the meeting of the purposes of sentencing as set forth in section 3553(a)(2) of title 18, United States Code;

(B) provide certainty and fairness in meeting the purposes of sentencing, avoiding unwarranted sentencing disparities among defendants with similar records who have been found guilty of similar criminal conduct while maintaining sufficient flexibility to permit individualized sentences when warranted by mitigating or aggravating factors not taken into account in the establishment of general sentencing practices; and

(C) reflect to the extent practicable, advancement in knowledge of human behavior as it relates to the criminal justice process; and

(2) develop means of measuring the degree to which the sentencing, penal, and correctional practices are effective in meeting the purposes of sentencing as set forth in section 3553(a)(2) of title 18, United States Code (18 U.S.C. Sec. 991, 1988).

[18 U.S.C. Sec. 3553(a)(2) specifies that "The court, in determining the particular sentence to be imposed, shall consider . . . (2) the need for the sentence imposed (A) to reflect the seriousness of the offense, to promote respect for the law, and to provide just punishment for the offense; (B) to afford adequate deterrence to criminal conduct; (C) to protect the public from further crimes of the defendant; and (D) to provide the defendant with needed educational or vocational training, medical care, or other correctional treatment in the most effective manner.]

MEMBERSHIP OF THE COMMISSION

Under the provisions of 18 U.S.C. Sec. 992, "The voting members of the United States Sentencing Commission shall be appointed for six-year terms, except that the initial terms of the first members of the Commission shall be staggered so that (1) two members, including the Chairman, serve terms of six years; (2) three members serve terms of four years; and (3) two members serve terms of two years." Section 992 further specifies that no voting member may serve more than two full terms.

DUTIES AND POWERS OF THE COMMISSION

There is a wide range of duties and powers of the Commission as set forth in 18 U.S.C. Sec. 994 and Sec. 995. The major duties of the Commission include but are not limited to (1) establishing sentencing guidelines which include determinations whether to impose sentences of probation, fines, or terms of imprisonment; (2) developing general policy statements regarding the present and future application of these guidelines; (3) establishing criteria whereby a convicted offender's probation may be revoked; (4) assuring that the guidelines and policy statements are entirely neutral as to the race, sex, national origin, creed, and socioeconomic status of offenders; and (5) periodically reviewing and revising established sentencing guideline criteria.

The powers of the Commission include but are not limited to (1) establishing general policies, rules, and regulations for the Commission to follow; (2) making data and report requests from any Federal agency; (3) monitoring the performance of probation officers in relation to sentencing recommendations and issuing instructions to them regarding the application of Commission guidelines; (4) establishing a research and development program to serve as a clearinghouse for the dissemination of information about Federal sentencing practices and publishing these results; (5) collecting and disseminating information about the effectiveness of sentences imposed; (6) studying the feasibility of developing sentencing guidelines for juveniles; and (7) make recommendations to Congress about modifications or enactments of statutes relating to sentencing, penal, and correctional matters that the Commission finds to be necessary and advisable to carry out an effective, humane and rational sentencing policy.

Bibliography

ABA Journal 1987. "Should Congress Adopt Sentencing Guidelines?" July 1, 1987.

ABA Journal 1988. "Sentencing Guidelines Under Fire." April 1, 1988.

Administrative Office of the U. S. Courts 1986. *Federal Offenders in the United States*. Washington, DC: Administrative Office of the U. S. Courts.

Albonetti, Celeste 1987. "Prosecutorial Discretion: The Effects of Uncertainty." *Law and Society Review*, 21:291–313.

Allen, H., C. Eskridge, E. Latessa, and G. Vito 1985. *Probation and Parole in America*. New York, NY: Free Press.

Allen, H. and C. Simonsen 1989. *Corrections in America*. New York, NY: Macmillan.

Allinson, Richard 1982. "Crisis in the Jails: Overcrowding is Now a National Epidemic." *Corrections Magazine*, 8:18–24.

Alschuler, Albert W. 1968. "The Prosecutor's Role in Plea Bargaining." *University of Chicago Law Review*, 36:50–112.

Alschuler, Albert W. 1978. "Sentencing Reform and Prosecutorial Power: A Critique of Recent Proposals for 'Fixed' and 'Presumptive' Sentencing." *University of Pennsylvania Law Review*, 126:550–577.

Alschuler, Albert W. 1980. "Sentencing Reform and Parole Release Guidelines." *University of Colorado Law Review*, 51:237–245.

Alschuler, Albert W. 1981. "The Changing Plea Bargaining Debate." *California Law Review*, 69:652–730.

Alschuler, Albert W. 1988. "Departures and Plea Agreements Under the Sentencing Guidelines." *Federal Rules Decisions*, 117:459–476.

American Law Institute 1962. *Model Penal Code Official Draft*. Chicago, IL: American Law Institute.

American Law Institute 1985. *The Model Penal Code and Commentaries*. Philadelphia, PA: The American Law Institute.

Andenaes, J. 1975. "General Prevention Revisited: Research and Policy Implications." *Journal of Criminal Law and Criminology*, 66:338–365.

Austin, James and Barry Krisberg 1981. "Wider, Stronger, and Different Nets: The Dialectics of Criminal Justice Reform." *Journal of Research in Crime and Delinquency*, 18:165–196.

Austin, James and Barry Krisberg 1982. "The Unmet Promise of Alternatives to Incarceration." *Crime and Delinquency*, 28:374–409.

Babst, D. V., M. Koval, and M. G. Neithercutt 1972. "Relationship of Time Served to Parole Outcome for Different Classifications of Burglars Based on Males Paroled in Fifty Jurisdictions in 1968 and 1969." *Journal of Research in Crime and Delinquency,* 9:99–116.

Barak, Gregg 1980. *In Defense of Whom? A Critique of Criminal Justice Reform.* Cincinnati, OH: Anderson.

Beck, J. L. and Peter B. Hoffman 1976. "Time Served and Release Performance: A Research Note." *Journal of Research in Crime and Delinquency,* 13:127–132.

Berecochea, J. E. and D. R. Jaman 1981. *Time Served in Prison and Parole Outcome: an Experimental Study.* Report No. 2. Sacramento, CA: California Department of Corrections.

Berke, Sarah F. and D. Loseke 1981. "Handling Family Violence: Situational Determinants of Police Arrest in Domestic Disturbances." *Law and Society Review,* 15:314–344.

Bishop, D. M. 1984a. "Deterrence: A Panel Analysis." *Justice Quarterly,* 1:311–328.

Bishop, D. M. 1984b. "Legal and Extralegal Barriers to Delinquency: A Panel Analysis." *Criminology,* 22:403–419.

Bittner, Egon 1967. "The Police on Skid Row: A Study in Peace Keeping." *American Sociological Review,* 32:699–715.

Black, Donald 1970. "Production of Crime Rates." *American Sociological Review,* 35:733–748.

Black, Donald 1971. "The Social Organization of Arrest." *Stanford Law Review,* 23:1087–1111.

Black, Donald 1980. *The Mannners and Customs of the Police.* New York, NY: Academic Press.

Black, Donald and Albert J. Reiss, Jr. 1970. "Police Control of Juveniles." *American Sociological Review,* 35:63–77.

Blackmore, John 1978. "Minnesota's Community Corrections Act Takes Hold." *Corrections Magazine,* 4:46–56.

Block, Michael K. and William M. Rhodes 1987. *The Impact of the Federal Sentencing Guidelines.* Washington, DC: National Institute of Justice.

Blumberg, A. 1967. *Criminal Justice.* Chicago, IL: Quandrangle Books.

Blumstein, Alfred 1982. "On the Racial Disproportionality of United States Prison Populations." *Journal of Criminal Law and Criminology,* 73:1259–1281.

Blumstein, Alfred 1983a. "Selective Incapacitation as a Means of Crime Control." *American Behavioral Scientist,* 27:87–108.

Blumstein, Alfred 1983b. "The Impact of Changes in Sentencing Policy on Prison Populations." in Alfred Blumstein, et al. (eds.) *Research on Sentencing: The Search for Reform,* Vol. II, pp. 460–489. Washington, DC: National Academy Press.

Blumstein, Alfred 1984a. "Planning for Future Prison Needs." *University of Illinois Law Review,* 2:207–230.

Blumstein, Alfred 1984b. "Sentencing Reforms: Impact and Implications." *Judicature,* 68:129–139.

Blumstein, Alfred 1987. "The Search for the Elusive Common 'Principle.' " *Northwestern University Law Review,* 82:43–51.

Blumstein, Alfred et al. 1983. *Research on Sentencing: The Search for Reform.* Washington, DC: National Academy Press.

Blumstein, Alfred et al. 1986. *Criminal Careers and "Career Criminals."* Washington, DC: National Academy Press.

Blumstein, Alfred, J. Cohen, J. Roth, and C. Visher 1986. *Criminal Careers and "Career Criminals."* Washington, DC: National Academy Press.

Blumstein, Alfred and Richard C. Larson 1971. "Problems in Modeling and Measuring Recidivism." *Journal of Research in Crime and Delinquency*, 8:124–132.

Breed, A. 1984. "Don't Throw the Parole Baby Out with the Justice Bath Water." *Federal Probation*, 48:ll–15.

Brewer, David, Gerald E. Beckett, and Norman Holt 1981. "Determinate Sentencing in California: The First Year's Experience." *Journal of Research in Crime and Delinquency*, 18:200–231.

Brookhart, Duane E., J. B. Ruark, and Douglas E. Scoven 1976. "A Strategy for the Prediction of Work Release Success." *Criminal Justice and Behavior*, 3:321–324.

Bureau of Justice Statistics 1985. *Examining Recidivism.* Washington, DC: U. S. Department of Justice.

Bureau of Justice Statistics 1987. *Federal Offenses and Offenders: Sentencing and Time Served.* Washington, DC: U. S. Department of Justice.

Bureau of Justice Statistics 1988a. *Prisoners in 1987.* Washington, DC: U. S. Department of Justice.

Bureau of Justice Statistics 1988b. *Profile of State Prison Inmates, 1986.* Washington, DC: U. S. Department of Justice.

Carney, Robert 1982. "New Jersey: Overcrowding is Blamed on the States." *Corrections Magazine*, 8:24–27.

Carroll, Leo 1974. *Hacks, Blacks, and Cons.* Lexington, MA: Lexington Books.

Carter, R. M. and L. R. Wilkins 1967. "Some Factors in Sentencing Policy." *Journal of Criminal Law, Criminology, and Police Science*, 58:503–514.

Casper, J. D. and D. Brereton 1984. "Evaluating Criminal Justice Reforms." *Law and Society Review*, 18:121–144.

Chaiken, Jan and Marcia Chaiken 1982. *Varieties of Criminal Behavior.* Santa Monica, CA: Rand.

Chambliss, William 1969. *Crime and the Legal Process.* New York, NY: McGraw-Hill.

Christianson, Scott 1981. "Our Black Prisons." *Crime and Delinquency*, 27:364–375.

Church, Thomas W., Jr. 1976. "Plea Bargaining, Concessions, and the Courts: Analysis of of a Quasi-Experiment." *Law and Society Review*, 10:377–410.

Clark, D. 1988. "The Future of Federal Parole: Interview with Benjamin F. Baer." *Corrections Today*, 50:32–36.

Clarke, R. V. G. 1966. "Approved School Boy Absconders and Corporal Punishment." *British Journal of Criminology*, 6:364–375.

Clarke, Stevens H. 1984. "North Carolina's Determinate Sentencing Legislation." *Judicature*, 68:140–152.

Clear, Todd R. and George F. Cole 1986. *American Corrections*. Monterey, CA: Brooks/Cole Publishing Company.

Cochran, D., R. Corbett, and J. Byrne 1986. "Intensive Probation Supervision in Massachusetts: A Case Study in Change." *Federal Probation*, 50:32–41.

Coffee, John C. and Michael Tonry 1983. "Hard Choices: Critical Trade-Offs in the Implementation of Sentencing Reform through Guidelines" in Michael Tonry and Franklin E. Zimring (eds.), *Reform and Punishment: Essays on Criminal Sentencing*. Chicago, IL: University of Chicago Press.

Cohen, Jacqueline 1983a. "Incapacitation as a Strategy for Crime Control: Possibilities and Pitfalls." in Alfred Blumstein et al. (eds.), *Research on Sentencing: The Search for Reform, Volume II* (pp. 1–84). Washington, DC: National Academy Press.

Cohen, Jacqueline 1983b. "Incapacitation as a Strategy for Crime Control." in M. Tonry and N. Morris (eds.) *Crime and Justice: an Anual Review of Research, Vol. 5*. Chicago, IL: University of Chicago Press.

Cohen, Jacqueline and Michael H. Tonry 1983. "Sentencing Reforms and Their Impacts." in Alfred Blumstein et al. (eds.) *Research on Sentencing: The Search for Reform*, Vol. II, pp. 305–459.

Coleman, James W. 1985. *The Criminal Elite: The Sociology of White Collar Crime*. New York, NY: St. Martin's Press.

Cullen, Francis, William Maakestad, and Gray Cavender 1987. *Corporate Crime Under Attack: The Ford Pinto Case and Beyond*. Cincinnati, OH: Anderson.

Davis, David S. 1983. "The Production of Crime Policies." *Crime and Social Justice*, 20:121–137.

Davis, Kenneth C. 1969. *Discretionay Justice: A Preliminary Inquiry*. Baton Rouge, LA: Louisiana State University Press.

Davis, Kenneth C. 1975. *Police Discretion*. St. Paul, MN: West Publishing Company.

Decker, Scott H. 1985. "A Systematic Analysis of Diversion: Net Widening and Beyond." *Journal of Criminal Justice*, 13:207–216.

Decker, Scott H. and C. W. Kohfeld 1984. "A Deterrence Study of the Death Penalty in Illinois, 1933–1980." *Journal of Criminal Justice*, 12:367–378.

Doerner, William G. and Ben S. Wright 1990. "Federal Sentencing Reform in Light of Incapacitation and Recidivism." (forthcoming)

Dowling, John 1988. "Sentencing Discretion in Pennsylvania: Has the Pendulum Returned to the Trial Judge?" *Duquesne Law Review*, 26:925–939.

Eakin, J. Michael 1987. "Sentencing Guidelines Are Needed to Assure Uniformity." *The Prosecutor*, 21:5–6.

Ehrlich, I. 1977. "Capital Punishment and Deterrence: Some Further Thoughts and Additional Evidence." *Journal of Political Economy*, 85:741–788.

Ehrhardt, Charles W. et al. 1973. "The Aftermath of Furman: The Florida Experience." *Journal of Criminal Law and Criminology*, 64:2–21.

Eisenstein, James 1977. *Counsel for the United States: Attorneys in the Political and Legal System*. Baltimore, MD: Johns Hopkins University Press.

Eisenstein, James 1988. *The Contours of Justice: Communities and Their Counties.* Boston, MA: Little Brown.

Eisenstein, James and Herbert Jacob 1977. *Felony Justice: An Organizational Analysis of Criminal Courts.* Boston, MA: Little, Brown.

Erickson, M. L., J. P. Gibbs, and G. F. Jensen 1977. "The Deterrence Doctrine and the Perceived Certainty of Legal Punishments." *American Sociological Review,* 42:305–317.

Eskridge, Chris W. 1986. "Sentencing Guidelines: To Be or Not To Be." *Federal Probation,* 51:7076.

Federal Bureau of Prisons 1984. *Comprehensive Crime Control Act of 1984: Inmate Systems Management.* Washington, DC: U. S. Department of Justice.

Feeley, Malcolm 1979a. "Plea Bargaining in the Lower Courts." *Law and Society Review,* 13:461–466.

Feeley, Malcolm 1979b. *The Process is the Punishment: Handling Cases in a Lower Criminal Court.* New York, NY: Russell Sage Foundation.

Feinberg, Kenneth 1984. "Selective Incapacitation and the Effort to Improve the Fairness of Existing Sentencing Practices." *Review of Law and Social Change,* 12:53–66.

Fennel, S. A. and W. N. Hall 1980. "Due Process at Sentencing: An Empirical and Legal Analysis of the Disclosure of the Presentence Report in Federal Courts." *Harvard Law Review,* 93:1615–1697.

Fine, R. A. 1986. *Escape of the Guilty.* New York, NY: Dodd Mead.

Fischer, Daryl R. 1987. "Parole Risk Assessment: A Tool for Managing Prison Populations and Recidivism" in Edward E. Rhine and Ronald W. Jackson (eds.) *Observations on Parole.* Boulder, CO: National Institute of Corrections.

Fisher, Franklin M. and Joseph B. Kadane 1983. "Empirically Based Sentencing Guidelines and Ethical Considerations" in Alfred Blumstein et al. (eds.), *Research on Sentencing: The Search for Reform, Volume II.* Washington, DC: National Academy Press, pp. 184–193.

Forst, Brian E. 1977. "The Deterrent Effect of Capital Punishment: A Cross-State Analysis of the 1960s." *Minnesota Law Review,* 61:743–767.

Forst, Brian E. 1983. "Selective Incapacitation: An Idea Whose Time Has Come?" *Federal Probation,* 46:19–23.

Forst, Brian E. 1984. "Selective Incapacitation: A Sheep in Wolf's Clothing?" *Judicature,* 68:153–160.

Forst, Brian E. and William M. Rhodes 1982. "Structuring the Exercise of Sentencing Discretion in the Federal Courts." *Federal Probation,* 46:3–13.

Forst, Martin 1982. *Sentencing Reform: Experiments in Reducing Disparity.* Beverly Hills, CA: Sage.

Forst, Martin and J. Brady 1983. "Effects of Determinate Sentencing on Inmate Misconduct in Prison" in N. Parisi (ed.) *Coping with Imprisonment.* Beverly Hills, CA: Sage.

Fox, James G. 1982. *Organizational and Racial Conflict in Maximum Security Prisons.* Lexington, MA: Lexington Books.

Fox, James G. 1983. "The New Right and Social Justice: Implications for the Prisoners' Movement." *Crime and Social Justice,* 20:63–75.

Fox, James G. 1986. "Conservative Social Policy, Social Control, and Racism: The Politics of New York State Prison Expansion, 1975–1985." *Working Papers in European Criminology*, 7:93–111.

Gardiner, John A. 1969. *Traffic and the Police: Variations in Law Enforcement Policy*. Cambridge, MA: Harvard University Press.

Gatz, Nick and Gennaro F. Vito 1982. "The Use of the Determinate Sentence— An Historical Perspective: A Research Note." *Journal of Criminal Justice*, 10:323–329.

Geerken, M. R. and Walter R. Gove 1977. "Deterrence, Overload, and Incapacitation: An Empirical Evaluation." *Social Forces*, 56:424–447.

Gibbs, J. P. 1968. "Crime, Punishment, and Deterrence." *Social Science Quarterly*, 48:515–530.

Gibbs, J. P. 1975. *Crime, Punishment, and Deterrence*. New York, NY: Elsevier.

Goldkamp, J. 1979. *Two Classes of Accused: A Study of Bail and Detention in America*. Cambridge, MA: Ballinger Publishing Company.

Goldstein, Herman 1977. *Policing in a Free Society*. Cambridge, MA: Ballinger.

Goldstein, Joseph 1969. "Police Discretion Not to Invoke the Criminal Process: Low-Visibility Decisions in the Administration of Justice." *Yale Law Journal*, 69:556–562.

Goodstein, Lynne 1980. "Psychological Effects of the Predictability of Prison Release: Implications for the Sentencing Debate." *Criminology*, 18:363–384.

Goodstein, Lynne 1982. "Quasi-Experimental Test of Prisoner Reaction to Determinate and Indeterminate Sentencing" in N. Parisi (ed.) *Coping with Imprisonment*. Beverly Hills, CA: Sage.

Goodstein, Lynne and John Hepburn 1985. *Determinate Sentencing and Imprisonment: A Failure of Reform*. Cincinnati, OH: Anderson.

Gottfredson, Don M. 1987. "The Problem of Crowding: A System Out of Control" in Stephen D. Gottfredson and Sean McConville (eds.) *America's Correctional Crisis*, pp. 137–159. Westport, CT: Greenwood Press.

Gottfredson, Don M., Michael R. Gottfredson, and James Garofalo 1977. "Time Served in Prison and Parole Outcomes Among Parolee Risk Categories." *Journal of Criminal Justicei*, 5:1–12.

Gottfredson, Don M. et al. 1975. "Making Paroling Policy Explicit." *Crime and Delinquency*, 21:34–44.

Gottfredson, Michael R. 1979. "Parole Guidelines and the Reduction of Sentencing Disparity: A Preliminary Study." *Journal of Research in Crime and Delinquency*, 16:218–231.

Gottfredson, Michael R. and Don M. Gottfredson 1980. *Decision Making in Criminal Justice: Toward the Rational Exercise of Discretion*. Cambridge, MA: Ballinger Publishing Company.

Gottfredson, Stephen D. and Don M. Gottfredson 1985. "Selective Incapacitation?" *The Annals*, 478:135–149.

Gottfredson, Stephen D. and Sean McConville (eds.) 1987. *America's Correctional Crisis: Prison Populations and Public Policy*. Westport, CT: Greenwood Press.

Greenburg, David and Drew Humphries 1980. "The Cooperation of Fixed Sentencing Reform." *Crime and Delinquency*, 26:206–225.

Greenwood, Peter W. (with Allan Abrahamse) 1982. *Selective Incapacitation*. Santa Monica, CA: Rand.

Greenwood, Peter W. and Andrew von Hirsch 1984 "Selective Incapacitation: Two Views of a Compelling Concept." *NIJ Reports*. Washington, DC: U. S. Department of Justice, National Institute of Justice.

Griswold, David B. 1978. "A Comparison of Recidivism Measures." *Journal of Criminal Justice*, 6:247–252.

Griswold, David B. 1985. "Florida's Sentencing Guidelines: Progression or Regression?" *Federal Probation*, 49:25–32.

Griswold, David B. 1987. "Deviation from Sentencing Guidelines: The Issue of an Unwarranted Disparity." *Journal of Criminal Justice*, 15:317–329.

Grunin, S. K. and J. Watkins 1987. "The Investigative Role of the United States Probation Officer Under Sentencing Guidelines." *Federal Probation*, 51:43–47.

Hagan, J. 1985. "The Social and Legal Construction of Criminal Justice: A Study of the Presentence Process." *Social Problems*, 22:620–637.

Hepburn, John R. 1978. "Race and the Decision to Arrest: An Analysis of Warrants Issued." *Journal of Research in Crime and Delinquency*, 15: 54–73.

Hepburn, John R. and Lynne Goodstein 1986 "Organizational Imperatives and Sentencing Reform Implementations: The Impact of Prison Practices and Priorities on the Attainment of the Objective of Determinate Sentencing." *Crime and Delinquency*, 32:339–365.

Heumann, Milton 1978. *Plea Bargaining: The Experience of Prosecutors, Judges, and Defense Attorneys*. Chicago: University Chicago, IL: University of Chicago Press.

Hewitt, John D. and Bert Little 1981. "Examining the Research Underlying the Sentencing Guidelines Concept in Denver, Colorado: A Partial Replication of a Reform Effort." *Journal of Criminal Justice*, 9:51–62.

Hoffman, Peter B. and James L. Beck 1984 "Burnout—Age at Release from Prison and Recidivism." *Journal of Criminal Justice*, 12:617–623.

Hoffman, Peter B. and Barbara Stone-Meierhoefer 1980 "Reporting Recidivism Rates: The Criterion and Follow-Up Issues." *Journal of Criminal Justice*, 8:53–60.

Hoffman, Peter B. et al. 1986. "Sentencing Reform, Sentencing Guidelines, and Related Issues: A Partial Bibliography." *Journal of Criminal Justice*, 14:545–569.

Hollinger, R. C. and J. P. Clark 1983. "Deterrence in the Workplace: Perceived Certainty, Perceived Severity of Employee Theft." *Social Forces*, 62:398–419.

Hussey, Frederick A. 1978. "Parole: Villian or Victim in the Determinate Sentencing Debate?" *Crime and Delinquency*, 24:81–88.

Hutto, D. 1988. "Corrections Partnership—the Public and Private Sectors Work Together." *Corrections Today*, 50:20–22.

Jacobs, James 1977. *Stateville: The Penitentiary in Mass Society*. Chicago, IL: University of Chicago Press.

Jacobs, James 1979. "Race Relations and the Prison Subculture" in N. Morris and M. Tonry (eds.) *Crime and Justice: An Annual Review of Research*, Vol. 1. Chicago, IL: University of Chicago Press.

Jacobs, James 1984. "The Politics of Prison Expansion." *New York University Review of Law and Social Change*, 12:1.

Janus, Michael 1985. "Selective Incapacitation—Have We Tried It? Does It Work?" *Journal of Criminal Justice*, 13:117–129.

Jensen, G. F., M. L. Erickson, and J. P. Gibbs 1978 "Perceived Risk of Punishment and Self-Reported Delinquency." *Social Forces*, 57:57–78.

Johnson, Perry 1978. "The Role of Penal Quarantine in Reducing Violent Crime." *Crime and Delinquency*, 24:465–485.

Kadish, Sanford 1962. "Legal Norm and Discretion in the Police and Sentencing Process." *Harvard Law Review*, 75:25–32.

Kitchener, Howard, Annesley K. Schmidt, and Daniel Glaser 1977. "How Persistent Is Post-Prison Success?" *Federal Probation*, 41:9–14.

Kittrie, Nicholas 1971. *The Right To Be Different*. Baltimore, MD: Penguin Books.

Klockars, Carl B. 1985. *The Idea of Police*. Beverly Hills, CA: Sage (pp. 92–121).

Knapp, Kay A. 1982. "Impact of the Minnesota Sentencing Guidelines on Sentencing Practices." *Hamline Law Review*, 5:237–256.

Knapp, Kay A. 1984a. *The Impact of The Minnesota Guidelines*. St. Paul, MN: Minnesota Sentencing Commission.

Knapp, Kay A. 1984b. "What Sentencing Reform in Minnesota Has and Has Not Accomplished." *Judicature*, 68:181–189.

Knapp, Kay A. 1986. "Proactive Policy Analysis of Minnesota's Prison Populations." *Criminal Justice Policy Review*, 1:37–57.

Kozol, Henry, Richard Boucher, and Ralph Garofalo 1972. "The Diagnosis and Treatment of Dangerousness." *Crime and Delinquency*, 18:371–392.

Kramer, John H. and R. L. Lubitz 1985. "Pennsylvania's Sentencing Reform: The Impact of Commission Established Guidelines." *Crime and Delinquency*, 31:461–480.

Kramer, John H., R. L. Lubitz, and C. Kempinen 1987. *The Impact of Pennsylvania Sentencing Guidelines: An Analysis of System Adjustments to Sentencing Reform*. University Park, PA: Pennsylvania Commission on Sentencing.

Krauth, Barbara A. 1987. "Parole: Controversial Component of the Criminal Justice System" in Edward E. Rhine and Ronald W. Jackson (eds.) *Observations On Parole*. Boulder, CO: National Institute of Corrections.

Lab, Steven P. 1988. "Analyzing Change in Crime and Delinquency Rates: The Case for Cohort Analysis" *Criminal Justice Research Bulletin*, Volume 10, No. 3. Huntsville, TX: Criminal Justice Center, Sam Houston State University.

LaFave, Wayne R. 1965 *Arrest*. Boston, MA: Little, Brown and Company (pp. 75–82).

Lagoy, Stephen P., Frederick A. Hussey, and John H. Kramer 1978. "A Comparative Assessment of Determinate Sentencing in the Four Pioneer States." *Crime and Delinquency*, 24:385–400.

Lanza-Kaduce, L. 1988. "Perceptual Deterrence and Drinking and Driving Among College Students." *Criminology*, 26:321–342.

Levin, Marshall A. 1984. "Maryland's Sentencing Guidelines: A System By and For Judges." *Judicature*, 684–5:172–180.

Liman, Lewis J. 1987. "The Constitutional Infirmities of the U. S. Sentencing Commission." *Yale Law Journal*, 96:1363–1388.

Lipson, Albert J. and Mark A. Peterson 1980. *California Justice Under Determinate Sentencing: A Review and Agenda for Research.* Santa Monica, CA: Rand.

Lowe, Chip J. 1987. "Modern Sentencing Reform: A Preliminary Analysis of the Proposed Federal Sentencing Guidelines." *American Criminal Law Review*, 25:1–58.

Lubitz, R. and C. Kempinen 1987. *The Impact of Pennsylvania Sentencing Guidelines: An Analysis of System Adjustments To Sentencing Reform.* University Park, PA: Pennsylvania Commission on Sentencing.

Lundman, Richard J. 1979. "Organizational Norms and Police Discretion: An Observational Study of Police Work with Traffic Law Violators." *Criminology*, 17:159–171.

Lundman, Richard J., Richard E. Sykes, and John P. Clark 1978. "Police Control of Juveniles: A Replication." *Journal of Research in Crime and Delinquency*, 15:74–91.

Maltz, Michael 1984. *Recidivism.* Orlando, FL: Academic Press, Inc.

Mather, L. 1979. *Plea Bargaining On Trial? The Process of Criminal Case Disposition.* Lexington, MA: Lexington Books.

Maynard, Douglas 1984. "The Structure of Discourse in Misdemeanor Plea Bargaining." *Law and Society Review*, 18:75–104.

Maynard, Douglas 1984. *Inside Plea Bargaining: The Language of Negotiation.* New York, NY: Plenum Press.

Mays, G. Larry and Frances P. Bernat 1988. "Jail Reform Litigation: The Problem of Rights and Remedies." *American Journal of Criminal Justice*, 12: (forthcoming).

Mays, G. Larry and Joel A. Thompson 1988a. "Mayberry Revisited: The Characteristics and Operations of America's Small Jails." *Justice Quarterly*, 5:421–440.

Mays, G. Larry and Joel A. Thompson 1988b. "The Political and Organizational Context of American Jails." Paper presented at the annual meeting of the Academy of Criminal Justice Sciences. San Francisco, CA, April 4–9.

McCloskey, J. 1985. "The Effectiveness of Independent Sentencing Commission Guidelines: An Analysis of Appellate Court Decisions in Two Jurisdictions." Unpublished paper presented at the annual meeting of the American Society of Criminology. San Diego, CA.

McCoy, Candace 1984. "Determinate Sentencing, Plea Bargaining Bans, and Hydraulic Discretion in California." *Justice System Journal*, 9:256–275.

McFarland, S. G. 1983. "Is Capital Punishment a Short-Term Deterrent to Homicide?: A Study of the Effects of Four Recent American Executions." *Journal of Criminal Law and Criminology*, 74:1014–1032.

McGahey, R. M. 1980. "Dr. Ehrlich's Magic Bullet: Economic Theory, Econometrics, and the Death Penalty." *Crime and Delinquency*, 26:485–502.

McKelvey, Blake 1977. *American Prisons: A History of Good Intentions.* Montclair, NJ: Patterson-Smith.

Menard, Scott and Herbert Covey 1983. "Community Alternatives and Rearrest in Colorado." *Criminal Justice and Behavior*, 10:93–108.

Michalowski, Raymond 1981. "The Politics of the Right." *Crime and Social Justice*, 15:29–35.

Michalowski, Raymond 1985. *Order, Law, and Crime.* New York, NY: Random House.

Miethe, Terance D. 1987. "Charging and Plea Bargaining Practices Under Determinate Sentencing: An Investigation of the Hydraulic Displacement of Discretion." *Journal of Criminal Law and Criminology*, 78:155–176.

Miethe, Terance D. and Charles A. Moore 1985. "Socioeconomic Disparities Under Determinate Sentencing Systems: A Comparison of Preguideline and Postguideline Practices in Minnesota." *Criminology*, 23:337–363.

Miethe, Terance D. and Charles A. Moore 1988. "Officials' Reactions to Sentencing Guidelines." *Journal of Research in Crime and Delinquency*, 252:170–187.

Miller, Rod and Bill Clark 1987. *Maine's Jails: Progress Through Partnership.* Washington, DC: National Institute of Justice.

Monahan, John 1981. *Predicting Violent Behavior.* Beverly Hills, CA: Sage.

Monkkonen, Eric H. 1975. *The Dangerous Class: Crime and Poverty in Columbus, OH, 1860–1885.* Cambridge, MA: Harvard University Press.

Moore, Charles A. and Terance D. Miethe 1986. "Regulated and Unregulated Sentencing Decisions: An Analysis of First-Year Practices Under Minnesota's Felony Sentencing Guidelines." *Law and Society Review*, 20:253–277.

Moore, Mark, et al. 1984. *Dangerous Offenders: The Elusive Target of Justice.* Cambridge, MA: Harvard University Press.

Morris, Norval 1977. "Towards Principled Sentencing." *Maryland Law Review*, 37:267–285.

Morrison, Alan 1986. "Guidelines Under Fire." *National Law Journal.* (June):46–48.

Morrison, Alan B. 1987. "A Fatal Flaw." *The National Law Journal*, (January):27–29.

Nacci, Peter L. 1978. "The Importance of Recidivism Research in Understanding Criminal Behavior." *Journal of Criminal Justice*, 6:253–260.

Nagin, Daniel 1979. "The Impact of Determinate Sentencing Legislation on Prison Population and Sentence Length: A California Case Study." *Public Policy*, 27:69–98.

Nardulli, Peter F., Roy B. Flemming, and James Eisenstein 1985. "Criminal Courts and Bureaucratic Justice: Concessions and Consensus in the Guilty Plea Process." *Journal of Criminal Law and Criminology*, 76:1103–1131.

National Institute of Justice 1984. *Corrections and The Private Sector.* Washington, DC: U. S. Department of Justice.

National Institute of Justice 1987a. "The Impact of the Federal Sentencing Guidelines." *NIJ Reports: Research in Action.* Washington, DC: U. S. Department of Justice.

National Institute of Justice 1987b. *Contracting for The Operation of Prisons and Jails.* Washington, DC: U. S. Department of Justice.

Padgett, J. 1985. "The Emergent Organization of Plea Bargaining." *American Journal of Sociology*, 90:753–800.

Palmer, John W. 1985. *Constitutional Rights of Prisoners (3rd ed.)*. Cincinnati, OH: Anderson.

Parent, D. 1988. *Structuring Criminal Sentences*. Stoneham, MA: Butterworth Legal Publications.

Parisi, Nicolette 1981. "A Taste of the Bars?" *Journal of Criminal Law and Criminology*, 72:1109–1123.

Passell, P. 1975. "The Deterrent Effect of the Death Penalty: A Statistical Test." *Stanford Law Review*, 28:61–80.

Passell, P. and J. B. Taylor 1977. "The Deterrent Effect of Capital Punishment: Another View." *American Economic Review*, 65:445–451.

Paternoster, Raymond and Tim Bynum 1982. "The Justice Model as Ideology: A Critical Look at the Impetus for Sentencing Reform." *Contemporary Crisis*, 6:7–24.

Paternoster, Raymond et al. 1982. "Causal Ordering in Deterrence Research: An Examination of the Perceptions-Behavior Relationship." in J. Hagan (ed.) *Deterrence Reconsidered: Methodological Innovations*, pp. 55–70. Beverly Hills, CA: Sage.

Paternoster, Raymond et al. 1985. "Assessments of Risk and Behavioral Experience: An Exploratory Study of Change." *Criminology*, 23:417–436.

Pearson, F. S. 1987. "Taking Quality into Account: Assessing the Benefits and Costs of New Jersey's Intensive Supervision Program" in B. McCarthy (ed.) *Intermediate Punishments: Intensive Supervision, Home Confinement, and Electronic Surveillance*. Monsey, NY: Willow Tree Press.

Pearson, F. S. and D. Bibel 1986. "New Jersey's Intensive Supervision Program: What is It Like? Is It Working?" *Federal Probation*, 50:25–31.

Pepinsky, Harold E. 1976a. *Crime and Conflict: A Study of Law and Society*. New York, NY: Academic Press.

Pepinsky, Harold E. 1976b. "Police Offense-Reporting Behavior." *Journal of Research in Crime and Delinquency*, 13:33–47.

Pepinsky, Harold E. 1978. "Discretion and Crime Legislation" in Margaret Evans (ed.) *Discretion and Control* (pp. 27–40). Beverly Hills, CA: Sage.

Pestello, H. F. 1984. "Deterrence: A Reconceptualization." *Crime and Delinquency*, 30:593–609.

Petersilia, Joan M. 1980. "Criminal Career Research: A Review of Recent Research" in M. Tonry and N. Morris (eds.) *Crime and Justice: An Annual Review of Research*. Chicago, IL: University of Chicago Press.

Petersilia, Joan M. 1985. *Probation and Felony Offenders*. Washington, DC: Bureau of Justice Statistics.

Petersilia, Joan M. 1987. *Expanding Options for Criminal Sentencing*. Santa Monica, CA: The Rand Corporation.

Petersilia, Joan M. and Susan Turner 1985 *Guideline-Based Justice: The Implications for Racial Minorities*. Santa Monica, CA: Rand.

Phillips, D. P. 1980. "The Deterrent Effect of Capital Punishment." *American Journal of Sociology*, 86:139–148.

Phillips, L., S. Ray, and H. L. Votey 1984. "Forecasting Highway Casualties: The British Road Safety Act and a Sense of Déja Vu." *Journal of Criminal Justice*, 12:101–114.

Piliavin, Irving and Scott Briar 1964. "Police Encounters with Juveniles." *American Journal of Sociology*, 70:206–214.

Platt, Tony 1982. "Crime and Punishment in the United States: Immediate and Long-Term Reforms from a Marxist Perspective." *Crime and Social Justice*, 18:38–45.

Ploscowe, Morris 1935. "The Investigative Magistrate (Juge D'Instruction) in European Criminal Procedure." *Michigan Law Review*, 33:1010–1036.

Pritchard, David A. 1979. "Stable Predictors of Recidivism: A Summary." *Criminology*, 17:15–21.

Randall, Sharon 1989. "Sensible Sentencing." *State Legislatures*, 15:14–18.

Rankin, A. 1964. "The Effect of Pretrial Detention." *New York University Law Review*, 39:641–655.

Reckless, Walter C. 1967. *The Crime Problem* (4th ed.). New York, NY: Appleton-Century- Crofts (pp. 673–674).

Reiman, Jeffrey 1979. *The Rich Get Richer and The Poor Get Prison*. New York, NY: Wiley.

Reiman, Jeffrey and Sue Headlee 1981. "Marxism and Criminal Justice Policy." *Crime and Delinquency*, 27:24–47.

Reiss, Jr., Albert J. 1971. *The Police and The Public*. New Haven, CT: Yale University Press.

Remington, F. J. et al. 1969. *Criminal Justice Administration: Materials and Cases*. Indianapolis, IN: Bobbs-Merrill.

Rhodes, William M. and Catherine Conly 1981. "Federal Sentencing Guidelines: Will They Shift Sentencing Discretion from Judges to Prosecutors?" in James A. Cramer (ed.) *Courts and Judges. Sage Criminal Justice System Annuals, Vol. 15*. Beverly Hills, CA: Sage.

Robbins, I. 1988. *The Legal Dimensions of Private Incarceration*. Washington, DC: American Bar Association.

Robinson, Paul H. 1986. "Dissent from the United States Sentencing Commission's Proposed Guidelines." *Journal of Criminal Law and Criminology*, 77:1112–1125.

Robinson, Paul H. 1987a. *Dissenting View of Commissioner Paul H. Robinson on The Promulgation of Sentencing Guidelines by The United States Sentencing Commission*. Washington, DC: U. S. Government Printing Office.

Robinson, Paul H. 1987b. "Hybrid Principles for the Distribution of Criminal Sanctions." *Northwestern University Law Review*, 82:19–42.

Robinson, Paul H. 1988. "Legality and Discretion in the Distribution of Criminal Sanctions." *Harvard Journal On Legislation*, 25:393–460.

Rosecrance, John 1985. "The Probation Officer's Search for Credibility: Ball Park Recommendations." *Crime and Delinquency*, 31:539–554.

Rosecrance, John 1988. "Maintaining the Myth of Individualized Justice: Probation Presentence Reports." *Justice Quarterly*, 5:235–256.

Rosett, A. and Donald R. Cressey 1976. *Justice By Consent*. Philadelphia, PA: Lippincott.

Ross, H. L. 1982. "Interrupted Time Series Studies of Deterrence of Drinking and Driving" in J. Hagan (ed.) *Deterrence Reconsidered: Methodological Innovations*, pp. 71–98. Beverly Hills, CA: Sage.

Rossi, Peter H. et al. 1974. "The Seriousness of Crimes: Normative Structure and Individual Differences." *American Sociological Review*, 39:224–237.

Rothman, David 1983. "Sentencing Reform in Historical Perspective." *Crime and Delinquency*, 29:631–647.

Rubinstein, Jonathan 1973. *City Police*. New York, NY: Farrar, Straus, and Giroux.

Rusche, Georg 1978. "Labor Market and Penal Sanctions: Thoughts on the Sociology of Criminal Justice." *Crime and Social Justice*, 10:2–8.

Rush, C. and J. Robertson 1987. "Presentence Reports: The Utility of Information to the Sentencing Decision." *Law and Human Behavior*, 11:147–155.

Saltzman, L. et al. 1982. "Deterrent and Experiential Effects: The Problem of Causal Order in Perceptual Deterrence Research." *Journal of Research in Crime and Delinquency*, 19:172–189.

Sampson, R. J. 1986. "Crime in Cities: The Effects of Formal and Informal Social Control" in A. J. Reiss and M. Tonry (eds.) *Communities and Crime (Crime and Justice*, Vol. 8), pp. 271–312. Chicago, IL: University of Chicago Press.

Sanborn, J. B. 1986. "A Historical Sketch of Plea Bargaining." *Justice Quarterly*, 3:111–138.

Saxton, S. 1988. "Contracting for Services—Different Facilities, Different Needs." *Corrections Today*, 50:16–18.

Schulhofer, Stephen J. 1980. "Due Process in Sentencing." *University of Pennsylvania Law Review*, 128:733–828.

Senate Report 1980 No. 96–553, pp. 378, 662.

Shane-Dubow, Sandra, Alice P. Brown, and Erik Olsen 1985 *Sentencing Reform in The United States: History, Content, and Effect*. Washington, DC: National Institute of Justice.

Sherman, Lawrence 1985. "Causes of Police Behavior: The Current State of Quantitative Research" in Abraham S. Blumberg and Elaine Niederhoffer (eds.) *The Ambivalent Force: Perspectives on the Police (3rd Ed.)* (pp. 183–195).

Sherman, L. W. and R. A. Berk 1984. "The Specific Deterrent Effect of Arrest for Domestic Assault." *American Sociological Review*, 49:261–272.

Shoham, S. G. 1974. "Punishment and Traffic Offenses." *Traffic Quarterly*, 28:61–73.

Shover, Neal and Werner Einstadter 1988. *Analyzing American Corrections*. Belmont, CA: Wadsworth Publishing Company.

Silets, Harvey M. and Susan W. Brenner 1986. "Commentary on the Preliminary Draft of the Sentencing Guidelines Issued by the U. S. Sentencing Commission in September, 1986." *Journal of Criminal Law and Criminology*, 77:1069–1111.

Simon, David and D. Stanley Eitzen 1986. *Elite Deviance (2nd Ed.)*. Boston, MA: Allyn and Bacon.

Sleffel, Linda 1977. *The Law and the Dangerous Criminal: Statutory Attempts At Definition and Control*. Lexington, MA: Lexington Books.

Smith, Douglas A. and Christy A. Visher 1985 "Street-Level Justice: Situational Determinants of Police Arrest Decisions." *Social Problems*, 29:167–177.

Social Psychiatry Research Associates 1968. *Public Knowledge of Criminal Penalties: A Research Report.* Washington, DC: Social Psychiatry Research Associates.

Sparks, Richard F. 1983. "The Construction of Sentencing Guidelines: A Methodological Critique" in Alfred Blumstein, et al., *Research on Sentencing: The Search for Reform, Volume II.* Washington, DC: National Academy Press, pp., 194–264.

State of Pennsylvania 1986. *Sentencing Guidelines Implementation Manual.* State College, PA: Pennsylvania Commission on Sentencing.

State of Washington 1983. *Sentencing Guidelines Commission: Report to the Legislature.* Olympia, WA: Sentencing Guidelines Commission.

Steadman, Henry 1972. "The Psychiatrist as a Conservative Agent of Social Control." *Social Problems,* 20:263–271.

Steadman, Henry 1977. "A New Look at Recidivism among Patuxent Inmates." *The Bulletin of the American Academy of Psychiatry and the Law,* 5:200–209.

Steadman, Henry 1982. "A Situational Approach to Violence." *International Journal of Law and Psychiatry,* 5:171–186.

Stier, Serena 1987. "Hybrids and Dangerousness." *Northwestern University Law Review,* 82:52–63.

Strasser, Fred 1989. "Making the Punishment Fit the Crime. . .And the Prison Budget." *Governing,* 2:36–41.

Sudnow, David N. 1965. "Normal Crimes: Sociological Features of the Penal Code in a Public Defender's Office." *Social Problems,* 12:255–276.

Sullivan, Michael P. 1987. "Parole Guidelines: An Effective Prison Population Management Tool" in Edward E. Rhine and Ronald W. Jackson (eds.) *Observations on Parole.* Boulder, CO: National Institute of Corrections.

Sutherland, Edwin 1950. "The Diffusion of Sexual Psychopath Laws." *American Journal of Sociology,* 56:142–148.

Sykes, Richard F., James C. Fox, and John P. Clark 1976. "A Socio-Legal Theory of Police Discretion" in Arthur Niederhoffer and Abraham S. Blumberg (eds.) *The Ambivalent Force (2nd Ed.)* (pp. 171–183). Hinsdale, IL: Dryden Press.

Taft, Philip B. Jr. 1979. "Backed Up in Jail." *Corrections Magazine,* 5:26–33.

Taylor, Elizabeth L. 1979. "In Search of Equity: The Oregon Parole Matrix." *Federal Probation,* 43:52–59.

Terry, Robert M. 1967. "Discrimination in the Handling of Juvenile Offenders by Social Control Agencies." *Journal of Research in Crime and Delinquency,* 4:218–230.

Thomas, Jim 1988. "Inmate Litigation: Using the Courts or Abusing Them?" *Corrections Today,* 50:124–127.

Thompson, Joel A. 1986. "The American Jail: Problems, Politics, Prospects." *American Journal of Criminal Justice,* 10:205–221.

Thornberry, Terence and Joseph Jacoby 1979. *The Criminally Insane: A Community Follow-Up of Mentally Ill Offenders.* Chicago, IL: University of Chicago Press.

Tinker, John H., John Quiring, and Yvonne Pimentel 1985 "Ethnic Bias in

California Courts: A Case Study of Chicano and Anglo Felony Defendants." *Sociological Inquiry*, 55:83–96.

Tillman, Robert 1987. "The Size of the 'Criminal Population': The Prevalence and Incidence of Adult Arrest." *Criminology*, 25:561–579.

Tilton, Peter J. 1987. "The Status of Parole in Maine" in Edward E. Rhine and Ronald W. Jackson (eds.) *Observations on Parole*. Boulder, CO: National Institute of Corrections.

Tittle, C. R. 1969. "Crime Rates and Legal Sanctions." *Social Problems*, 16:408–423.

Tittle, C. R. and A. R. Rowe 1974. "Certainty of Arrest and Crime Rates: A Further Test of the Deterrence Hypothesis." *Social Forces*, 52:455–462.

Tobias, Jerry J., Bruce Danto, and Robert H. Robertson 1980 "The Role of the Police in Dealing with Sexually Abused Children." *Journal of Police Science and Administration*, 8:464–473.

Tonry, Michael 1982. "Criminal Law: The Missing Element in Sentencing Reform." *Vanderbilt Law Review*, 35:607–641.

Tonry, Michael 1988a. "Sentencing Guidelines and the Model Penal Code." *Rutgers Law Journal*, 19:823–848.

Tonry, Michael 1988b. "Structuring Sentencing" in M. Tonry and N. Morris (eds.) *Crime and Justice*, Vol. 10, pp. 267–337. Chicago, IL: University of Chicago Press.

Tonry, Michael and J. C. Coffee 1987. "Enforcing Sentencing Guidelines: Plea Bargaining and Review Mechanisms." in A. Von Hirsch, K. A. Knapp, and M. Tonry (eds.) *The Sentencing Commission and Its Guidelines*, pp. 142–176. Boston, MA: Northeastern University Press.

Tonry, Michael and Norval Morris (eds.) 1983. *Crime and Justice: An Annual Review of Research, Vol. 5*. Chicago, IL: University of Chicago Press.

Tonry, Michael and Norval Morris 1988. *Crime and Justice: A Review of Research*. Chicago, IL: University of Chicago press.

U. S. Department of Justice 1984. *Handbook on the Comprehensive Crime Control Act of 1984 and Other Criminal Statutes Enacted by the 98th Congress*. Washington, DC: U. S. Government Printing Office.

U. S. Sentencing Commission 1987a. *Federal Sentencing Guideline Manual*. St. Paul, MN: West Publishing Company.

U. S. Sentencing Commission 1987b. *Guidelines Manual*. Washington, DC: U. S. Government Printing Office.

U. S. Sentencing Commission 1987c. *Preliminary Observations of the Commission on Commissioner Robinson's Dissent*. Washington, DC: U. S. Government Printing Office.

U. S. Sentencing Commission 1987d. *Sentencing Guidelines and Policy Statements*. Washington, DC: U. S. Government Printing Office.

U. S. Sentencing Commission 1987e. *Supplementary Report on the Initial Sentencing Guidelines and Policy Statements*. Washington, DC: U. S. Sentencing Commission.

U. S. Sentencing Commission 1988. *Supplementary Report to Congress*. Washington, DC: U. S. Sentencing Commission.

Van Dine, Stephen, Simon Dinitz, and John Conrad 1977 "Incapacitation of the Dangerous Offender—A Statistical Experiment." *Journal of Research in Crime and Delinquency*, 14:22–34.

Visher, Christy A. 1983. "Gender, Police Arrest Decisions, and Notions of Chivalry." *Criminology*, 21:5–28.

Visher, Christy A. 1987. "Incapacitation and Crime Control: Does a 'Lock 'Em Up' Strategy Reduce Crime?" *Justice Quarterly*, 4:513–543.

Vito, Gennaro F. 1978. "Shock Probation in Ohio: A Re-Examination of the Factors Influencing the Use of an Early Release Program." *Offender Rehabilitation*, 3:123–132.

Vito, Gennaro F. 1984. "Developments in Shock Probation: A Review of Research Findings and Policy Implications." *Federal Probation*, 48:22–27.

Vito, Gennaro F. 1986. "Felony Probation and Recidivism: Replication and Response." *Federal Probation*, 50:17–25.

von Hirsch, Andrew 1976. *Doing Justice: The Choice of Punishments*. New York, NY: Hill and Wang.

von Hirsch, Andrew 1981. "Desert and Previous Convictions in Sentencing." *Minnesota Law Review*, 65:591–634.

von Hirsch, Andrew 1982. "Constructing Guidelines for Sentencing: The Critical Choices for the Minnesota Sentencing Guidelines Commission." *Hamline Law Review*, 5:164–215.

von Hirsch, Andrew 1984. "The Ethics of Selective Incapacitation: Observations on the Contemporary Debate." *Crime and Delinquency*, 30:175–194.

von Hirsch, Andrew 1987a. "The Sentencing Commission's Functions" in A. Von Hirsch, K. A. Knapp, and M. Tonry (eds.) *The Sentencing Commission and Its Guidelines*, pp. 3–15. Boston, MA: Northeastern University Press.

von Hirsch, Andrew 1987b. "Numerical Grids or Guiding Principles?" in A. Von Hirsch, K. A. Knapp, and M. Tonry (eds.). *The Sentencing Commission and Its Guidelines*, pp. 47–61. Boston, MA: Northeastern University Press.

von Hirsch, Andrew 1987c. "Hybrid Principles in Allocating Sanctions: A Response to Professor Robinson." *Northwestern University Law Review*, 82:64–72.

von Hirsch, Andrew 1984. "Selective Incapacitation: Some Queries About Research Design and Equity." *New York University Review of Law and Social Change*, 12:11–51.

von Hirsch, Andrew and Kathleen Hanrahan 1981. "Determinate Penalty Systems in America: An Overview." *Crime and Delinquency*, 27:289–316.

von Hirsch, Andrew, Kay Knapp, and Michael Tonry 1987. *The Sentencing Commission and Its Guidelines*. Boston, MA: Northeastern University Press.

Walker, Samuel 1980. *Popular Justice: A History of American Criminal Justice*. New York, NY: Oxford University Press.

Walker, Samuel 1985. *Sense and Nonsense About Crime: A Policy Guide*. Monterey, CA: Brooks/Cole.

Waller, Irvin 1974. *Men Released from Prison*. Toronto, Can: University of Toronto Press.

Walsh, A. 1985. "The Role of the Probation Officers in the Sentencing Process." *Criminal Justice and Behavior*, 12:289–303.

Webb, Vincent J. et al. 1976. "Recidivism: in Search of a More Comprehensive

Definition." *International Journal of Offender Therapy and Comparative Criminology*, 20:144–147.

Weinstein, Michael B. 1987. "Put Sentencing Discretion Back in the Hands of Judges." *The Prosecutor*, 21:5–6.

Wilkins, Leslie T. 1968. *Evaluation of Penal Measures*. New York, NY: Random House.

Wilkins, Leslie T. 1981. *The Principles of Guidelines for Sentencing: Methodological and Philosophical Issues in Their Development*. Washington, DC: U. S. Department of Justice.

Willis, Cecil L. and Richard H. Wells 1988. "The Police and Child Abuse: An Analysis of Police Decisions to Report Legal Behavior." *Criminology*, 26:695–716.

Wilson, James Q. 1968. *Varieties of Police Behavior: The Management of Law and Order in Eight Communities*. New York, NY: Atheneum.

Wilson, James Q. 1983. *Thinking About Crime (Revised ed.)*. New York, NY: Basic Books.

Wisconsin Law Review 1986. "Insuring the Accuracy of the Presentence Investigation Report in the Wisconsin Correctional System." *Wisconsin Law Review*, 1986:613–631.

Witte, A. D. 1980. "Estimating the Economic Model of Crime with Individual Data." *Quarterly Journal of Economics*, 94:57–84.

Wolfgang, Marvin E., Robert M. Figlio, and Thorsten Sellin 1972. *Delinquency in A Birth Cohort*. Chicago, IL: University of Chicago Press.

Wolfgang, Marvin 1985. "Longitudinal Research as a Tool of Criminal Policy." *Unafei Annual Report*. New York, NY: United Nations.

Wormith, J. Stephen and Colin S. Goldstone 1984. "The Clinical and Statistical Prediction of Recidivism." *Criminal Justice and Behavior*, 11:3–34.

Zatz, Marjorie S. 1984. "Race, Ethnicity, and Determinate Sentencing: A New Dimension to an Old Controversy." *Criminology*, 22:147–171.

Zimring, Franklin E. 1981. "Making the Punishment Fit the Crime" in H. Gross and A. Von Hirsch (eds.) *Sentencing*, pp. 327–335. New York, NY: Oxford University Press.

Zimring, Franklin E. 1987. "Principles of Criminal Sentencing, Plain and Fancy." *Northwestern University Law Review*, 82:73–78.

Zimring, Franklin E. and G. J. Hawkins 1973. *Deterrence: The Legal Threat in Crime Control*. Chicago, IL: University of Chicago Press.

Cases Cited

Avery v. Johnson, 398 U.S. 483 (1969)

Baxter v. Palmigiano, 425 U.S. 308 (1976)

Bell v. Wolfish, 441 U.S. 520 (1979)

Bivens v. Six Unknown FBI Agents, 403 U.S. 387 (1971)

Bounds v. Smith, 430 U.S. 817 (1977)

Commonwealth v. Mourar, 504 A.2d 197 (PA. Super.) (1986)

Connecticut Board of Pardons v. Dumschat, 449 U.S. 898 (1981)

Cooper v. Pate, 378 U.S. 546 (1964)

Cruz v. Beto, 405 U.S. 319 (1972)

Cuyler v. Adams, 449 U.S. 433 (1981)

Enomoto v. Clutchette, 425 U.S. 153 (1976)

Estelle v. Gamble, 429 U.S. 97 (1976)

Furman v. Georgia, 408 U.S. 238 (1972)

Gagnon v. Scarpelli, 411 U.S. 778 (1973)

Gilmore v. Lynch, 404 U.S. 15 (1971)

Greenholtz v. Inmates of the Nebraska Penal and Correctional System, 442 U.S. 1 (1979)

Hewitt v. Helms, 459 U.S. 460 (1983)

Houchins v. KQED, 438 U.S. 1 (1978)

Howe v. Smith, 452 U.S. 473 (1981)

Hutto v. Finney, 437 U.S. 678 (1978)

Inmates of Attica Correctional Facility v. Rockefeller, 453 F.2d 12 (2nd Cir. 1971)

Jones v. North Carolina Prisoner's Labor Union, Inc., 433 U.S. 119 (1977)

Jones v. Wittenberg, 330 F. Supp. 707, (N.D. Ohio 1971), aff'd 456 F.2d 12 (6th Cir. 1971)

Meachum v. Fano, 427 U.S. 215 (1976)

Mistretta v. U. S., 109 S.Ct. 647 (1989)

Montanye v. Haymes, 427 U.S. 236 (1976)

Moody v. Daggett, 429 U.S. 78 (1976)

Morrissey v. Brewer, 408 U.S. 471 (1972)

Olim v. Wakinekona, 461 U.S. 460 (1983)

O'Lone v. Estate of Shabazz, 482 U.S. 342 (1987)

Parratt v. Taylor, 449 U.S. 527 (1981)

Pell v. Procunier, 417 U.S. 817 (1974)

Procunier v. Martinez, 416 U.S. 396 (1974)

Rhodes v. Chapman, 452 U.S. 337 (1981)

Richardson v. Ramirez, 418 U.S. 24 (1974)

Santobello v. New York, 404 U.S. 257 (1971)
State v. Evans, 311 N.W. 2d 481 (Minn. 1981)
Saxbe v. Washington Post Company, 417 U.S. 843 (1974)
State v. Hernandez, 311 N.W. 2d 478 (Minn. 1981)
State v. Schantzen, 308 N.W. 2d 484 (1981)
Turner v. Safley, 482 U.S. 78 (1987)
United States v. Ammidown, 497 F.2d 615 (D.C. Cir.) (1973)
United States v. Bean, 564 F.2d 700 (5th Cir.) (1977)
Vitek v. Jones, 445 U.S. 480 (1980)
Williams v. New York, 337 U.S. 241 (1949)
Wolff v. McDonnell, 418 U.S. 539 (1974)

Name Index

Subject Index

Crime Control Act of 1984 66, 75
Cruel and unusual punishment 49

"Dangerous classes" 144
Dangerousness, risk 141–144 (*see also* Selective Incapacitation) factors in prediction of 141; "high risk" offenders 141; social control 143
"Date bargaining" (*see* Plea Bargaining)
Death penalty 4–5, 35
Delaware 235
Denver, CO 22
Department of Housing and Urban Development (HUD) 9
Deputy Attorney General 16
Determinate sentencing (*see* Sentencing)
Deterrence 32–46, 234; and sentencing guidelines 37–45, 234–235; general deterrence 34–35, 41; influencing by fear 34; perception 35–36; plea bargaining 44–45; public perceptions of 42–44; research 35–36; specific 34–35, 41
Discretion (*see* specific topics)
Diversion 162; influence of guidelines on 162
Drug Enforcement Administration (DEA) 13
Drug laws 69–71, 74, 87–88, 114–115, 153
Drug prosecutions 16, 66
Drug Quantity Table 115
Drug trafficking 114, 156

Eastern District of Pennsylvania 160–161
Edna McConnell Clark Foundation 51
Electronic surveillance 131; cost 131; influence of guidelines 131
Embezzlement 93, 236
Enforcement of laws 105
Extralegal factors 33, 38–39, 102, 141–142, 221, 232

False positives 142
False statements 9
Federal Bureau of Investigation (FBI) 13
Federal Bureau of Prisons 49, 72, 75, 177, 182, 198
Federal Constitutional Tort Theory 213
Federal Judges Association 89
Federal Judicial Center 75
Federal jurisdiction 3–4, 12–13
Federal prison population (*see* Prison Populations)
Federal Rules of Criminal Procedure 103, 107
Federal Tort Claims Act 210, 213
Feinberg, Kenneth 64
Fines 130; neglect by guidelines 130

"Flat time" 156, 235
Florida 5–6, 14, 22, 176; presumptive guidelines 5–6
Fraud 220
Freed, Daniel 51, 59

Gaes, Mr. 73, 88
Gambling 12
General Accounting Office 73, 75, 233–234, 239
General deterrence (*see* Deterrence)
Good conduct time (GTC) 184
"Good time" 5, 156, 168–169
Guidelines 119; application 114–116; federal 98–99; judicial restrictions 119; mandatory nature 98–99; state 6; "shopping" 119–120

Habeas corpus filings 207, 210 (*see also* Inmate Rights)
Habitual offenders 136
Halfway houses 160, 175
"Hands-off" doctrine 208
Hijacking 4
Hinckley, John 4
Hobbs Act 4
Home detention 130, 160, 163
Homicides 9, 217
House Criminal Justice Subcommittee 51; Albert W. Alschuler's statement 52–61
"Hydraulic effect" 132, 166, 233

Illinois 187, 189
Immigration 4, 12
Immigration and Naturalization Service 13
Incapacitation 33, 54–55, 146, 173, 222–225, 235–236; collective 222; "low growth scenario" 54–55; selective (*see* Selective Incapacitation)
Indeterminate sentencing (*see* Sentencing)
Inmate litigation 202, 204–213; administrative remedies 206; administrative search warrants 204; conditions of confinement 206; discipline 204; health services 204; in forma pauperis suits 206; jailhouse lawyers 204, 214; mail censorship 203–204; petitions filed, state and federal 211–212; possession of obscene material 204; postconviction remedies 207, 210; pro se filings 213–214; reasons for 206–205; scope of 210–213; use of force by correctional officers 204
Inmate rights 202–206; access to courts 208; access to legal materials and aid 208–209; cruel and unusual punish-

Case Index

About the Contributors

ALBERT W. ALSCHULER is currently Wilson-Dickinson Professor of Law, University of Chicago Law School. He received his A.B. from Harvard College and his LL.B. from Harvard Law School. He has held professorial posts at the University of Pennsylvania, University of Texas, and University of Colorado. His numerous articles have appeared in the *Michigan Law Review, University of Chicago Law Review, Harvard Law Review, National Law Journal, Law and Society Review, Yale Law Journal,* and *Texas Law Review* among others. His recent research and writings have focused upon sentencing, plea bargaining, preventive detention, jury selection, civil settlement, and search and seizure. Among his peers and throughout the academic community, Professor Alschuler is widely recognized as an authority on plea bargaining. He has taught criminal law and procedure, constitutional law, jurisprudence, and professional responsibility, and he has formerly held visiting professor posts in several universities.

DEAN J. CHAMPION received his Ph.D. in Sociology from Purdue University with B.S. and M.A. degrees from Brigham Young University. He is Professor of Sociology at the University of Tennessee, Knoxville. He has authored *Basic Statistics for Social Research* (Macmillan), *Sociology of Organizations* (McGraw-Hill), *Felony Probation: Problems and Prospects* (Praeger), *Methods and Issues of Social Research* (w/James A Black) (Wiley), *Corrections in the United States: A Contemporary Perspective* (Prentice-Hall), *Probation and Parole in the United States* (Merrill), *Criminal Justice in the United States* (Merrill), and *Basic Methods and Statistics for Criminal Justice and Criminology* (Prentice-Hall). He has numerous articles in the *Journal of Criminal Justice, The Prosecutor, The American Journal of Criminal Justice, Criminal Justice Review, Journal of Crime and Justice* and many others. His current research interests include plea bargaining and the federal judiciary, juvenile transfer hearings and criminal outcomes, and interregional prosecutorial discretion.

WILLIAM G. DOERNER is currently an Associate Professor in the School of Criminology at the Florida State University. He received his Ph.D. from the University of Tennessee and the M.A. from Emory University. His past research interests have included homicide and the regional culture of violence thesis, police training, the link between child maltreatment and juvenile delinquency, and victim compensation. At this time he is engaged in a project which analyzes police shooting behavior. He is also a part-time law enforcement officer with the Tallahassee Police Department and is preparing an introductory text on policing. He has authored numerous articles and *Delinquency and Justice* (w/William E. Thornton and Lydia Voigt) (Random House).

JAMES G. FOX received his Ph.D. in Criminal Justice from the State University of New York at Albany in 1976. He is Associate Professor of Criminal Justice at the New York State University College at Buffalo, where he holds appointments with the graduate and undergraduate faculty. He has also served on the faculty at the Pennsylvania State University and has held visiting appointments at the University of Toronto and the University of Oregon. His publications include *Organizational and Racial Conflict in Maximum Security Prisons* and numerous articles in journals including *The Prison Journal, Crime and Social Justice,* and *Widerspruche..*

LYNNE GOODSTEIN received her Ph.D. from the City University of New York. She is currently Associate Professor in the Administration of Justice Program at the Pennsylvania State University. She has contributed numerous articles to criminal justice journals including *Justice Quarterly, Criminal Justice and Behavior, Journal of Research on Crime and Delinquency, Law and Policy Quarterly,* and she has published book chapters in *The Criminal Justice System and Blacks* (D. E. Georges-Abeyie, Ed.) (Clark Boardman) and *Coping with Imprisonment* (Nicolette Parisi, Ed.) (Sage). She also has co-authored a book, *Determinate Sentencing and Imprisonment: A Failure of Reform* (w/John Hepburn) (Anderson). Her research interests include the impact and implications of sentencing systems on offenders and the criminal justice system.

DENIS J. HAUPTLY received his B.A. in American Studies from St. Michael's College in 1968 and a J.D. degree from the University of Notre Dame in 1972. He is currently serving as a Special Master for the United States Claims Court. He has previously served as Associate Director of the Office of Legislation (Criminal) in the United States Department of Justice and as General Counsel of the United States Sentencing Commission, as well as in a variety of positions in the

Judicial Branch. He is the author of four works of non-fiction for adolescents.

KAY A. KNAPP has worked in the area of sentencing reform for the past ten years. Ms. Knapp was Research Director and then Director for the Minnesota Sentencing Guidelines Commission during the development, implementation, and evaluation of its guidelines. During that period, she worked extensively with the Minnesota State Legislature on sentencing issues and matters related to prison populations. Ms. Knapp has consulted with twenty other states (as well as two foreign countries) on sentencing reform and prison population issues, working with legislative committees and executive branch staffs. Ms. Knapp served as Staff Director for the U. S. Sentencing Commission and worked at the Federal Judicial Center developing training programs on sentencing for the federal judiciary and probation officers. Ms. Knapp is currently the President and Director of the Institute for Rational Public Policy, Inc. and works with states to develop structured sentencing and to improve criminal justice information systems.

JOHN H. KRAMER is Associate Professor of Sociology at the Pennsylvania State University and Executive Director of the Pennsylvania Commission on Sentencing. His research interests have focused on the effect of legal sanctions on self-concept and neutralizations, and recent developments in criminal sentencing. Besides three texts in *Criminal Justice,* he has published numerous articles in journals including *Justice Quarterly, International Journal of Sociology* and *Journal of Crime and Delinquency.*

STEVEN P. LAB received his Ph.D. in Criminology from Florida State University and is currently Assistant Professor in the Criminal Justice Program at Bowling Green State University, Ohio. His primary areas of interest are crime prevention and juvenile delinquency/justice. He is author of *Crime Prevention: Approaches, Practices and Evaluation* (Anderson) and *Juvenile Justice* (w/John Whitehead) (Anderson). His articles have appeared in *Criminology, Justice Quarterly, Journal of Criminal Justice, Journal of Police Science and Administration, Criminal Justice Review* and many others.

FRANKLIN H. MARSHALL was appointed as a U. S. Probation Officer, Eastern District of Pennsylvania (Philadelphia) in 1976. He is presently assigned to the Presentence Report Unit and is responsible for a variety of report types from individual to corporate. Mr. Marshall has been involved with the implementation of the U. S. Sentencing Guidelines within his district, including training and evaluation. He has a Bachelor's degree in Sociology and a Master's degree in Public Administration from Ohio State University. Formerly he was a Graduate Research Assistant in the Program for the Study of Crime and Delinquency at Ohio State University and is the author of numerous research monographs and articles. He is also an adjunct faculty member in the Department of Criminal Justice Administration at Temple University.

G. LARRY MAYS is Professor of Criminal Justice and Head of the Department of Criminal Justice at New Mexico State University. He has taught at Appalachian State University, East Tennessee State University, and was formerly a police officer with the Knoxville, Tennessee Police Department. He received his Ph.D. from the University of Tennessee. Dr. Mays has authored *Juvenile Delinquency and Juvenile Justice* (w/Joseph W. Rogers) (Wiley), and he has published articles in the *Journal of Criminal Justice, Justice Quarterly, Judicature, Justice System Journal, American Journal of Criminal Justice,* and *Policy Studies Review.* His teaching and research interests are in the areas of criminal and juvenile justice policy development, implementation, and evaluation.

JOHN W. PALMER received his B.A. degree from Oberlin College and J.D. degree from the University of Michigan Law School. He was a Fulbright Scholar at the University of Stockholm, Sweden, and has studied at the Institute of Comparative Law, Luxembourg, The Hague Academy of International Law, Netherlands, and at the Advocacy Institute, U. S. Department of Justice. He is the former Dean of Capital University Law School, Columbus, Ohio, and a former Assistant U. S. Attorney, Southern District of Ohio. Dr. Palmer is currently Professor of Law, Capital University Law School. His publications include *Constitutional Rights of Prisoners* (Anderson) and numerous articles and reports. He is also Publisher and Editor-in-Chief of the *Ohio Evidence Review* and the *Ohio Criminal Law Review.* He received a commendation from FBI Director William Webster in 1978 and is a Fellow of the American Bar Foundation.

ELLEN HOCHSTEDLER STEURY received her Ph.D. in Criminal Justice from the State University of New York at Albany in 1980 and currently holds the position of Associate Professor of Criminal Justice at the University of Wisconsin-Milwaukee. Her academic research interest centers on both the theoretical and operational definition of criminal responsibility. Examining the operational definition of criminal responsibility has led her to focus on the adjudication process in criminal (and lower civil) courts. In that vein, she has conducted original research and published papers on the prosecution of the mentally disordered, and she has edited a book entitled *Corporations as Criminals* (Sage).

W. CLINTON TERRY III received his Ph.D. in sociology from the University of California, Santa Barbara. He has taught at California State University, Fresno, the University of Florida, and Florida International University, where he is currently associate professor and chairperson of the Department of Criminal Justice. He is the author of *Policing Society: An Occupational View* (Wiley) and has written widely on law enforcement and criminal justice topics, especially within the areas of police organization, administration, and stress as well as the use of video technologies in the courtroom and crimes against the elderly. He is formerly editor of the *Journal of Justice Issues*. His articles have appeared in *Journal of Criminal Justice, Journal of Police Science Administration, Law and Human Behavior, Judicature, Journal of Crime and Justice* and many others. He has consulted with a number of local, regional, and national organizations on police-related topics, including the cities of Miami, Ft. Lauderdale, West Palm Beach, the National Urban League, and the Police Foundation. Currently he is studying the impact of immigration upon the provision of municipal services within South Florida and is involved in conducting crime analysis, victimization surveys, and safe neighborhood planning for several cities within South Florida.

DEBORAH G. WILSON is Policy Advisor, Kentucky Attorney General, and Associate Professor, School of Justice Administration, University of Louisville. She received her M.S. and Ph.D. degrees from Purdue University. She has taught at Purdue University and Auburn University and was a former Branch Manager of Research and Research Consultant for the Kentucky Corrections Cabinet. She has published articles in many journals including *Justice Quarterly, Federal Probation, Journal of Criminal Justice Policy Review,* and *Correctional Monograph*. Her books include *The American Juvenile Justice System* (1985) and *Introduction to Criminal Justice Research* (forthcoming).

BENJAMIN S. WRIGHT is an Assistant Professor of Criminal Justice at Louisiana State University. He received a B.S. degree from the University of South Carolina and M.C.J. and Ph.D. degrees from the Florida State University. He has taught at South Carolina State College. Between 1982–1985, he was a Patricia Roberts Fellow while studying at Florida State University. Dr. Wright has contributed to research inquiries that have addressed such diverse issues as the use of psychological tests as predictors of recruit police performance and an examination of how book reviews published in criminology journals are utilized in the tenure process. His current research interests include identifying relevant police productivity measures, the use of psychological tests in the police selection process, and the adjudication of minority suspects.